MW00511093

THE BUDGET
AND
RESPONSIBLE GOVERNMENT

A Description and Interpretation of the Struggle for Responsible Government in the United States, with Special Reference to Recent Changes in State Constitutions and Statute Laws Providing for Administrative Reorganization and Budget Reform

BY
FREDERICK A. CLEVELAND
AND
ARTHUR EUGENE BUCK

INTRODUCTION BY
WILLIAM HOWARD TAFT

New York
THE MACMILLAN COMPANY
1920
All rights reserved

EDITOR'S NOTE

ALONG with the discussion of a budget system and budgetary procedure in city, state and nation, which has progressed with growing intensity during the past fifteen years, there has been a wide range of practical experimentation in the application of the budget idea, especially in municipal and state governments in the United States. It seemed a few months ago when the National Budget Committee was organized and incorporated under the laws of the District of Columbia, as a citizens' movement, that the time had come to have this experience summarized and interpreted by competent authorities, especially when the appointment of select committees of inquiry in both houses of Congress indicated that we were likely to have national legislation in the near future looking to the establishment of some kind of a national budget system.

The editor of this series was gratified to find that he could get Dr. Frederick A. Cleveland and Mr. Arthur E. Buck to undertake the task, and former President William Howard Taft to furnish an introduction to the volume. Dr. Cleveland is not only a pioneer but also the foremost authority in America on the subject of the budget. He has had an exceptional professional training and experience in the underlying political theories of democracy, and the technical problems of public accountancy. The whole budget movement in the United States owes much to his persevering activities, since he planned and installed the budget system of the great municipal government of New York City ten years and more ago, on a scale that almost rivalled in complexity and size of operations the business of the Federal Government not many decades ago. Later he was the Chairman of Presi-

v

dent Taft's Commission on Economy and Efficiency, and in that capacity directed and made the first and only comprehensive catalogue and survey of the operations of the Federal Government. In connection with the Constitutional Convention of 1915 in New York State he directed and made a similar survey of the organization of the government of the Empire State.

President Taft was the first chief executive of the nation, or of any American state, who fully grasped and presented the issues of the budget principle in relation to legislation and public administration in any government.

Mr. Buck was not only trained under Dr. Cleveland as a member of the staff of the New York Bureau of Municipal Research, with which Dr. Cleveland had been connected from its organization and of which he was sometime Director, but had also had notable experience as adviser to Governor Harrington of Maryland, in the preparation of the first Maryland state budget, and in other states as well. Mr. Buck was therefore exceptionally qualified to deal with the subject matter of Parts II and III of this volume, for which he is chiefly responsible.

This volume is dedicated to the proposition that the foundations of all democratic institutions must rest on an effective means of making government responsive to public opinion. The method of exposition is historical and descriptive of the devices developed in response to the popular demand that public business shall be " visible " and that leadership shall be " responsible." After laying down the commonly accepted proposition of popular control (right of election, acquiescence in the decision of a majority, and the need for a forum before which the responsible heads of the public service may be arraigned), Dr. Cleveland, as author of Parts I, IV, and V of the text, maintains this thesis:

(1) That the outstanding need, which our federal con-

stitution was designed to meet, was a need for executive leadership, which vested in the President "the executive power" and gave to him the means for making his leadership effective;

(2) That the "visibility" of leadership is provided for by requiring "a regular statement and account of receipts and expenditures of all public monies," and making it the duty of the President "from time to time to give to Congress information of the State of the Union and recommend to their consideration such measures as he shall deem necessary and expedient";

(3) That means of enforcing "responsibility" were put in the hands of Congress, and the electorate, by giving to Congress the control over the purse, and making both the President and the controlling representative and appropriating body answerable to the people for the manner in which their powers are exercised;

(4) That immediately after this new federal government had been set up, these underlying principles of popular control were violated, by Congress insisting on retaining to itself the leadership which during the revolutionary period had been exercised by committees and refusing to permit Hamilton, as President Washington's representative, to come before them to give an account of stewardship and to submit plans and proposals to be financed — the result being the centralized government by standing committees administrated by a bureaucracy, with a board of strategy organized outside of the government by irresponsible political parties.

The constructive proposals in this part of the book are largely those which will be found in the report of President Taft's Commission on Economy and Efficiency. They may be summarized as follows:

1. "That the President shall each year get before the

country what it is that the administration desires to do: shall indicate in a budget message wherein action is necessary to enable the administration adequately to meet public needs. . . . That the President, under the powers given to him by the constitution is in a better position than any one else to dramatize the work of the Government, to so impress this upon the attention of the people through the public press . . . as to arouse discussion and elicit comment such as will keep the Congress, as well as the administration in touch with public opinion when deciding whether or not the proposals are such as will best meet welfare demands."

2. That " as an incident to such procedure it is thought that there must necessarily develop a system of representation which will consistently support the administration program which is submitted,"— The same idea being elaborated and the report continuing to show that " a budget system necessarily carries with it means for developing an administrative program and means for presenting it and defending it before the legislative branch of the government and the country."

3. Having provided adequately for executive leadership the exercise of effective control over this leadership, both by the representative branch and the electorate, depend on the development of a procedure of inquest, criticism, and discussion in Congress before the whole body as an open forum, in which each member shall be called upon to vote for or against the plan or program to be financed, section by section and as a whole. In this connection it is claimed that the recognized purpose of committees of Congress should be to find out what is being proposed and to bring every proposal into critical review before the members and the country. In other words, the committees should be of two kinds, those acting as attorneys for the administration, and those as its critics. Therefore, the committee assuming leadership for the

budget should be taken from the pro-administration party
and the committee assuming critical leadership should be
made up chiefly from the opposition.

In the ranks of the National Budget Committee there
developed differences of opinion almost from the start
concerning the relative merits of the proposals for a national budget system, especially with respect to the location of the budget bureau and the concentrating of responsibility for the initiation of the budget in the office
of the President, as provided for in the Good bill which
passed the House of Representatives almost unanimously
Oct. 21, 1919, and the plan of the McCormick bill introduced in the Senate but not yet reported out by the
Select Committee of which Senator McCormick is chairman. Senator McCormick's plan puts the budget bureau
under the Secretary of the Treasury and divides responsibility for revision of the estimates and preparation of
the budget between that officer and the President who,
however, must transmit and assume financial responsibility for the initiation of the budget. The difference of
opinion on this point is largely one of emphasis.

Mr. Taft is primarily interested in seeing executive
responsibility fixed and strengthened and therefore naturally prefers the Good plan, while Dr. Cleveland is so
much attracted by other features of the McCormick plan
which seems to him to spell executive representation before the legislature and the putting of the " opposition "
where it can make clear-cut issues and public debate of
budget questions, that he seems to prefer it as a whole
and to think that the Good bill, even with the revision of
rules contemplated by separate resolutions not yet acted
upon by the House, would mean the perpetuation of many
evils of the present committee system.

The National Budget Committee's position is that a
combination of the two plans in a McCormick-Good bill,

which may finally be enacted by Congress, will give us the advantages of a budget system in which the responsibility of the President for the initiation of the budget, and for the correction of the evils which any budget system is sure to reveal in the business organization of the Government, through some such powers as were conferred on the President as a war measure by the Overman Act, but practically unused by him hitherto, will be made unquestionably secure, and Congressional responsibility for criticism and decision of clear-cut issues of policy will be made equally clear and effective.

Samuel McCune Lindsay.

Columbia University,
March 17, 1920.

PREFACE

This volume was begun as a report to the National Budget Committee. Much has been written and published on the subject of budget since 1912, when propaganda for a national budget was seriously begun by President Taft in a special message to Congress urging the adoption of the recommendations of his Commission on Economy and Efficiency. In the seven years following Congress did nothing. Meanwhile action was taken looking toward the introduction of a budgetary procedure by forty-four of the states and scores of cities. And now, out of the entanglements of war finance the question has come back to bother Congress.

During the last year a volume was brought out by Dr. W. F. Willoughby, descriptive of the budget legislation passed in the several states. The story of how these laws have worked, where they have been in operation long enough to judge, was still to be written. In undertaking this task, it at once became evident that, since a budget is only a method or mechanism of control, judgment as to the value of one budget system or another must take into account the working relations between the representative or controlling body on the one hand and the administrative leadership over which control is to be exercised on the other. This in turn led to a consideration of the manner in which leadership is organized and expressed. In other words, a study of the organic laws of the several states was found to be an essential part of a report on budgetary procedure.

Upon taking stock of what had been done in this particular it was found that in addition to the wealth of published materials made available by state boards and commissions, a report was in course of preparation by the Governor's Reconstruction Commission of the State of New York, dealing with, among other things, the subject of administrative reorganization in the several states. Mr. Buck of the New York Bureau of Municipal Research was a member of the staff of this commission and was immediately responsible for the preparation of these materials. He was, therefore, asked to collaborate in the collection of further materials dealing with the budget experience in the states. Chapters IX, X, XI and XII in this book contain the materials, in modified form, which have appeared in the Commission's Report on Retrenchment and Reorganization in the State Government. Chapter XIII was prepared with the assistance of Mr. Luther H. Gulick of the New York Bureau of Municipal Research, who as secretary of the Joint Special Committee on Finance and Budget Procedure of the Massachusetts Legislature was particularly qualified to make this contribution. I take this opportunity also to acknowledge indebtedness to Dr. Samuel McCune Lindsay, Vice-Chairman of the National Budget Committee, and editor of the Series in which this volume appears.

F. A. C.

Norwood, Mass.
February 1, 1920.

INTRODUCTION

I am glad to write a Foreword to this book. Mr. Cleveland I have known for a number of years. He is a pioneer in the reform of the wasteful methods of government finance in municipal, state and the federal field. He is not a mere public accountant — he is a student of government, and he has thought out methods for avoiding the ordinarily sloppy and irresponsible manner of managing the public business in a Democracy, by giving to our ubiquitous sovereigns, the people, the knowledge which they should have of the numerous monetary transactions of their agents in which they are interested. The great problem of popular government on its practical side is to create machinery by which those for whom government is carried on, and who should control and direct government in a large way, shall be advised of the facts, and upon those facts, correctly interpreted, shall exercise discriminating criticism and ultimate decision. Mr. Cleveland rightly conceives that one of the great defects in the past which has led to wastefulness and ineffectiveness in government finance is the failure to keep the public thus advised. This leads to invisible government which does not make for either efficiency, economy or honesty. Mr. Cleveland regards a proper governmental budget as very important in eliminating " invisible government."

The budget system for governments has had its fullest and most successful development in Great Britain, and it has squared with the whole structure of government in that country. When therefore we attempt to adapt the results there attained to our own case we are somewhat

embarrassed by the constitutional differences between the
British governmental system and ours.

In English history, the King was the Executive, and
Parliament and the House of Commons, as the originator
of financial legislation, were the donors of the funds with
which the King was to conduct his government. He applied to Parliament for enough to run the nation. Parliament considered his application and determined whether
he was not asking too much. In order to induce compliance with his request, he found it wise to elaborate
the details of his needs and prove them to the satisfaction
of the representatives of the people who were to be bur-
dened with the cost. Each year Parliament had to determine how much it thought the King needed of what he
asked, and the particular methods of taxation by which
the money could be taken from the people. It was this
statement which constituted the budget. It showed how
much was to be spent in detail and showed the source
from which and method by which what was to be spent
should be secured. The natural attitude in such an
arrangement of the representatives of the people was
that of closest scrutiny of the petition of the King for
appropriation and of reluctance and opposition toward too
great expenditure. It did not enter into the early idea of
the relation between the executive and legislative branches
that the legislative branch could be a factor in increasing
the appropriations. Hence in the reign of Queen Anne it
became a standing order of the House of Commons that
no motion to increase any item in the supplies should be
in order except upon motion of the Crown. Of course
the relations between the executive and the legislative
branches have had a revolutionary change in Great Britain, so that the King has ceased to be the executive, and
the Government is carried on by a Premier and a Cabinet,
who are the real executive and, as leaders of the majority
in the House of Commons, also constitute the moving

party in the legislative and appropriating branch. But whatever changes the constitutional changes in the British government have made, the important features of the budget remain. Detailed estimates are made by the government and furnished for examination and determination by the committees in Parliament and the Chancellor of the Exchequer as a representative of the Crown ultimately presents to Parliament, in a succinct, graphic way, the general financial condition of the Treasury, what is needed to run the Government for another year, and the taxation method by which it is to be raised. It is a comprehensive speech, adapted to popular understanding, and the result of expert work in the executive offices and in committee, and is presented in such a way as a whole that the press and other instruments of publicity can bring it to the people and present the issues arising out of its important factors clearly and with a sense of proportion. The people can judge from such a budget how much each important item costs and how they could be relieved from taxation if the item were omitted.

Except in the very early days of the Republic, when Hamilton, with his wonderful genius, was inaugurating the business side of our Government, we never had anything like a proper budget. We have never had concentrated in one capable body the duty of detailed calculation of what is needed to run the Government for a year and the systematic fixing of the taxation sources from which the money needed is to be procured. It is true that the General Appropriation Committee of the House, until within some decades, did have the function of making all the appropriations for the Government, and it is also true that earlier the function of determining the ways and means was united with that of fixing the expenditures; but we never have had executive responsibility for the preparation of the expense plan of the Government, with a suggestion of the means by which it could be met. The Executive spends the money. The Executive operates the machinery of government. Therefore, the Executive is much more intimately associated with the facts upon which the cost of government is to be determined than the legislative branch can be, and if it is so minded, is better qualified to determine where real economy can be effected and where apparent economy will be wasteful. This is not to be regarded as an argument in favor of taking away from the legislative branch the ultimate decision as to the expenditure of the funds of the Government and the methods of taxation to raise them, but it is a strong reason why the legislative branch of the Government in its work of ultimately determining how much should be spent and where it should be raised should have the benefit of the assistance of the executive department in an elaborate statement of how much the Government can be run for and where the money can be had.

What should be the machinery to secure it? From my personal experience I have no doubt that the responsibility and power should be given directly to the President; that he should be allowed funds from which to create a budget bureau, and that the estimates prepared by the heads of departments should be subjected to the pruning and veto power of the President, as assisted by his Budget Bureau. There is a difference between the House and the Senate over the pending bill as to whether the Secretary of the Treasury should have the Budget Bureau as a part of the Treasury Department and should himself exercise the pruning and limiting power. The Senate bill relieves the secretary from some of his duties in order to enable him to discharge this additional burden. Supporters of the Senate bill object that the President has not the time to do this thing. I venture, in the light of the experience I have had, to differ radically with this latter view. The preparation of the budget is going to be one of the most important functions that the whole Administration performs. Therefore the President may well devote all the time that is needed to giving general form to the budget and deciding the questions that are certain to arise between his Budget Bureau and the departments whose estimates are to be subjected to a pruning. The Secretary of the Treasury will not have sufficient prestige with the other departments to avoid the effect of the jealousies that any one familiar with the working of departments knows must exist. The President himself will have sufficient difficulty in adjusting the differences between his own Bureau and the various departments, but he can do it with his power — I doubt if the Secretary of the Treasury can. The conservatism of chief clerks and those who have been long in the service and under whose influence the heads of departments must come is a very difficult obstacle to overcome in seeking proper economy and a change of method. When one-third of the expenditures of the Government is to be through the Treasury Department itself, the expenses of that department should be passed upon by a higher power. The Good House bill, therefore, in providing for a Presidential budget, is much to be preferred to the McCormick Senate bill. The former bill gives the President an unusually effective method of keeping proper watch on the departments and of stimulating the heads of the various departments to greater detailed care in the saving of public money. More than this, the budget will necessarily contain recommendations involving high and important governmental policies, and it is right that the head of the Administration should be directly responsible for such recommendations. Of course all these matters will be considered in Cabinet and in respect to all of them the President must be the ultimate judge. He can be saved detail, but he can not be saved and ought not to be saved the duty of exercising deliberate judgment on the main issues which the budget will necessarily present.

Mr. Cleveland in this work deals with another feature that can not be suppressed in the consideration of a budget system, and that is the way in which Congress shall discharge its duty in respect to the executive budget after it has been presented. The mere publication of an executive budget and its submission to the committees of Congress is not enough to give it proper weight and effect. Improved as the means of publicity and information have been, the spoken word, with its accompanying incidents, is still a most important factor in bringing home to the people the critical points in any measure, especially in that of a budget. The Administration as the proponent of the budget should have an opportunity to be heard in the court to which it submits its case — that is, in Congress. The President should make the same kind of a speech to Congress as the Chancellor of the Exchequer in Great Britain makes to Parliament, and then his Cabinet ministers should be given the opportunity on the floor of each House to support and defend the features of the budget for which they are responsible and with which they are familiar. There is not the slightest reason why the heads of the departments should not be given seats in both Houses, with an opportunity to take part in any debate. In the discussion of the budget, both in the explanation before it shall be referred to the committees, and in criticism of the action of the committee after the committee has made its report, the Administration should be heard.

It is suggested that the heads of departments could hardly support and defend estimates which had been pruned down or changed by the President. This is a reason of no substance whatever. The heads of departments are and should be loyal to the Administration, and should take and support the view which the President has adopted as the Administration view in respect to the budget. They will have no difficulty in so doing. If any head of a department does, then his place is not in the Cabinet.

Just after the Civil War, the leading statesmen of both political parties recommended that the heads of departments be given seats in each House and an opportunity to join in the debate. Some twenty years later, men equally prominent in the Government, experienced in Congress, made a similar recommendation. Such an arrangement would greatly facilitate the business of Congress in getting at the facts through the interrogation of members of the Administration on the floor of each House; and it would give the members of each House a clear conception of the needs of the Government as the Administration thinks them to be, backed by arguments of men who must by reason of their duties know what they are talking about. Indeed the very function thus added to the others of the Cabinet ministers will stimulate them to a closer attention to their departments and a more intimate knowledge of their working.

But more important even than giving the Administration a chance to explain and defend its budget in the very forum where questions are to be decided is the reform of the two Houses of Congress themselves by creating a committee whose functions shall cover the whole field of expenditures and receipts. The division of authority in making up appropriation bills between a dozen committees in each House is a travesty which necessarily leads to expansion of governmental expenditure far beyond what it would be restrained to, if all expenses were in the control of one body which at the same time was vested with the duty and power of arranging for the raising of the money. Congress, as Mr. Good, the Chairman of the Appropriation Committee says, must put its own house in order before it shall have a right to criticise the executive for extravagance.

One may note in opposition to the budget the claim that Congress always cuts down and never adds to the estimates of the various departments.   Doubtless the statistics will prove this in respect to what may be called routine expenses, but that is due to the complete absence of restraint upon executive estimates.   Each bureau chief and each department head now make estimates and nobody curbs them.   The executive budget places responsibility on the President to do this.   The custom has grown among executive chiefs of bureaus and departments to ask for much more than it is expected will be appropriated in order to avoid their being cut below actual requirements. Such a haphazard method of estimates and their pruning is certain to be wasteful and often misdirected and likely to hamper governmental operation.   The President with his control may easily see to it that only that is asked which is needed, and he and his Administration can explain why.   Congress can then exercise the discretion that it should have in either approving the judgment of a responsible maker of a budget or in differing from him. In such a case Congress will be dealing with real estimates and a real plan and their judgment will be based on the best judgment which the Administration can furnish them.

Never before in the history of the country has reform of its ridiculous system of spending and raising money been so critically important.   For years we shall have to raise enormous amounts and the dangers of interfering with our prosperity by the stifling weight of taxation must convince everyone who thinks, of the imperative necessity of improving our national business system.

Mr. Cleveland was a chief participant in the great work done for the city of New York by the Bureau of Municipal Research which after a struggle of fourteen years has brought about a radical improvement in the management of the finances and expenditures of New York City.   He was the Chairman of the Economy and Efficiency Commission which under the authority of an appropriation from Congress I appointed during my Administration to investigate the proper methods of introducing economy in the business of the Government through a budget system and in many other ways. That commission made reports which I transmitted to Congress, which ought to be of great value in assisting the present Houses in the preparation of a proper bill. The recommendations and reports of the commission did not meet the favor of leading Congressmen and all the work done, contained in printed reports and unprinted manuscripts, has been dust covered until now. Of course the bureaus and divisions of governmental work have been vastly increased in number and expanded in function since that time, due to the war. Still those reports are instructive. The discussions and researches of that commission reflect the highest credit on its very able members, of whom Mr. Cleveland was the official head. Mr. Cleveland had much to do in aiding the very thorough investigation of the proper methods of budget reform embodied in the proposed New York Constitution of 1915. It is for these reasons that we may welcome this book from Mr. Cleveland.

WILLIAM HOWARD TAFT.

CONTENTS

CHAPTER XII

PART III. DETAILED ACCOUNTS OF THE CHARACTERISTICS AND OPERATION OF RECENT STATE ENACTMENTS PROVIDING FOR A BUDGET PROCEDURE

CHAPTER XIII

Contents

CHAPTER XIV

THE "EXECUTIVE BUDGET" IDEA AS EXEMPLIFIED IN ILLINOIS —
ITS ACCOMPLISHED RESULTS 240

CHAPTER XV

THE "COMMISSION BUDGET" IDEA AS EXEMPLIFIED IN WISCONSIN 256

CHAPTER XVIII

CHAPTER XIX

Contents xxxiii

PART I. HISTORIC BACKGROUND AND INTER-
PRETATION OF THE RECENT MOVE-
MENT FOR ADMINISTRATIVE
REORGANIZATION AND
BUDGET PRO-
CEDURE

THE BUDGET AND RESPONSIBLE GOVERNMENT

CHAPTER I

THE PRINCIPLES AND ESSENTIALS OF POPULAR CONTROL

THERE is no human phenomenon more depressing, no political condition more fraught with peril to society, than a government unsupported by the good will of the people — a condition which, unabated, causes increasing distrust and social unrest, leading, when long continued, to popular despondency or acts of violence. Under such circumstances no permanence can be given to the institutions to which society looks for its ministry of justice and service, except as such institutions can be maintained by an overriding and overruling militarism — the discipline enforced by a dominant autocracy.

Popular Good Will — the only Safe Foundation for Institution Building

Class rule in any form is autocratic. Autocracy in any form violates the most persistent and compelling ideals of group consciousness. And when group consciousness is awakened there is no resort for the maintenance of the established order except to corruption or terrorism. Both of these methods of control, when exercised by persons in authority, carry with them the seeds of destruction of the very institutions which autocracy seeks to protect.

3

Whether the governing class be an established nobility, a legalized aristocracy, an extra-legal plunder-bund, a privileged plutocracy, or a soviet of terrorists acceptable to a misguided proletariat, the continuing consent of other classes cannot be assumed. Every institution so set up rests upon a smoldering volcano.

Class Domination — the Cause of Social Unrest

The reason for this uncertainty and unrest is obvious. Both the *motive* and the *underlying assumption* of class rule are hostile to the ideals that move the masses. The usual motive of class rule is *exploitation*. The underlying assumption in every case is *superiority of the ruling class* — an assumption which, in the end, arouses the organized opposition of the masses. Both the motive and the assumption breed distrust in the government and resentment toward the governing class. For this reason any government which does not provide a means for the peaceable abatement of class rule as a condition which arouses continuing popular distrust and resentment must be prepared to meet its doom. The end is either economic and social degeneration, with corresponding political weakness, or revolution.

Need for Means of Peaceable Adjustment

The need for providing means of peaceable adjustment of institutions to social environment finds another justification — it is a condition essential to survival. Political institutions grow and are subject to much the same conditions as other living organisms. In the process of growth, class rule at some time or other asserts itself because of its temporary superiority — a superiority gained through leadership. But class rule is advantageous only so long as class leadership can appeal to, and obtain the support of, the masses, and the favoring condition is the absence of a nation-wide popular consciousness of desire for individual equality of opportunity. When such a consciousness is present class rule gives way to democracy, for the reason that only democratic leadership can command the confidence and support of the people. From class rule to democracy, however, is a long and devious road. Changes at best must come slowly. But politically organized peoples ultimately insist on change, when they become conscious of the need. Revolution cannot operate as a positive principle; its only service is negative. It may be highly serviceable, just as a great conflagration at times has proved to be. But constructively, as a method of adjustment, it is unfavorable to democracy. It is unfavorable because a revolution can be brought about only by class conflict; and, left to itself, in the end it establishes class rule — the danger being that the dominant class will seek to intrench itself in the newly established order.

Revolution — the Result of Lack of Means of Peaceable Adjustment

A war of defense against foreign aggression contributes to national unity of purpose and action, but revolution does not. Civil war may be necessary to break the domination of a ruling class which has become intrenched; but, as has been said, the immediate result, if the insurgents are successful, is to set up at least a temporary domination of another ruling class. The best that can come from revolution is a leadership, and a following favorable to the holding of governing powers in trust for all the people, till peace conditions may be reëstablished conformable to democratic ideals.

Realization of Ideals of Democracy — Essential to Peace

On the other hand, the ideals of democracy operating under conditions which admit of peaceable adjustment of existing institutions to meet social needs are such that, if realized, they make civil war impossible; for they contain in themselves the principles essential to the reconciling of class conflict and the inspiring of mutual confidence. They are ideals of social optimism. The vision of democracy is a vision of a society ruled by " justice." Peace is assured by a good will that rests on the consciousness that every man is ready to do his bit for the benefit of all — a concept of brotherhood that means that each person is a member of a family having common rights and opportunities.

What Is a Democracy?

A democracy is a politically organized society the members of which undertake, one with another, to accept, for purposes of control, the deliberate judgment of a majority. Institutionally, democracy means that the public agencies of the politically organized society shall be controlled by the will of a majority of its members and conducted for their benefit; or, to use the words of Lincoln, the demands of a democracy are that the " government of the people " shall in the last analysis be " by the people " and at all times be " for the people." In the exercise of popular control over the government, democracy means the decision of every question of public policy in accordance with the dictates of social conscience; it means that there must be a meeting of the minds of not less than a majority of the whole society as determined by a plebiscite or representative body, or both, instead of the society being subject to the dictates of a personal sovereign or the consensus of the minds of a minority as a dominant privileged class. It means rule by the consensus of public opinion, including all classes, arrived at after due deliberation; *i. e.*, after each question at issue has been clearly stated, the facts supporting the claims and contentions of all parties are made known, and the arguments of the recognized leaders of all parties have been heard. Democracy assumes, as a condition precedent to its successful operation, that means must be employed to give to its people full knowledge of facts and conditions, and the benefits of full discussion and interpretation, before a consensus of opinion is taken. Public opinion to be just, must be deliberate; and it is a primary duty of all democratic society to provide the means to make it such.

Where Justice Resides

Given adequate means of enlightenment, democratic justice rests on the superior rights of the whole people to sit in judgment. This superior right is insisted on, in order that the politically organized society may be assured that each decision will be consistent with commonly held ideals of " liberty," " equality," and " fraternity," as against the selfish desires of a class to establish an order of things favorable to an assumption of its own superiority — the notion that an individual or a class has a right to claim advantages and opportunities not enjoyed by others.

The language of democracy — that is, the terms in which the consensus of opinion shall express itself — needs no definition or elucidation because it proceeds from the thought of the people; the very essence of which is that they, the people who make the decision, shall insist on their own interpretation. For judgment, democracy assumes to need no guidance in arriving at conclusions consistent with group conscience other than that of its own chosen leadership. It only insists that it be informed and provided with a means of arriving at a consensus of opinion; that it be permitted to express its will; and that its decision, when reached, may be enforced.

By long experience it has been found that the most

human, the most just, the most socially sound, judgment on matters of right and duty is not the judgment of an individual or the judgment of a class, but the judgment of a majority of the whole society affected. Never has the question as to where justice resides, what is the best test to be applied to any matter of public policy, been more ably expressed than by Alexander Hamilton when discussing the virtues of democracy in a letter written to a farmer in 1775. He said: " The sacred rights of mankind, are not rummaged for among old parchments or musty records. They are written as with a sunbeam in the whole volume of human nature . . . and cannot be erased or obscured by mortal power."

There is a universal longing among mankind for " justice "— a justice which satisfies the desires of the human heart. And the most fundamental of all human desires is for that respect and opportunity which is expressed in demands for " equality." Equality of opportunity requires that each individual shall be free — hence the demand for " liberty." The most complete expression of this ideal is found in the common notion of " brotherhood."

Wherever there is class domination and exploitation this popular ideal of justice is violated and organized opposition is aroused. Individuals may object to popular notions of justice, carping critics may endeavor to show that in human society there can be no such thing as liberty, equality, and fraternity; but nevertheless these ideals persist and are made the basis for every appeal to group endeavor. They have been, are to-day, and ever will be the dominating motive in every democratic social action.

Present-day Meaning of " Liberty "

The voice of democracy speaks in terms of the highest inspiration of the human race. These ideals form the basis of social ethics. Under conditions of inequality enforced through institutional restraint, liberty has been given a negative meaning. But with slavery abolished, and the harshness of the law abated liberty becomes constructive. In our democratic society, liberty is interpreted as "the right of self-determination," and this right is given an unselfish meaning.

By "the right of self-determination" we mean the right of every individual to choose his own career and make the most of it, so long as thereby he does something that is serviceable to society. That is to say, democracy has no place for slackers; it demands service. And the liberty longed for by a democratic society is that each person must be free to choose how he shall undertake to serve himself by serving others.

In other words, the free will and choice of each man must always be subject to the right of the society of free men of which he is a part to decide what is serviceable and what is not. Thus the only restriction placed on the individual is the mandate of society that each man, in order to gain his liberty, shall go through the service gate; that he shall gain his freedom by service to his fellow men. This is the only view which is consistent with democratic notions of human happiness and common well-being.

Adopting this definition of liberty, only those who are not socially minded are not free. This view sets up no barriers except to those who would claim for themselves privileges which they would not accord to others. This is the ideal which marks the distinction between autocracy and democracy. Autocracy insists that a "divinely appointed" person or a privileged class must decide what is serviceable; democracy insists on the judgment of the whole political society, leaving to the individual, however, the fullest freedom to employ and develop his faculties and to express his deepest longings within the ever widening range of serviceable activities made possible by social coöperation.

Meaning of " Equality " and " Fraternity "

In our democratic society " equality " is interpreted to mean that each person shall have a like opportunity to achieve success in whatever specialized field of service to mankind he may choose; and " fraternity " is interpreted to mean that, by common consent, all are members of a political family whose supreme law is mutual consideration and a desire to serve others carrying with it acceptance of the principle that the individual shall at all times be ready and willing to subordinate self to the common good.

Democracy, in its present-day interpretation, therefore, carries with it the notion that service to one's fellows stands above self.   Or to put it in another way, each shall be free to find his greatest happiness in his own choosing to do things which are serviceable to the society of which he is a member, claiming for himself the success which those who are served may award.   It is in this concept of justice that the ideals of democracy begin and end.   In this philosophy there is no room for class domination and class exploitation.   Every individual and group accomplishment or success is the accorded measure of service, whether the rewards are material or otherwise; they are, nevertheless., the rewards to man by man for benefits conferred.

Practical Application of Concepts of Democracy

Making practical application of this concept of social justice to everyday affairs, it is insisted that society has the right, by well-considered majority opinion, to decide not alone what is serviceable and what is not, but also to decide what services can best be rendered through the government as its organ, and what can best be left to private arrangements or contract between individuals. Having decided that certain services can best be rendered through the government, it is for the society served to determine what shall be performed by national, state or local agencies, and how each shall be organized and controlled. With respect to that broad domain left to private initiative, it is for society to decide what may be performed by corporate and what by noncorporate agencies; what shall be regulated as public utilities and what left to private arrangements; what services offered to society shall have professional technical qualifications prescribed by law; what shall be regulated to insure health and safety and what not; what provision shall be made to prevent profiteering through capitalistic monopoly and control. In fact, every relation of life must come within the rule of democratic justice to have any status or right at all; and the rule of justice having been established no one has any right or reason to complain. He may seek change in the order of things, but unless and until his proposal meets with favorable consideration he must accept the judgment of mankind that what is, is right.

Thus the solid foundations of government and of all human institutions and all vested rights are to be found in the laws and customs of a contented people; in laws which express the will of a majority; in constitutions which leave to the people as a whole the right of self-determination, giving them the means of gradual growth in adaptation of their institutions to an ever changing environment. Accepting this as the paramount justice to be attained through adequate and effective means of popular control, it is conceived that every constituent part of society may find a place and be an element of strength in the structure reared for the continuing service and happiness of the people,— that the " government of the people, by the people, and for the people shall not perish from the earth," and that in even more perfect adaptation the spirit and the institutions of democracy may go on forever.

Need for Providing Organs of Volition as well as of Action

The practical problems of democracy lie in providing institutional means of self-expression: self-expression on matters of social justice; self-expression in the choice of effective instruments and agencies for individual and group accomplishment; self-expression in control over its corporate and governmental servants, its organs of collective action.

Wherever government rests on the popular will there must be organs of volition as well as for action — organs of popular perception, resolution, and control as well as agencies for rendering community service. That is to say, the mind of the nation must be organized as well as the body — a personnel must be provided for deliberation and expression of opinion, as well as a personnel for performing physical ministerial acts. In these two fields, the one for successful functioning of organs of volition, the other for the successful functioning of organs of administration, lie every problem of politics and government — every consideration which has to do with the formulation and outworkings of rules of justice and social conveniences as interpreted by group conscience and translated in action by the politically organized people — the state.

Two types of Organization and Leadership

Organization is a means; its success depends on adaptation to an end to be achieved. The whole purpose of organized effort is to get things done, which could not be so well done or at all if left to individual effort. The problem of democratically organized group action is to enable society to avail itself of the benefits of teamwork, and at the same time to enable the membership to control the team. Therefore, in a democracy there is something more to be done than in an autocracy; in an autocracy it is only necessary to provide the means for getting things done; in a democracy means must be found for making the doing organization responsive to the will of the people. To this end all democratically controlled group activities, whether political, industrial, social, or otherwise, must provide:

1. An organization and leadership which is effective for action, for teamwork in rendering service, for achieving results.
2. An organization and leadership for enabling the membership to determine what service or results are desired and to know whether the results which are achieved through teamwork are consistent with their determining will.

The first provision is essentially administrative, its end is ministerial; the second is a deliberative and inquisitional function. For the first, the form of organization and procedure must be suited to teamwork or effective group action; for the second, the form of organization and procedure must be suited to deliberation and inquisition — deliberation and inquisition which has for its purpose the arriving at conclusions through membership control. For the first, the leadership must be executive, directive — leadership in planning for the development of a subordinate organization for the execution of plans, in imposing a discipline which will assign to each man a part and make him promptly responsive to every executive order given; for the second, the leadership must be inspirational, and suggestive or critical as the case may require — leadership which foresees needs

for adaptation, proposes change, arrays facts and argu·
ment in an appeal to reason to win the approval or disapproval of a majority of the deliberative body with a
view to making this reflect the popular will.

This means that every coöperative body, if it is to
succeed in the achievement of its ends, must provide for
itself two groups of servants; that is, it must provide servants who are responsible as *doers*, and it must provide
servants who are responsible as *determiners*. It must
organize each of these groups of servants in a different
way, must arrange and dispose of the personnel of each
group in a manner adapted to performing these two essentially different functions. The one must be adapted
to rendering service — administration; and the other must
be adapted to ascertaining the will of members and impressing this will on the service group — the exercise of
popular or membership control.

The present purpose is to point to the principles and
essentials of popular control. But before doing so, it
may be helpful first to note the distinguishing characteristics of the organization upon which the will of the membership is to operate.

Essential Characteristics of Organization and Leadership for Action

The ministerial service, the organization of the mobile
service group, in order that it may achieve the purpose
for which the institution exists, must be so developed
that its leadership may be effective. The controlling law
of administration must be the law of obedience; its discipline must aim to develop in each member ability to
act in coöperation. And to accomplish this every individual and working group must respond to a dominating directive will. The rank and file must be made up of
superiors and subordinates, each subordinate in the organization being responsive and responsible to executive

authority.   There must be an attitude of respect; there
must be personal loyalty.   Such organization and discipline is necessary to get things done through teamwork
whether the institution, of which the serving group is a
part, be autocratic or democratic.

The difference between an autocracy and a democracy
lies not in its administrative organization, but in the absence or presence of a controlling electorate or representative body outside of the administration with power
to determine the will of the membership, and to enforce
the will on the administration.   To satisfy the requirements of a democracy, this nonadministrative controlling
group must be a voting personnel, an electorate, broad
enough to include all classes.   The working or administrative group must be controlled for the benefit of the
whole membership as its needs are adjudged by a majority.   To serve the purposes of a democracy, the administrative group has the same need of a directing executive, single or multiple, as in an autocracy.   Effective
coöperation is possible only when there is a supreme authority to command; but in a democracy this must be
amenable to a group not under the domination of the
executive but which rises superior to it in its power to
decide what the service organization shall be and who
shall be responsible for leadership.   But if the controlling
group is not to be destructive of its own purpose, it must
be able to enforce its decisions upon the service group
without interfering with its discipline.   Therefore the
controlling group must speak to the service organization
through its executive leadership.

*Essential Characteristics of Democratic Agencies for
      Deliberation and Decision*

Coming now to the principles which govern the organization and leadership of a popular controlling group,— to
be effective and at the same time democratic, each mem-

ber of it must be free, a law unto himself — the purpose
being through individual freedom to arrive at a group
opinion on any question brought up for decision, whether
it be a question ·of group policy, or a matter of inquest
into the acts and proposals of the executive,. or determination as to whether the executive is worthy of the
confidence and the authority reposed.   The purpose of
the organization and leadership of this controlling group
is: (1) to find out and state in form for consideration
what are the questions with respect to which the collective
judgment of a numerous voting membership is to be had;
(2) to provide a method of inquiry and discussion which
will get the question fully before this numerous membership with all its social and institutional implications;
(3) to put the question, after consideration, in such form
that it may be answered "yes" or "no," and to record
accurately the opinion of each person authorized to vote;
(4) to devise an effective procedure for impressing and
enforcing this collective judgment — the ascertained will
of the membership.

Essentials of Popular Control as Exemplified in Popular Assembly

In the outworking of a small local democracy the
problem of devising an organization and procedure to
make the controlling group effective is a simple one.
Nevertheless, its essentials are the same as must govern
the organization and procedure of the controlling group
in a populous, widely scattered democratic society.   For
this reason it seems worth while first to consider what
these essentials are as they find expression in the small
political unit.

In a simply democratic society the entire voting membership, or electorate, meet and organize themselves into
a deliberative, inquisitorial, and determining body.   Such
an organization is found in the New England township;

such were the folkmoots of the ancient Teutons and early English; such was the controlling group as first constituted by agreement on the *Mayflower* before the Pilgrim fathers set about founding a colony at Plymouth. In a controlling body of this kind the first business is to organize and to provide for leadership for purposes of deliberation. To this end a chairman or moderator is appointed to conduct the proceedings and to keep order, in which purpose he is assisted by one or more sergeants at arms. There is also a secretary to keep a record. Leadership is provided for by having matters of business brought forward in one of two ways: (1) by executives or officers of the administrative group who are called to account by having them appear before the controlling body to report on their stewardship — and to submit proposals for change in administrative law and grants of authority; (2) by members of the controlling group itself, each of whom on his own initiative may submit proposals for discussion and action.

In case a report or proposal is brought forward by an executive officer, it is presented to the whole body of voting members by the officer in person. After making his presentation he submits himself to questioning by any members of the controlling body who may desire further information. If the proposal comes from a member it is expected that it will be explained and defended by that member; and if the proposal calls for a committee as an aid to deliberative action it is usual to make the proposer the chairman of the committee — unless the motion for a reference to a committee comes from the opposition when the opposition leader should be in control of the committee. If opposition is developed which calls for action, the opposition or criticism must be offered in the presence of the leader criticized in order that he may be given full opportunity to explain and defend. In any case, every proposal must be presented by its sponsor in the form of a motion or resolve so stated that there can be no question about its meaning; and so stated that decision may be reached by a " yes " or " no " vote.

When issue is joined on any proposal, great care is taken not to have any uncertainty about it, a special procedure being used so as not to confuse the opposition or criticism with the original motion. An issue presented by an opposition must therefore be clearly set forth in the form of an amendment and a vote must be taken on the amendment before the main question is put. The purpose of this special procedure is to make the leaders take sides — to enable each member to know what each leader stands for when he makes an appeal for votes. Before a vote is taken, arguments are heard from the leaders of each party — those who are sponsors for the measure, and those who lead the opposition being required to submit to questioning by the voting members. It is only after each member of the deliberative body has had every chance to become informed that the matter in hand is then brought to a vote and decided. Thus every provision is made in order that every action by the controlling group may be taken after due consideration, and that the group opinion may be an act of deliberate judgment.

Procedure of Deliberation as Exemplified in Trial by Jury

This procedure, developed for insuring that group action shall be based on deliberation, is not alone confined to controlling bodies which sit in judgment on questions of social and political justice, as in a town meeting or a folkmoot; it is exemplified in Anglo-Saxon courts of justice for the application of rules of law and equity to controversies between individuals and the adjudication of vested rights. For this purpose a jury is chosen to sit as a small body of citizens so selected that they may act for, and express the opinion of, the community. This jury, together with a presiding officer, a judge, constitutes the popular forum. To the end that the court thus constituted may act with due deliberation, the following are considered as essentials:

(1) Before the trial or hearing begins, each party must be " in court; " *that is,* each must submit a carefully prepared statement of his claims, and, if there is any opposition, issue must be joined — there must be no doubt in the mind of the presiding officer and the parties concerned as to what is the question to be decided; in case motions and counter-motions are interposed those are taken up and disposed of by the court, one at a time.

(2) When the case is ready for hearing on its merits, each party has a right to be confronted by his adversary in order that he may hear his statements and criticisms, and answer them. The jury has the right to hear the evidence, and to listen to cross-examination of witnesses to test the creditability of the evidence submitted for its information.

(3) Before the jury is asked to vote each has a further right to be fully informed as to all pertinent facts and to hear arguments of the moving parties on the application of recognized and accepted principles of justice, to the facts as developed at the hearing.

(4) The hearing having been closed, each member of the jury, being fully informed as to the facts and contentions of parties, has a right to vote according to his own consciousness of right — the consensus of opinion arrived at thus being taken as the will of the whole political society,

> unless appeal is permitted and taken in a manner prescribed.

The jury system is a departure from the methods of direct democratic control in that a representative body takes the place of a meeting of the whole voting membership of the political society served. But the principles governing the deliberations of the jury are in effect the same as those governing the folkmoot. In fact, they are the recognized essentials of every deliberative body which is controlled by democratic ideals.

Procedure of Deliberation in Representative Government

It is only in a very small political society that all the voting members can get together personally to participate in deliberations which lead up to an expression of group opinion. It is found, however, that, when political societies grow beyond the possibility of such participation by the whole electorate, the representative principle, as in the case of the jury, may be effectively used. That is, practical application is given to democratic principles of control by creating an intermediate representative body to sit as a court of political inquest and deliberation in place of the electorate, the proceedings being so conducted that what takes place in the court may be known to, and reviewed by, the whole membership. In other words, a representative body is created to assist the electorate and to act for them on matters delegated to it. Thus the representation principle does not change the function of the electorate; it only changes the method of procedure whereby the electorate may be informed. The whole voting membership still retains the power of ultimate or supreme control. When inquest is made into the acts and purposes of an executive officer, the electorate, in theory at least, still retains the right to settle all issues on matters of public policy; it still retains the right to enforce its decisions and make the administrative organization and leadership subservient through " election " and " control of the purse." In a democracy, the electorate is the organ of society for giving voice to the will of the people; and where a representative body is interposed for purposes of inquest and discussion, it serves as a court of first instance, the electorate being the court of last resort.

Whether the practice coincides with the theory depends on the procedure developed and used (1) in the conduct of the deliberations of the representative body; (2) in provision made for giving publicity to its inquiries and discussions; (3) in the opportunity given to leaders for appeal to the electorate, and (4) in the methods employed for the conduct of the appeal to the people.

Procedure for the Conduct of Deliberation in Representative Assembly

Wherever the representative principle is applied, these proceedings are found by practical experience to be essentials to effective popular control; they are essentials because they are the processes by which the motor centers of the body politic are brought under the domination of the will of the people — the only processes by which popular sovereignty can be made real. It is important, therefore, that each of these processes be carefully worked out, reduced to a definite procedure, and that this procedure be protected and maintained, otherwise the processes of popular control may be prostituted to the purposes of class rule, and action taken of the people will not be deliberate.

It is necessary that all of the essentials of deliberative procedure be developed for the conduct of the business of the representative political branch of the government that by experience has been found necessary to the enlightenment of voting members of a folkmoot or a repre-

sentative court of justice. By no other process can the
members of the representative political body act intelligently in an effort to voice their own opinion or to voice
the will of their constituencies. For purposes of inquest into matters of administration, it is necessary that
the executive or responsible directing officer be brought
before those who are to sit in judgment: unless this is
done the members are deprived of opportunity to question them; unless this is done they must accept hearsay
evidence as to the facts; unless this is done no opportunity is given to members sitting as a political grand
jury to listen to cross-examination to test the creditability of witnesses; unless this is done the case of administration must be tried on information by star-chamber
proceedings — without opportunity to explain and defend
when changes are made, the purpose of which is to con-
vict them of malfeasance or nonfeasance or breach of
trust and to rob them of their " character " as public servants in the interest of persons of selfish design.   These
are essentials not alone to the protection of the public
servant, but also to the whole morale of institutions of
political and social justice.

How Publicity can be Given to Acts of Government

Provision must be made by the representative body for
giving publicity to its inquests and deliberations, for this
is the only way that a large and widely scattered electorate may become informed.   It is only through such
a procedure in the representative body as has been described, and a means of publicity which will make its acts
known to the people, that an informed public opinion
can be developed.   And in making such provision this
fact is to be borne in mind, that the only way that a city,
state, or nation can be kept informed is through the news
columns.   The proceedings of the representative body,
therefore, must be so staged and so conducted as to make

news. This means that the proceedings of inquest and deliberation of the representation must be conducted as a public forum in order that the whole people may " listen in " through the public press. This means that every issue must be dramatized; it means that the chief actors must be persons who will be listened to — that the great leaders must be brought upon the stage where those who are the recognized advocates of the people in the trial of issues of political and social justice may be pitted against each other. The scene in the forum in the trial of issues joined on questions of common welfare and justice, must be a battle of giants — recognized champions ultimately must stand before the whole electorate for a verdict of thumbs up or thumbs down. This is the purpose for which the representative body is created: to sit in council as the duly constituted forum of the people and try causes of political and social justice, and to do this in such a manner as not only to make the decision one of deliberative judgment, but to make every act and expression " visible " to the whole people. A primary essential, therefore, is a procedure which will make news of the inquiries, and deliberation of the causes which are being heard by the deliberative branch of the government involving questions of welfare and social justice.

The Need for Responsible Leaders

An opportunity must be given for appeal from the decision of the representative body to the whole electorate — that is, when the chosen leader of a majority in the deliberation body or responsible head of the administration whose acts are under review, may not deem the action taken to be to the highest interest of the public, opportunity should be given to sound public opinion though the electorate. It is only by giving an opportunity to leaders to make an appeal to the electorate as the final authority in a democracy that popular opinion can control. Nothing short of this will enable the people to express their will on issues that they have not already passed on, nothing short of this can prevent representative government being controlled by an oligarchy — a designing minority. Since group opinion organizes itself around the proposals of leaders in the representative body, it is only by giving to leaders the right of appeal that they can be made responsible to the people. In no other way can action or proposals for action be brought to a final test. And the appeal must be taken at the time when a question at issue is under discussion, when the facts and the arguments may be voted on without confusion. This is a recognized rule in every deliberative proceeding. It is even more important in making an appeal to the country than it is for obtaining a vote in the representative body.

Another principle must also be borne in mind: that in taking a vote on any question which involves executive responsibility or leadership, the continuing confidence of the people in the man is quite as important as the measure or act in controversy. Responsibility is a personal thing. The vote to be taken must therefore be a vote for or against the officer whose act or proposal has been the subject of inquest and deliberation in the forum of the people where the issue may first be tried. The initial proceeding must be had in a duly constituted forum, in order that the decision may be based on evidence, with full opportunity given for hearing and argument. It is only by such proceeding that a deliberate decision may be reached by the representatives. It is only after such a proceeding, with full publicity given, that judgment on appeal may be deliberate; it is only by process of appeal on a record thus developed that the electorate may act as a positive constructive force in voicing the popular will.

Appeals to the People

Appeal to the people must be taken before them and conducted by recognized advocates. If leadership is to be made responsible, these advocates before the people must be leaders; and the issues must be those actually developed in the transaction of the public business. This is vital to effective exercise of popular control. The process of appeal must necessarily be one of " election "—of choice between men who stand for measures. If the real leaders are not the ones who go before the people and if the issues which the people are asked to decide are framed *in camera*, by irresponsible persons or groups who have not been required to stand up in a forum constituted by the people for inquest, trial, and discussion, if the contest is not framed under such conditions that evidence can be adduced, witnesses examined and cross-examined, the whole process of popular appeal is degraded to a mock trial, and action by the people decides nothing except who, among irresponsible leaders, shall be given a chance to work out his selfish designs. Under such conditions the electorate has no opportunity to exercise its true constitutional function; and the Constitution itself, by which popular control is sought to be established, becomes a dead letter.

CHAPTER II

AMERICANS have been characterized as "a good-
natured people dominated by an irresponsible political
boss." This observation may have been apt in times
past, but it is not to-day. We are still dominated by an
irresponsible political boss, but we are no longer good-
natured about it. We resent the fact of this autocratic
control; we resent any characterization which assumes
that we willingly accept autocracy in any form — although we can not and do not deny that we are still a
boss ridden people. Every page of our political history
since the days of Jackson fairly shouts boss rule. And
it is a part of the personal experience of every citizen
that when one boss has been overthrown another has
stepped into his waiting shoes. Following every campaign to crush boss rule, "the system" has insidiously
found its way to the forefront of political organization
and leadership, first to surprise and later to madden the
people.

Attempts made to Account for "Social Unrest"

Many attempts have been made to account for this
most persistent of all our political phenomena. Some
have thought of it as an inherent weakness of democracy
— the only alternative remaining after monarchy and
aristocracy have been laid aside. Others have explained
it as an Americanism — the necessary political result of
a dominant commercialism. Still others have attributed
it to lack of public spirit on the part of our citizenry and

to an effort on the part of impractical reformers to detract from American institutions. Again it has been ascribed to a too rapid influx of foreign peoples.

Appeals to Patriotism to Maintain the Status Quo

In this time of great social unrest, not infrequently appeals are made to the patriotism of citizens to preserve the *status quo*. The value of such appeals is questioned. For, it is said, is not the fact of such widespread dissatisfaction in itself sufficient evidence that the *status quo* should not be preserved? In other words, when it is urged that institutions as they exist, in some important particulars, are not in keeping with common ideals of justice when they do not serve as instruments or means of expressing and serving those common purposes which give to the people their impulse to group action — in these circumstances all effort made to induce men to close their eyes to the things which offend common sense can have no other result than to weaken the government at is foundation.

Popular Concept of Right

This harks back to the principle laid down by Professor Giddings in his illuminating volume of lectures published under the title of " The Responsible State ": That the people insist on distinguishing between what is established by law and what is *right;* and that the " liberty " to make this distinction, to assert the judgment of the individual and the group as to what is *right* as distinguished from the *status quo,* is the fundamental on which responsible government rests. It is by reason of this fact that popular control is insisted on.

Evidence of Institutional Maladjustment

Instead of drawing our inspiration from those who appeal for the maintenance of the *status quo* as a patriotic duty at a time like this, instead of seeking to pillory those who point to institutional defects and maladjustments, it would seem the part of wisdom to heed the voice of popular protest, and to take the best advice which may be had for determining what is wrong — not with results, for the people themselves insist on being the judge of results — but with the institutions that have produced these results.

To make sure that our advisers have not lost perspective, let us go back to a period before the war, and before the days when those who ventured to criticize the government were labeled, when honest criticism was not considered dangerous, when the voice of dissent was a voice of protest that carried with it no threat of violence. And in looking back, let us go over again the pictures drawn by men of known conservatism and highest standing.

American Institutions as Appraised by James Bryce

First let us read again the pages of Bryce's "American Commonwealth." In this he repeatedly points to what we know to be institutional weaknesses in that they have developed inadequate means for recording public opinion, for impressing the will of the people on real issues. He points to what we know to be maladjustment in state and Federal Government and characterizes the government of our cities as a byword and a shame for Americans all over the world.

Shortcomings Described by President Wilson

In 1885, Woodrow Wilson, in a popular rendition of his scientific treatise on our Federal system, a work that gave to him a national reputation, said:

"For a long time this country of ours has lacked one of the institutions which freemen have always and everywhere held fundamental. For a long time there has been no sufficient opportunity of counsel among the people; no place or method of talk, of exchange of opinion, of parley. . . . Congress has become an institution which does its work in the privacy of committee rooms and not on the floor of the chamber. . . . Party conventions afford little or no opportunity for discussion; platforms are privately manufactured."

The Picture Drawn by Senator Hoar

And in support of this conclusion Mr. Wilson quotes from Senator Hoar, one of the oldest and best informed men in American public life. · After describing the Congress as a body which had lost its character as a national public forum — as having abdicated its powers and turned over the work of deliberation to its standing committees — to a large number of " little legislatures " that do business behind closed doors — he says:

" Hundreds of measures of vital importance receive — near the close of an exhausted session, without being debated, printed, or understood — the constitutional assent of the representatives of the American people."

Mr. Wilson, commenting on the results of this evident perversion of representative government, further says:

" Our legislation is conglomerate, not homogeneous. The doings of one and the same Congress are foolish in pieces and wise in spots. They can never, except by accident, have any common features. . . . Only a very small part of its most important business can be done well; the system provides for having the rest of it done miserably and the whole of it taken together done haphazard."

Since that time he has continued to hold this picture

up before the American people.   In 1912, in his campaign
for the presidency, this portrayal was repeatedly used.
with new setting, and the lesson was drawn therefrom
— that the people had lost control over their government; that this was a system which lent itself to the
uses of persons seeking and enjoying special privilege;
that it was undemocratic; that it could lead to nothing
but lack of confidence in our government, popular distrust, and discontent.

President Roosevelt's Stand

President Roosevelt, differing widely from Mr. Wilson
both in temperament and in politics, spent his whole life
in calling the people to a realization of their duties and
opportunities as citizens; and his whole life stands out
as a protest against the practices and methods which had
deprived the people of their right to control the government.   And as he ripened in years and experience it was
this moral aspect of public duty that led him to stand
forth as leader of a new party — in doing which he was
vigorously condemned by his opponents as leading a
popular movement which, if successful, would undermine
and destroy American institutions.

Proposals of Governor Hughes

But even the most conservative have recognized that
the basis for criticism was sound — that there was serious
need   for   institutional   change.   In   1910,   Governor
Hughes of New York in his annual message to the legislature pointed to cogent reasons why the people of that
state had irresponsible government.   And in doing so was
among the first of a long line of governors who rendered
a like service.

Defects Described by President Taft

President Taft, whose judicial mind led him to consider

the problem of administration and the discharge of executive duty as consciously as if he were sitting in a court of equity, in a special message to Congress, transmitting one of the reports of the commission appointed by him " to inquire into the methods of transacting the public business " in June, 1912, said:

" Generally speaking, however, the only conclusions which may be reached from all this are that:

" No regular or systematic means has been provided for consideration of the detail and concrete problems of the government.

" A well-defined business or work program for the government has not been evolved. . . .

" The committee organization is largely the result of historic development, rather than of a consideration of present needs."

Causes of Popular Resentment Described by Senator Root

With respect to the political aspects of institutional maladjustment in this country, no one has more faithfully portrayed the causes of popular resentment and social unrest than Senator Elihu Root. Standing before the Constitutional Convention of New York in the summer of 1915, after weeks had been spent by members considering what changes should be made to make the government more responsive to public opinion, and to provide the means of enforcing accountability, Mr. Root stepped out of the chair to present what to him seemed an outstanding fact — a condition that could not be overlooked by men who had been sent to Albany by the people to readjust the governmental organization. In the course of his remarks, he went to the very vitals of the problem by making the following statement:

"I am going to discuss a subject now that goes back to the beginning of the political life of the oldest man in this convention, and one to which we cannot close our eyes, if we keep the obligations of our oath. We talk about the government of the constitution. We have spent many days in discussing the powers of this and that and the other officer. What is the government of this state? What has it been during the forty years of my acquaintance with it? The government of the constitution? Oh, no; not half of the time, nor halfway. When I ask what do the people find wrong in our state government, my mind goes back to those periodic fits of public rage in which the people rouse up and tear down the political leader, first of one party and then of the other party. It goes back to the public feeling of resentment against the control of party organizations, of both parties and of all parties.

"Now, I treat this subject in my own mind not as a personal question to any man. I am talking about the system. From the days of Fenton, and Conkling, and Arthur, and Cornell, and Platt, from the days of David B. Hill, down to the present time, the government of the state has presented two different lines of activity, one of the constitutional and statutory officers of the state, and the other of the party leaders — they call them party bosses. They call the system — I do not coin the phrases, I adopt it because it carries its own meaning — the system they call 'invisible government.' For I do not remember how many years, Mr. Conkling was the ruler of the states; the governor did not count, the legislature did not count, comptrollers and secretaries of state and what not did not count. It was what Mr. Conkling said; and in a great outburst of public rage he was pulled down.

"Then Mr. Platt ruled the state; for nigh upon twenty years he ruled it. It was not the governor; it was not the legislature; it was not any elected officers; it was Mr. Platt. And the capitol was not here [at Albany]; it was at 49 Broadway, with Mr. Platt and his lieutenants. It makes no difference what name you give, whether you call it Fenton or Conkling or Cornell or Arthur or Platt, or by the names of men now living. The ruler of the state during the greater part of the forty years of my acquaintance with the state government has not been any man authorized by the constitution or by the law; and, sir, there is throughout the length and breadth of this state a deep and sullen and long-continued resentment at being governed thus by men not of the people's choosing. The party leader is elected by no one, accountable to no one, bound by no oath of office, removable by no one."

This was in 1915. It is the statement of a man who was an honored member of Mr. Roosevelt's cabinet, and who, though he has always been clear of vision, incisive in analysis, and outspoken in the advocacy of institutional adaptations, when needed, is considered as without any of the aberrations of an emotionalist — at all times " safe and sane." And what was his vision of the pressing need, the remedy demanded to cure this " deep and sullen and long-continued resentment "? He did not prescribe palliatives or narcotics; he did not propose to take away the constitutional guaranties of free speech and free press; he prescribed surgery — some far-reaching orthopedic surgery to be performed on the government itself. He also proposed breaking up the adhesions that had been established between the " irresponsible party " organization and the agencies of public service; he proposed the normal functioning of the body politic and to this end the reëstablishing of the nerve centers of popular control. The high purpose which he urged upon American citizenship and American statesmanship was " to destroy autocracy and restore power so far as may be to the men *elected* by the people, *accountable* to the people, *removable* by the people."

The Need for an Institutional Means of Obtaining Expression of Popular will based on "Deliberation"

This is a vision that goes back to Jefferson, "America's great prophet of democracy," who before the advent of this malignant growth on the body politic which has come to be popularly described as the "boss and his machine," laid down what he regarded as the laws of democratic institutional hygiene.   The ideals of democracy have not been misunderstood.   At no time when any great issue has been presented has there been any uncertainty about what was conceived by the people as *right*. There has been no cause for questioning the right-mindedness of the people.   The great problem of democracy has been and ever will be to develop an organization and a leadership which is serviceable — institutions by and through which the servants of the people may be made responsive and responsible to the will of the people.   How may the *will of the people* be an expression of *deliberate judgment* instead of an outburst of passion after "deep and sullen and long-continued resentment" has destroyed faith and given to the institutional firebrand a dangerous following?   This is the real problem before us.

Standard for Judgment of Institutional Fitness

For Americans there can be but one standard for judgment as to whether, amid the shifting scenes of an ever-widening pluristic life, their welfare institutions need modification, and that is the standard laid down by every great interpreter of democracy.   It is the standard which Edmund Burke had in mind when he said:

" If any one ask me what a free government is, I reply it is what the people think so."

This is the standard which President Hadley of Yale had in mind when he said:

" The thing that governs us is public opinion — not the nominal public opinion of creed and statute book, but the real public opinion of living men and women.

" Liberty is essential to progress, democracy is needed to prevent revolution, constitutional government is requisite for that continuity and orderliness of living without which no worthy life is possible.

" Democracy is right when it is used as a means of keeping the government in touch with public opinion, it is wrong when it encourages a temporary majority to say that their vote, based on insufficient information or animated by selfish motives, can be identified with public opinion concerning what is best for society as a whole.

" Constitutional safeguards are absolutely necessary to make any measure of liberty or democracy possible; but when they are used to protect the liberties of a class bent on its own interest rather than on the general interest of society, they cease to be a safeguard and become a source of peril."

Wanted — an Effective Mechanism of Popular Control

For democratic institutions there can be but one foundation — the common sense of justice, the right-mindedness of an intelligent, patriotic people, who believe in what is because they have the institutional means of expressing their will and impressing it on their governmental and service agencies through an outstanding, farsighted, clear-thinking leadership, whose acts and proposals are at all times open to public scrutiny, and whose powers rest on the confidence and support of a majority of the people.

The present-day problem of democracy is primarily a problem of institutional mechanics — or to use a figure which carries with it the notion that institutions are living organisms, a problem of hygiene. It is only when a mechanism or an organism is kept in constant repair and adjustment, that it may be of continuing service and saved from an appraisal which condemns it as unfit. The American people know that their institutions are right in principle and fundamentally sound; they also know that in the conflicts of contending interest, the efforts of some to maintain the *status quo* and of others to bring about readjustment, there can be only one place where the power to decide questions of policy can safely reside, namely: in the people themselves. They know that whatever be the cost of overhauling or readjustment, American institutions cannot be reconciled with the demands of a right-minded nation unless they provide for an effective means of popular control. This is a part of the mechanics of institution building to which too little attention has been given.

This is a matter to which the conservative well wishers of America should give prayerful consideration. In these days when men by the million are ready to make the supreme sacrifice to make the world safe for democracy there must be unrest until institutional adjustments are made whereby the voice of its people may be impressed on their leadership and through majority leadership on the government — until American institutions and rights may rest on the abiding faith of citizens that the prevailing ideals of right, the commonly accepted notions of individual, political, economic and social justice inspirit those who are entrusted with the exercise of the nation's sovereign powers.

CHAPTER III

FOUR conditions are essential to stable, effective
democratic government: (1) consciousness of *common
ideals and purposes* to be realized: (2) *organization to*
secure these ends; (3) *leadership*, as an essential to cooperation: (4) *popular control* to make the organization
and leadership consistent with the conscious ideals and
purposes of those who are served. The American
people as a whole have been moved by the highest ideals.
They have developed a genius for organization. But in
government they have purposely deprived themselves of
responsible leadership and, consequently, have not developed an effective mechanism of control over leadership.
In other words, the means for making popular control
effective being lacking, leadership has been irresponsible
and the government has not been popular.

Popular Control the Essence of Democracy

Popular control is the very essence of democracy. But
to make popular control effective it is necessary to provide a mechanism by which the popular will can function — an effective method of enabling the people to know
currently what is being done or proposed, of determining
what the popular will is and of impressing this will on
governing agents. This mechanism or procedure must
be developed not in the administrative branch, but outside of it, with a view to exercising control over it. There
is a distinction to be made between the machanism of a

people for developing power, and the mechanism for controlling its development and use. The *administrative branch* is the power mechanism. The *deliberative branch and the electorate* are the mechanism of control. The principle cannot be too much magnified, that the purpose of a mechanism of control is not to develop or to use power, but to regulate the development and use of power; in a democracy its purpose is to enable the people through their representatives to make their political engines and all the machinery of public service responsive to their will.

How Popular Control is Made Effective Through Representatives

The method by which this may be done effectively finds apt illustration in the method used by the Allied Powers during the World War. The movements of all the shipping of the world were controlled through " the bunker privilege." That is, the representatives of the Allied Powers having gained control over necessary supplies, the " council " did not take away from the shipping companies and agencies their leadership, but they undertook to control the companies and agencies by controlling their leadership. To do this the council required each captain of each ship, the active executive, to tell in such detail as was desired what he proposed to do before further supplies were made available. Then, if a satisfactory statement were made, he was given as much of each kind of supply needed as was deemed necessary to carry him to another port where supplies could be furnished subject to the same scrutiny and control. And in case he did not give a satisfactory account of his sailing or if he so conducted the vessel as to seem to be untrustworthy, further supplies were denied until some one else, in whom the representatives of the Allied Powers had confidence, was put at the helm. This method of enforcing accountability, it is to be noted, not only placed control of supplies in a representative council, but presumed that the captain was responsible for the crew under him and was able to protect his own responsibility through the authority which he had over his crew without any intermeddling with the discipline of the crew by the council.

The American people are sailing a large fleet, comprising a flagship, the Federal Government, and forty-eight regular line ships of state, each of which is accompanied by from fifty to five hundred lesser auxiliary craft. The organization and mechanism of control over this great fleet, the process of forcing responsibility upon the captain and crew of each craft, large or small, are of the utmost importance. The question of control over government is as important as " liberty " or " justice " or " general welfare." It involves the vital interests and opportunities of every citizen and every group.

Restatement of the Problem

Organization and leadership in a democracy must be of two kinds: 1. the organization and leadership for the flagship and each of these ships of state, *the administration;* 2. organization and leadership for purposes of citizen control — *a representative body and an electorate.* Budget making is only a process in the operation of the mechanism of popular control over government by which the people have given over to their representative councils control over all needed supplies; a means by which they expect the council to exercise control over the public service through the bunker privilege. Thus the budget comes to be a matter of supreme importance. To repeat the much-quoted statement of Gladstone, the greatest political mechanician that the Anglo-Saxon race has produced: " Budgets are not merely affairs of arithmetic, but in a thousand ways go to the root of the pros-

perity of individuals, the relations of classes and the
strength of kingdoms."

Budget making is something which, if made functional, must be integrated with that part of our moral
philosophy which concerns itself with the popular will.
That is, the budget making process, if it is to be made
effective for purposes of control in a democracy, must
be a means of enabling the representative branch of the
government to reach to the popular consciousness, find
its final authority in the will of the people, as it is given
expression by the electorate. This is what gives discussion of the mechanics of administration and the procedure of budget making a place in the literature of democracy.

An East Indian View

There is a point of more than passing interest in the
observation made by an East Indian philosopher while
visiting America. Being asked about the attitude of his
people toward the British rule, he said:

" The British do the rough work of government very
well. They seem to like that sort of thing and we are
glad to be rid of it. Other people gifted in the art of
organization have come down upon India and taken over
her public service. To some we paid very dearly and
got little in return. But the British — they are good
servants; they are courteous; and on the whole they have
proved to be honest. They do the rough work of keeping order; they protect our borders from invaders; they
carry the mail and parcels; they build and repair our
roads, clean our streets and do a lot of other useful things,
so that we are free to do pretty much as we choose."

Kipling in his " White Man's Burden " has stated the
most up-to-date British imperialistic theory of the service
rendered to dependent peoples.

The East Indian's idea of freedom was that he had a

white man working for him. It differs radically from ours in one respect, but it is quite consistent with it in another. The idea that government exists to serve the people is a fundamental principle of democracy. The individual member of a democratic society is usually glad enough to be rid of the "rough work" of satisfying those wants which common necessity and convenience create — glad to be rid of the need of carrying a gun and of bearing the burdens incident to life in a primitive society in which each man or family stands alone as an isolated protective and producing unit. He is glad to avail himself of broader and still broader coöperation made possible through a well-ordered and highly developed and centralized public service, provided this is subservient to public opinion — to the will of the majority.

Democracy Insists that Leadership shall be Subservient

But democracy has no sympathy with, or interest in, any philosophy which stops short of popular control over government. It insists upon political as well as individual freedom. It conceives that without the right of group self-determination, individual liberty has no guaranty; that members of the group have the right to organize and decide what laws they shall have for the regulation of their conduct, so that each may have equal opportunity and each may enjoy the full benefit of association; that members have a right to settle among themselves which services or activities shall be left to individual initiative and which shall be organized and conducted in common. These are matters to be determined by representative and electoral common sense and not by benevolent paternalism.

Democracy must possess and control all of the organized means of protecting its interests as it understands them. In other words, the people themselves must be master of those who master the ship; through the master

they must control the crew.   This is what must be done
if they act positively.   They may, however, act negatively
and tie up the ship.   When, therefore, those who are
employed or who by self-appointment undertake to do
" the rough work " in rendering common service incur
the displeasure and lose the confidence of those whom
they serve, it is time to change servants rather then stop
the service by embargo; and if those who are in possession of the implements and institutions of service use the
resources of the people to fortify themselves and remove
themselves from popular control, democracy claims the
right to tear down such part of their institutions, public
and private, as give them shelter, to enable the people to
put an end to practices hostile to concepts of justice.
This is the right of control by revolution — the fundamental doctrine of the Declaration of Independence.   But
democracy does not stop here.   Revolution, though justi-
fiable under circumstances such as are described in the
Declaration, is tyrannical and wasteful.   The only useful thing about it is the social impulse which it serves.

Jefferson's Four Principles of Popular Control

The highest welfare of the people depends on dis-
covering some method of control which will not require
a democracy to tear down its house in order to oust its
distrusted servants.   The author of the Declaration of
Independence did not stop in his thinking about democracy with a formulation of the right of revolution.   Just
twenty-five years after the Declaration was signed (July
4, 1776), lacking three months, on the fourth of March,
1801, Jefferson put forth another declaration of principles which, in his opinion, would, if applied, make revolution unnecessary.   Independence had then been won;
threatened war with France had been averted — and no
foreign foe threatened; a constitution of perpetual union
had been adopted; a new house of their own design had

been built by the people to live in; and for twelve years
(1789 to 1801) the same servants (the Federalists) had
been employed to run it.   But in this new house there
had been trouble between the servants and the members
of the household.   Many of the latter complained that the
former were seeking to free themselves from control.
There was growing discontent among the people, at
times bordering on revolt.

When in 1801, Jefferson, America's first great apostle
and prophet of democracy, on the occasion of his inauguration as President addressed his fellow country-
men he protested against the aristocratic tendencies of
those in control of the Federal Government.   He was
not, however, opposed to the federal idea; he urged
federal union.   On this occasion he urged its preservation "in its whole constitutional vigor."   He characterized the federal charter "as the sheet anchor of our
peace at home and safety abroad."   By him it was re-
vered as a holy creed, an object of high inspiration, a
vital thing set up by the fathers "to establish justice, to
insure domestic tranquillity, provide for the common
defense, promote the general welfare, and secure the
blessings of liberty to themselves and their posterity."
To make sure that the Federal Constitution might be preserved, he laid down in his inaugural address, at a time
when his political enemies had cast doubt on the sanity
of his views, what he understood to be the principles of
democracy.   Among these he gave voice to the following principles of popular control:

(1) "A jealous care of the right of election by the
people — a mild and safe corrective of abuses which are
lopped by the sword of revolution where peaceable
remedies are unprovided;

(2) "Absolute acquiescence in the decisions of the
majority, the vital principles of republics from which
there is no appeal but to force;

(3) " The diffusion of information and the arraignment of all abuses at the bar of the public reason."

Another principle, not listed by him, was included in the concluding paragraph of the address:

" Relying, then, on the patronage of your good will I advance with obedience to the work, ready to retire from it whenever you become sensible how much better choice it is in your power to make."

Jefferson's mind was not analytical, nor did he have Gladstone's faculty for institutionalizing ideals, but he was gifted with clear vision and sound instinct in things democratic, and in enumerating what he believed to be the fundamentals of democracy, he included the four principles which have subsequently been adopted and enlarged upon, recognizing them as essential to an effective mechanism of popular control over government. These essentials may be expressed as: (1) popular election; (2) acceptance of the judgment of the majority as a rule of political justice; (3) arraignment of persons at the head of the administration for trial on evidence; (4) the right of appeal to the electorate or popular recall — in the broad sense in which that term is hereinafter employed.

It must be remembered that not one of these four principles of control had been institutionalized up to that time either here in America or in any other country; neither had executive. leadership become fully institutionalized on lines adapted to popular control. A mechanism of efficient service was not as yet developed here; and the mechanism of popular control by any method other than revolution was as yet experimental or wholly undeveloped in any country. America was far in advance in devising a government which frankly rested on popular sovereignty, and Jefferson's administration went far to prove its ability to weather the storms of class conflict. In this, the newly founded government proved to be a success beyond the wisdom of its authors, and despite the predictions of contemporaries.

The Federal Constitution having been set up, an aristocracy reached out for and obtained control over the government; and Jefferson went before the public as the apostle of popular control — his preachment being that the masses, not the classes, should rule. Here were the principles that in his opinion were to be adhered to in order to make democracy safe. As in the case of the principles of mechanics, means had to be found for their integration into the scheme of things with which men work, in order to make them of practical consequence.

The Principle of Popular Elections

As suggestive of the fundamental importance of these four principles and also indicative of the time required for an institutional overhauling in the process of adjusting new devices, these facts should be noted: It was not until after a half century of agitation and two partisan overturnings here in America, the Jeffersonian and the Jacksonian, that manhood suffrage took electoral control out of the hands of the propertied classes. In most of our states where women have not yet been permitted to vote, the " right of election by the people " is still an issue. In Great Britain, electoral adjustment to a basis of manhood suffrage came later and more slowly, beginning with the Reform Act of 1832 and continuing to the present time.

Acceptance of the Principle of Majority Rule

Great Britain has long been schooled in the principle, " acquiescence in the decisions of the majority." But it has only a qualified meaning. The controversy over the right of the House of Lords to overrule the Commons — the representatives of the people — was not finally settled until the twentieth century, and even now, the

will of a majority of the representatives of the people
may be held in abeyance till confirmed by subsequent
expression. In America, at the time of the adoption
of the Constitution, there was great fear of majorities;
and it was not until after the failure of many efforts to
thwart the will of the majority, including the Whisky
Rebellion, the movements culminating in the Kentucky
and Virginia Resolutions, the Hartford Convention,
South Carolina's Nullification, and the Civil War, that
the operation of this principle, as far as provided for in
the Constitution, came to be accepted in its national application.

Arraignment of Administration in Representative Forum

The importance of the third principle (the "arraignment of all abuses at the bar of public reason" and the
"diffusion of information") can be fully appreciated
only as we weigh Jefferson's words. Jefferson was a
lawyer. To him the word "arraignment" must have
had a significance quite different from "accusation" or
"condemnation" or other words simply implying individual denunciation or public appeal. "Arraignment"
implies three things: A person or persons responsible
for some fault or abuse; an information or indictment
by a responsible person; a duly constituted tribunal for
the determination of the facts and application of rules
of justice.

Whether the Constitution was set up by an aristocracy
or a democracy, this was thought of as essential to responsible government, to the enforcement of political
as distinguished from legal responsibility. The Magna
Charta was forced upon King John by a group of aristo-
crats who commanded in their armed retainers the force
necessary to apply the principle of control by revolution,
if the principle of continuous control by peaceful means

was not accepted.   More than six hundred years after the
barons at Runnymede had made their experiment, in the
mechanics of control over government, after autocracy
had gradually yielded to democracy as the controlling
force in the English state, John Stuart Mill gave it as
his view that the following were the true functions of the
House of Commons:

"To watch and control the government; to throw the
light of publicity on its acts; to compel a full explanation and justification of all of them which any one considers questionable; to censure them if found condemna-
ble; to be at once the nation's committee on grievances;
an arena in which not only the opinion of the nation, but
that of every section of it, as far as possible, of every
eminent individual that it contains, can produce itself
in full sight and challenge full discussion."

In other words, Mill's view was that the representative, deliberative, appropriating body was not a mechanism for leadership but a mechanism for the exercise of
control over leadership.   This was his contribution to
a broad propaganda which was then in progress in England under the leadership of Gladstone, the aim of which
was to perfect the processes and institutional adjustments necessary to make the third Jeffersonian principle
of control effective in the English system of government.
Early in the century, about the time of Jefferson's inaugural, the first step in this direction was taken in England by establishing the principle of responsible leadership, the principle, namely, that if anything goes wrong,
some one must be answerable for it, some one must be
"arraigned at the bar of public opinion."   That person
was the prime minister.   And to make responsibility certain, it came to be accepted that his whole cabinet was
on trial, on the theory that the prime minister was responsible for them and that they must stand or fall to-

gether.   This was a measure of justice, since it at once
insured loyalty to leadership and provided for locating
responsibility.

The next step was to constitute the House of Commons
a court of inquest.   The rule of " Cabinet solidarity "
made certain that the prime minister would be brought
before this court to give an account of his stewardship
and that his colleagues must share in paying the penalty
if anything went wrong.   A regular form of accounting
and trial practice was provided for in the budget procedure.   When an accounting was to be had, the membership of the House was organized as a jury sitting as
a committee of the whole.   Provision was made which
required members of the administration requesting funds
to be present to explain past acts.   Provision was made,
also, for the three essentials of trial practice in a jury
proceeding: (1) the party arraigned had a right to be
confronted by his adversary — the accuser must be
brought face to face with the accused; (2) each party
had a right to be represented by counsel — their leaders;
(3) when Gladstone came to power and found that provision was lacking for trying the administration on evidence, he proposed, and during the later sixties his proposals became laws, that each member of the House
should be provided with the means for having every act
of the administration involving money transactions reviewed and reported on with approval or disapproval by
an officer of the House to be called Comptroller and
Auditor General.   This official was placed beyond the
reach of the administration by being given an independent
status with tenure for life.   Gladstone also insisted that
his political adversaries, the organized " opposition," be
given every facility for informing themselves in order
that the " indictment " or " information " on which the
administration was arraigned might come from a responsible party.   That is, he insisted that if the cabinet

was to be held responsible for its acts, through leadership, the opposition should also be made responsible for criticism through leadership, the Parliament and the nation to be the judges as to which leadership would be supported. But to make the opposition leadership responsible, as critic, it was necessary that every opportunity be given for obtaining information, and for arraignment of the administration — the only limitation being that the accuser should be required to confront the accused, and that the issue should be tried before the whole membership with both parties present. This procedure not only gave to England responsible leaders, but also responsible parties, since the parties consisted of those who stood for or against the leadership of the administration. In order that the opposition might be made responsible, Gladstone insisted that there should be a Committee on Public Accounts, the chairman of which was to be a member of the opposition, which would have power during sessions and between sessions to inquire into the acts of the administration — with access to public records and the right of subpœna. That enabled the members to have the best evidence. The Auditor's critical report filed at the beginning of the session was referred to this committee, the staff of the comptroller and auditor general being available to help the committee to a complete understanding of the facts. He also insisted that when the budget and the accounts of the administration were presented, each member of the House, the trial jury, should be given fullest opportunity to question, criticize, offer evidence, and propose votes of censure. All this was to be done openly, and with the members of the administration arraigned to answer all questions and defend, so that members of Parliament and the people would not be misinformed when the time came for them to vote. These where the institutional adjustments which were worked out largely under the leadership of

Gladstone to make the third Jeffersonian principle of popular control effective in England, while we in America were trying by civil war to establish the second.

The Right of Leaders to Appeal to the People from Decision of Representative Body

England was the first country to make effective the fourth principle, the right of appeal to the people — an effective means of recall in case it is found on appeal that the executive on the one hand or a majority of the representative body on the other did not have the support of the people in the issue on which appeal was taken. During the half century following Jefferson's statement of principles, coincident with the establishment of the solidarity of cabinet responsibility, the passage of the reform acts and the definition of trial practice before the committee of the whole, the crown was made a part of the machinery of control over the executive. After the cabinet became responsible, the crown, no longer the head of the administration, was made to represent sovereignty of the whole nation, so far as the king functioned at all politically; on the crown was placed responsibility for administering the principle of appeal to the people. To this end a rule was adopted, that, in case there should develop a deadlock between the executive (the prime minister and his cabinet) and the House (as a court of inquest representing the people), it was incumbent on the crown, with the consent of the prime minister, to ask some one else to organize a cabinet which would have the confidence and support of the majority; but if the prime minister thought that the majority in the House did not fairly represent the people on the issue in question, and that the people would support him and defeat the hostile majority in the House, then it was made the duty of the crown to call an election. This placed "the people" in control. It made popular sovereignty real. Thus it was by a gradual process that the millwrights of English democracy worked out a mechanism for making the last two of the four principles of popular control over their government effective.

Experience of Other Countries

As a further sidelight on these principles first stated by Jefferson, it is of interest to note what happened during this time in some of the other countries which adopted constitutional forms of government. In France, the principles of popular election, acceptance of the decision of a majority, and popular recall by dissolution administered through an elected president, were developed; but an effective procedure for the arraignment of the administration before the bar of public opinion for trial on evidence was not devised. There, as with us, the principle of responsibility is still confused; the cabinet is required to come before the assembly, but does not have to stand or fall as a man; the prime minister and cabinet are not responsible in the same direct way as in England through control over supplies, but the estimates of each minister go before a legislative budget commission, and the commission, selected from the whole House by lot, submits the financial plan for action. Leadership and responsibility for the project as presented is in the commission. Many eminent Frenchmen have long been working for a more effective trial practice which would place responsibility on the executive and hold him to account to the assembly as a court of inquest, and to insure that the action taken would be on evidence, instead of on gossip and impulse. The French practices have been severely criticized by men like M. Ribot as conducive to patronage and waste. Their criticisms translated into English might be mistaken for excerpts from our *Congressional Record*.[1]

In the German Empire none of the four principles of popular control were made effective.

In Canada the principles of popular election, acceptance of the decision of the majority, and recall, are in full and effective operation, but the third principle (the arraignment of the administration before the bar of public opinion to be tried on evidence) has been made ineffective. This has come about in a very interesting way. While all of the machinery developed under the leadership of Gladstone was imported into Canada, in the British North America Act and subsequent statutes, it has been so run as to defeat its purpose. The Committee on Public Accounts, instead of being made an effective agency for arguing the case against the administration, by being put under the leadership and control of the opposition has been subordinated to the control of the cabinet, the very persons to be investigated. Instead of being an effective means of enabling the representative body "to watch . . . the government; to throw the light of publicity on its acts; to compel full explanation of all of them which any one considers questionable," it has been appropriated by the majority and used to enforce " gag rule." The office of each minister, as a result, has become a political bargain counter for the dispensing of " patronage " and " pork," as it is called on this side of the line, with little opportunity given to the opposition leaders to let the people and their representatives know what the facts are before a vote is taken — and the vote has been largely a matter of testing irresponsible party loyalty.

Neglect of Last Two Principles in United States

Now to return to the outworkings of these principles

[1] See Réné Stourm, "Le Budget," translation published by Institution of Government Research, Washington, 1917, page 59.

in the United States.   As has been said, we have given
much thought to the first two principles of popular control laid down by Jefferson in 1801.   The vote-casting
mechanism has been worked out fairly well — by ex-
tension of the suffrage, corrupt practice acts, and adoption of the Australian and other systems of secret ballot;
and since the Civil War, the principle of majority rule,
so far as this is provided for or permitted under our
constitutions, has not been challenged by organized force,
although threatened on at least one occasion — that of
the Hayes-Tilden election.   The first two principles have
thus been developed in practice in a sufficiently satisfactory manner, but they have been ineffective for purposes of popular control for a very simple reason.   This
is because the other two necessary parts of the mechanism
of popular control have not been worked out; and those
which have been developed, being without the complementary parts, were geared up with the existing institution in such a way as periodically to put the stamp of
popular approval on the very thing that the mechanism
of control was designed to prevent — irresponsible government.

CHAPTER IV

A CONSTANT danger to democracy is to be found in those political neuropsychic disorders — the symptoms of which are class rule and the social demoralization which attends; it must be the constant care of statesmen to prevent these disorders.

The Boss — the Product of Conditions

Any study of political pathology must begin with knowledge of the anatomy and physiology of a healthy organism. Samuel P. Orth, discussing " The Boss and the Machine," makes an observation which is worthy of more than passing thought.

" It was discovered early in American experience that without organization, issues would disintegrate and principles remain but scintillating axioms. This necessity enlisted executive talent and produced a politician who, having achieved an organization, remained at his post to keep it intact between elections and used it for purposes not always prompted by public welfare " (p. 20).

Lack of Appreciation of Need for Leadership

It is a strange fact that it was left to the " boss " to impress on the American people the idea that social and political ideals can be made real and practical only through organization; and that leadership is essential to both. The very existence of the " boss " and the absence of responsible leadership in American political life speak of a condition and an environment which must produce disease. This condition and environment has been a mental attitude on the part of people — induced by their effort to get away from government as they knew it, and by experiences in a new continent which caused them to accept a philosophy of extreme individualism as a reasoning basis for appeals for support in a war for independence. In the one great enterprise before them, war, they recognized the need for leadership, and the need for organization and discipline to make such leadership effective. But with the War for Independence ended, it remained for an irresponsible oligarchy which had reached out and possessed itself of institutions of common welfare to bring to the people a consciousness of need for responsible leadership. It was this fundamental necessity for leadership of some kind which, being overlooked, finds organic accommodation in the growth of an irresponsible boss, supported by a privileged class.

Thus, in explaining a pathological condition, explaining why we in America have a " boss " and a " machine," the diagnosis has reference to a principle that inheres in group action — broader than democracy itself. The same observation might as well have been made in discussing the normal and abnormal outworkings of the political organization following the Norman conquest; of the upbuilding of the Christian Church; of the success of Harvard College; of the organization of the Carnegie Steel Company; of the New York *World;* namely, that strong, able, farsighted, commanding leadership is necessary to the success of every enterprise, public and private — to institutions both autocratic and democratic. The success of a democracy, however, depends in leadership being made responsible. Responsible leadership is the very keystone of the democratic institutional arch.

The causes which have produced the result (our " invisible " and " irresponsible " government) are clearly

seen in every period and at every point of our national
history.   They are seen in the growth of legislative domination in the colonies under conditions unfavorable to
responsible executive leadership; in the extra-govern-
mental and irresponsible committees of correspondence,
the aim of which was to create sentiment to overthrow the
foreign autocracy; in the temporary and interim agencies
of the Revolutionary War in which the governing bodies
sought to conduct public affairs through committees without a chief executive; in the methods and organization
of the Continental Congress and the discussions of the
convention of delegates which framed our Federal Constitution; in the writings of public men who showed a
profound distrust of the wisdom and right-mindedness of
a broad electorate, and who have urged a type of organization which would insure a form of self-government to
be worked out by an "aristocracy of refinement and
wealth"; in the fact that during the whole controversy
about rights of self-government from 1765 till the French
Revolution, almost no steps were taken to establish a
democratic electorate; in failure to invoke a plebiscite
for the adoption of revolutionary and of post-revolu-
tionary charters; in provision of the Federal Constitution for the election of senators by "councils of the wise"
(the state legislatures), for the election of members of
the House of Representatives by the propertied class,
and for the choice of the President by an electoral
college; in refusal of Congress to accord to the executive
branch a position of equality in its first session when it
denied Hamilton's request to come before it to present
and explain the plans of administration and financial
support which Washington had gone over and made his
own; in the treatment accorded Washington himself by
his constitutional advisers, the Senate, which caused him
to turn away in disgust.

The Leadership of Standing Committees

Bringing over from an older régime the idea of committee domination, and the preferability of a "council of the wise" to an effective plan of popular control, the "standing-committee" system was developed for the transaction of business in the representative branch; the committee of the whole procedure for purposes of inquest and informal discussion was permitted to degenerate or go into disuse; the "lobby," "logrolling" methods, the secret "party" caucus, and "gag rule" to muzzle opposition on the floor grew up as naturally as mushrooms grow around a compost pile. And out of all this came the irresponsible "boss" and the irresponsible "party" or the organization controlled by the boss. Or again to quote from Dr. Orth: these conditions "produced a politician who, having achieved an organization, remained at his post . . . and used it for purposes not always prompted by public welfare."

The secret lobby maintained by persons and corporations seeking special privileges; the domination of party organization by a boss and his "organization" for the nomination of representatives and executive officers to be chosen by the electorate after the suffrage had been broadened; the making of platforms to secure votes for the candidates of irresponsible parties; control of elections; the organization of legislative "committees on expenditure" to secure information for party use, with little or no regard for real issues; an irresponsible party controlled press; the "spoils system" and secret logrolling methods of obtaining public money, for distribution through contractors in order to maintain irresponsible party allegiance and enforce party discipline; the "party secret service," a system of district leaders and walking delegates organized first by Aaron Burr and his contemporaries as a *junta* for the control of the political underworld, later adopted and made more perfect as a means of finding out who are the faithful — these have been an integral part of our irresponsible " party " system, unwittingly aided and abetted by a territorially widening and ever more keenly conscious and correspondingly more distrustful democratic citizenship.

Acceptance of the Principle of Oligarchy

The hold which this idea of a determining " council of the wise," an oligarchy as opposed to a democracy, has had may be seen not alone in the forms mentioned but also in the methods and practices of discontented " independent " reform bodies as well.   When a protesting people have sought to overthrow the boss and his machine, the same methods have been used by them to obtain results as had been developed and were used by persons and the " party " whose acts had caused resentment.   These have been the only methods that have found a place in our political life except at times when a Jefferson or a Roosevelt has violated all " party " traditions and shown his confidence in the right-mindedness of the masses by direct appeal.

But in all this there have been evidences of the soundness of the foundations of our institutions.   While the need for providing institutionally for responsible leadership and an effective means of popular control has not been perceived until very recently, in every case where great leaders have gone to the people the principle has become operative.   The reason that no great national leader has labored for an effective mechanism of popular control seems to be the acceptance of the principle of paternalism.   In no class or political group has the operation of this principle been more strongly exemplified, the principle that a select few should determine what is best, than in those self-appointed civic committees and other agencies of humanitarian motive developed outside the government and in opposition to the "boss and his machine" for the guidance of the electorate. Instead of this opposition leadership insisting on the development of a procedure in the representative body, the established forum of the people, to make this organ of the popular government effective for inquiry, discussion and publicity — instead of seeking to provide within the government itself a means for the exercise of critical judgment and for informing the people, so that public opinion might be deliberately formed on current issues after *due consideration,* the uniform method had been both for "parties" and for persons interested in reform to organize irresponsible committees and to give to the people gratuitous advice. These committees, in so far as they have had any public function to perform, have undertaken gratuitously to do through irresponsible persons exactly what should have been done by the representatives and executive officers who by every tenet of democratic faith should have been made responsible by the adoption of a procedure suited to this purpose.

The Rise of Humanitarian Civic Leadership

In the absence of responsible leadership — and an open public forum composed of representatives of the people organized to inquire into, approve, and disapprove the acts and proposals of leaders, and to carry disputed issues to the people — in the absence of this, each community has accepted the leadership of irresponsible "party" leaders organized for patronage and spoils; either this or the communities have supported the hands of various irresponsible specialized civic agencies, whose motives were good but whose methods were the same as those of the "boss" and the corporation "lobbyist." The prevalence and persistence of this type of leadership is evident on every hand. For example, in Philadelphia there are some two thousand irresponsible detached organizations, each with its leader or committee, inquiring into some one or more subjects of interest, seeking to serve its special constituency with a view of making more intelligent citizens or to bring about some special improvement. New York has two or three times as many, Boston, St. Louis, Chicago, San Francisco, Cleveland — every city and town has its proportional share. Each in turn, when it has sought to bring about a change of law, establish a new branch of public service, or make one already established more serviceable, has worked through the "system" of irresponsible parties or irresponsible legislative committees; employs the lobby; has used log-rolling methods; has helped to make the irresponsible boss and his machine more powerful — not from preference, however, but because there has been no other way to get things done.

American citizenship instead of providing itself with responsible leadership and providing a means of control over the public service in the representative branch and the electorate, without realizing the significance of its habits and prejudices, first followed the leadership of the boss, then followed the leadership of a multitude of paid secretaries of independent civic agencies outside the government. That is, the people have not undertaken to take the steps necessary to prevent the breeding of a foreign malignant growth which has come to sap the vitality of the body politic; but have undertaken to make itself immune to infection by a benevolent culture. It has not resorted to hygiene but to the development of antibodies.

Three Groups of Irresponsible Leaders

Generally speaking, these irresponsible agencies which have grown up have been of three kinds, which in the order of their historic development may be characterized as following: (1) the kind which is so freely discussed as a thing quite undemocratic — i. e. irresponsible politi-

cal "parties" which aim to nominate and secure the
election of members of their organization so that those
who make " politics " a business may obtain the patronage
and the profit that attend an alliance of government with
private undertaking; (2) irresponsible civic societies and
committees, not interested in spoils — but organized to
promote specialized humanitarian projects each of which
has taken upon itself leadership to obtain action looking
toward the improvement of a particular governmental
service or activity; and, (3) irresponsible civic agencies,
not interested in spoils, and not interested in the promotion of any special humanitarian project — but which,
being opposed to waste and inefficiency, have undertaken
to obtain the information needed to arouse public opinion
to demand better public administration, more intelligent
executive planning, and effective execution of plans.
This third class of agencies were interested in economy,
efficiency, and budget making as a means of locating
and enforcing executive accountability. Let us get before us a little more clearly the conditions which gave rise
to these three kinds of irresponsible agencies:

The Irresponsible " Boss " and the Irresponsible " Party "

1. The first of these groups, *irresponsible political*
"parties," came into being after the Jefferson and Jackson influence had broadened the electorate and after control by a landed aristocracy had been overthrown.
Their forerunner had been the congressional caucus.
But this, with the broadened electorate, developed a vul-
nerable point in its protective armor. The caucus was
made up of representatives elected by the people. Its
doom was sealed when Jackson went out and won over
to his leadership the support of the unaristocratic majority
of the electorate.

Thus aristocratic control was first defeated by Jefferson, and its controlling body, " the legislative caucus,"

was killed by Jackson. With "the legislative caucus" died the last vestige of responsible leadership. Then it was that a new type of practical politician came to the front; men like De Witt Clinton of Jackson's time; and, after his time, men like Fenton, Quay and Hanna and Platt. There was an important function to be performed, for which no institutional means was provided. Their practical problem was to organize and make effective for purposes of nomination and election a " party "— and to organize in such manner that the controlling group would be fortified against the electorate. Having made their leadership safe through well-chosen devices like " platforms," a hand-picked hierarchy, and judicious distribution of spoils, they undertook to secure their ends by controlling the ever widening democratic electorate.

Having nominated his candidates and secured the election of men who were trusted by his " party," the boss found that the secret processes of the irresponsible legislative committees and the methods which had been inaugurated by the controlling aristocracy before the electorate had been broadened and the unaristocratic boss and his machine got control were admirably suited to his purposes. Therefore party managers fostered government by standing committees, the rule of seniority, and all that went with irresponsible leadership. When the people rebelled and demanded direct election of a multitude of executive officers, the bosses accepted the situation and made nomination and election of an increasing number of officers grist for their own mill. And from time to time, as one reform measure after another gained favor in appeals to the people to " overthrow the boss and his machine," they were able to accept each new proposal made in the interest of " reform " so long as they could control nominations and elections and remain the chief beneficiaries of the standing-committee system with its methods of dealing in the dark.

Irresponsible Humanitarian Leadership

2. The second group of civic agencies to take a significant part in our political life, the *irresponsible, specialized civic committee* interested in humanitarian projects, found an environment suited to their growth when the people began to look to the government for improved service. The prevailing political philosophy of the first half century after our independence was that government was an evil — necessary, to be sure, but an evil to be abated as far as possible. The average American felt independent. Except to protect his property rights and to secure personal safety he held the view that he did not need to look to the government. When any one lost out in his efforts to possess himself of ample means for working out his own salvation, all he had to do was to " Go West," possess himself of an allotted part of a great, unused fertile public domain and " grow up with the country." The chief demand on the government was to apportion the land to the citizenship which, collectively as sovereign, had become successors to the British Crown. Here was an empire wide and rich beyond human conception. The chief cost in the distribution was small. The only thing necessary was to drive the Indians back as fast as the white man wanted more land, and to provide for maintaining such police as were needed to protect the frontiersman from the uncivilized rage of aboriginal tribes.

But finally these rich lands ready for the ax and plow became scarce, and the inducements offered to collective capital to develop manufactories and commerce began to bring large populations together as urban dwellers. Then a new attitude toward the government began to assert itself. The government was found to be the only agency to which the urban dwellers could look for such common necessities as good water, sunshine, and pure air; for protection against contagious disease and epidemic; for defense against the exploitation of monopolists and profiteers.

Living conditions in the towns became very complex. Those who busied themselves making a living as wage earners and as small business men under these new conditions did not know and could not find out why their lot was made hard — but economic adversity, ill health, and physical suffering often was found in the midst of plenty. In this enviroment humanitarian instincts came to the front. Persons who had means of support and time to think interested themselves in these conditions, and in doing what they could to make the government more serviceable. Some interested themselves in the sick poor; others in the industrially disabled; others in the pauper; others in the insane; others in causes of crime and the treatment of prisoners; others in regulation of food supply; others in the prevention of disease; others in hours and conditions of work and so on. All sorts of conditions which constituted social ills were made the subject of special inquiry and care by benevolent-minded persons whose social vision went beyond their own family and set. To make their efforts more effective it became the fashion to inquire into causes, and in most instances this led to a knowledge of what the government was doing and to a consideration of what it could do to make it more serviceable. And as each of these various specialized civic agencies applied themselves each to its task, each found itself face to face with these two forces with which they had difficulty in coping: (1) the unaristocratic and also quite autocratic party leader, who, from choice, remained outside the government in order that he might fortify himself and build up an organization beyond the reach of the electorate; (2) an electorate which had come to be broadly democratic but which, having failed to provide the means of protecting itself by constitutional or other means of insuring responsible leadership, was being used to further the interests of the boss.

Out of this situation a new species of political propaganda came forth. Each of these specialized humanitarian civic agencies sought to get and keep the particular governmental activity in which it was interested "out of politics"—out from under the control of the irresponsible boss and his machine and also where it could not be reached by the electorate. In a political campaign, a quest for votes, these specialized humanitarian societies and their non-political leaders were no match for the party boss and his machine; but they could beat the party manager when it came to making a human appeal for service. They did find a public opinion favorable to their appeal in the democracy; and for this reason they did get a sympathetic response to the demand that the public service be taken "out of politics." The practical solution was that one service after another was by law set apart and placed under an appointed board or commission.

The arguments of the specialized civic agencies and of their secretaries ran like this: "By placing each of the particular public-service activities in which they were interested under a board with overlapping terms, the experience of the administrative body would be made continuous; by making the term of each member of the board longer than the term of office of the politically elected candidate who was made the appointing agent, the appointing agent would stand in fear of the effect of a bad appointment in the next election; by making the terms long enough even a venal political appointing agent could not control the board; by making the appropriation continuous the board would be relieved of going before a politically controlled standing committee of the legislature every time it needed funds; and finally, being thus relieved of the necessity for dealing with the boss and

his machine, the board could employ and retain the services of experts — men qualified to deal effectively with
the intricate questions of administration."

But there was another advantage which was not set
forth in the propaganda which gave to our states a multitude of administrative boards and commissions. The
standing committee system in the legislatures was not
touched. There was no effort made to dethrone the irresponsible leader outside the government by setting up a
method by which leadership would be responsible. The
many-headed, much-divided management did not take the
people at large into confidence in matters of administrative acts and proposals. This gave to the humanitarian
committees and their secretaries the same sort of advantage as had been used by the boss; in fact their organizations were patterned after the institutions of the boss
and his machine, being different only in the end which
they sought to achieve. And just to the extent that the
service was taken out from under the control of the boss
and his machine — to that extent it fell under the domination of the specialized civic committee and its secretary.
The people were relieved to a certain extent of the results of control of the bosses of irresponsible political
" parties " whose aims were spoils; they received the
benefits of a benevolent paternalism by putting their affairs under the domination of a multitude of bosses of
humanitarian, though irresponsible, specialized civic societies.

It is a fact to be squarely faced that while the prevailing spirit of America has always responded to appeals
to the highest ideals of democracy, this spirit has not
found an institutional means of expression in the form of
devices for controlling the motor system of the body
politic. The spirit of the people has been democratic.
But the movements of the body politic have been dominated by local and class impulses. Political action, ex-

cept in time of great national emergency, has not been a reflex of the soul of the people, but the reflex of localized or specialized class interests. To use a figure drawn from physical life: The mind of the people has not been *in coma*, it has been at all times alert to appeals of idealism; but with respect to all objective relations, the senses of sight and touch and hearing were linked up with local centers of control, which in turn linked up with an outside boss — humanitarian or venal as the case might be. They did not reach the reasoning and thinking of a responsible leadership. Popular sovereignty was not real, for there was a hiatus between the seat of the popular will and the local centers of motor control. Continuously operating means of communication with the mind of the people had not been established. The motor system, having adapted itself to being actuated by stimuli controlled by the party boss or latterly, in part at least, by stimuli furnished by a multitude of secretaries of independent humanitarian committees who got their desired results through the many independent nerve centers — the body members, even though they might be made to operate strongly, acted without coördination, except in so far as this might be brought about by command or agreement of the outside irresponsible leaders.

The political spinal cord that was provided for in the Constitution, automatically to link the mind of the people with the motor centers of the government, was attenuated or in a condition of temporary paralysis. It was constricted initially by the makers of the Constitution who distrusted the people; later this constriction was taken advantage of by those outside organizations who found it to their advantage not to have public opinion function except at the end of fixed terms and then in response to stimuli coming from irresponsible leaders; and the bosses spent their time devising ways and means whereby the people could have no choice at the end of the fixed terms except as between alternatives dictated by bosses.

This system has caused the people to grow more distrustful and resentful, so that when the electoral system acts independently it reflects only inhibitory or negative conclusions.   The system thus actuated has produced results which are a mockery to the spirit of democracy. The voice of the people has been a voice to condemn its servants to political death for conditions which have made for distrust and over which the servants of the people have had little or no control.   Time and again the people have commissioned a set of new servants, and because of these conditions the political boss has known that only the untried could be elected.   Then these new servants in turn have fallen victims to the system.   But the " boss " and the irresponsible " party " and the " standing committees " and " invisible government " have lived on.

The point made here is that while the servants of the people have been condemned, the system which makes for " invisible government " and " irresponsible " leadership, has gone on and on.

The contest between the outside irresponsible boss with his servile party and the opposition made up of outside irresponsible secretaries, both fortified by establishing their organizations on foundations beyond the reach of the electorate, who, " in periodic fits of popular rage," turned out their helpless servants and condemned them to political death — the contest between those two political forces has been a contest for control over the decentralized motor bodies of the government.   And, as has been said, in this struggle the civic secretaries had the advantage, because their motives were true to the ideals of democracy, although their methods were paternalistic and autocratic.   Whenever a definite humanitarian issue has come before the people, the party has usually lost out because the motives of the boss were known to be selfish. The civic secretary in each case has sought to make the specialized service in which he was interested more serviceable to the people, while the party boss was seeking to monopolize the commercial transactions of the government for the selfish advancement of members of the organization of which he was the head. Both the boss and the secretary were irresponsible. The one however has had a benevolent interest; the other has been dominated by the spirit of the profiteer.

Irresponsible Agencies to Promote Responsible Leadership within the Government

3. Now comes upon the stage a third group, another group of *independent, unofficial, irresponsible soviets* in whose eyes the need of the hour seemed to be lack of coördination of public functions; lack of planning for the government as a whole; lack of managing ability at the head. With this came loss of energy in the body politic because of the overlapping conflicting claims and jurisdictions of the scores of independent or semi-independent centers of administrative control, as they came to assert themselves through the efforts of social groups which favored decentralization.

The leadership in this third group of committees and societies came largely from two sources: the nonspecialized humanitarian and sociologist on the one hand; the taxpayers and economists on the other.

The nonspecialized humanitarian was born in the environment of those eleemosynary institutions which took a broad survey of social relations as expressed in human want — such as the charity organization societies. They had grown up under a leadership which had sought to render to society a service by better coördinating the activities of the various detached, unofficial, specialized, eleemosynary societies; they had sought to overcome some of the evils of social sectarianism and the efforts of social forces which had favored governmental decentralization.

The taxpayer and the economist gained their inspiration largely from the rapidly rising cost of government and the economic waste.

Both of these types of persons were aided and abetted by the student of political and social sciences in the universities.

When this third group of civic agencies entered the political arena, they did so on the assumption that the chief cause of the high cost of government was the waste and inefficiency which came from prostituting the public service to the selfish purposes of the irresponsible party boss and his machine — " graft," " patronage," " spoils." But as the work of these new bodies went on they found that quite as much, possibly more, of the inefficiency and waste was due to the headless, spineless system of government; they found that the incoördinate acts, the conflicts and the lack of coöperation were due to the fact that the administrative motor bodies were actuated from unrelated centers of control, each of which was made responsive to stimuli from the outside and did not record themselves at the political brain center — a chief executive that in turn was accountable to the whole people for leadership.

Or, to state the problem in terms of positive function, the chief executive was used as a convenience to affix the sign manual of authority to acts initiated in irresponsible standing committees of the representative branch; or to the designs initiated in unofficial bodies entirely beyond the reach of the electorate controlled by the " party " boss or secretaries of nonpartisan eleemosynary societies.

This third group of agencies therefore set themselves at work to develop processes whereby the local stimuli of social need and the experience derived from contact with the administrative problem might come to be known at the brain center of the government — become known to some one in chief authority who might stand before the people as responsible leader; processes which would enable the members of the representative body to act as a court of inquest for the people; processes which would enable the electorate to think and have a will in final determination of questions of public policy.

Thus it was that propaganda for better accounting, periodical reporting of conditions and results, budget making as a procedure of planning, and administrative reorganization as a means of locating and enforcing responsibility came to make itself felt. These measures were put forward for popular consideration and approval along with the propaganda for more effective, better social service.

CHAPTER V

TWELVE years ago the machinery of administration
was not a subject of popular interest, and the word
" budget " was seldom used by the American people.
When either subject was introduced into conversation, it
was almost without meaning. Now reorganization measures are being passed by every city and state, and
" budget " is a part of the vocabulary of every one — a
subject of common talk. We can scarcely pick up a mag-
azine without seeing something about scientific management, city planning, household economics, the wage
earner's budget, the housewife's budget, the city budget,
the state budget, or the national budget.

New York City a Center of Interest in Better Adminis-
tration

Twelve years ago, when a New York editor was asked
to make his " daily " a medium through which the public
might be kept in touch with administrative reorganization, budget and accounting work then in progress, his
answer was: " It can't be done. We do not *make* news;
we *print* news. The work of an editor is not to find out
what people ought to know, but what they will read.
News is made by persons who do things or by happenings
that the public are interested in. They are not interested
in methods of administration; they are not interested
in budgets; are not interested in accounting. Most of
them have never heard of a budget; and the rest of them

don't care to hear about management or budget methods."

This editor was right. Stories of current happenings to people and things that the public are interested in are news; and what the people think about the news topics of yesterday and to-day is public opinion. Community thought and talk about current happenings carried in the news columns, headlined in black face, is the thought and talk that controls the destinies of cities and nations. But the people themselves and those to whom the people look as leaders make news.

A Question of News

The sayings and doings of men who are looked to as leaders is always news. It is this interest in outstanding persons that gives to leadership its hold on public opinion, and makes the press a force in a community. A great leader is like a great newspaper in this respect; his greatness largely depends on his knowing what the people want. The leader is made by his following. He cannot go farther than his following will go. Whatever other qualities the leader must posses he must have ability to forecast popular approval. It is from this that he takes his reckonings. The fact that administrative reorganizations and budgets have come to be talked about means that through changed conditions and leadership the people have developed a new interest. What is news to-day was not news yesterday. The vital concerns of community life have taken on a new emphasis and leadership has a new basis for appeal.

The story of the recent movement for responsible government and budgets in America, of how this new interest has developed during the last ten years, is significant. A budget has come to mean a method of dealing with this question of vital concern. We have always accepted the theory that government should be responsible. This is one of the primary demands of democracy.

But the truth is America has not had enough of an interest in democracy before to think out what is needed to make the government responsible.   The Revolutionary War was not a war for democracy; it was a war for political independence.   The second war with Great Britain was necessary to make good the fruits of the first.   Our Mexican War was a war of aggression.   Our Civil War was to compel economic and political unity.   Our Spanish War was to abate a nuisance.   The campaigns waged by Roosevelt and Wilson against special privilege were the beginning of a national democratic awakening.   The war against Germany was our first war for democracy.   The twentieth century interest in democracy carried with it a demand for responsible government. Our recent movement for administrative reorganization and a budget procedure is one of the fruits of this demand.

A Question of Sick Babies and Padded Rolls

While the public cannot be interested in doing things through abstract discussion, it may be aroused by relating the methods to a result to be achieved, and abstract discussion follows.   Twelve years ago, when the happenings about work under way looking toward the introduction of new methods of administration and control in New York City had no news value, there was a deep-seated, long-enduring, and increasing resentment on the part of the people which had been provoked by old methods that made for popular unrest.   This long-enduring resentment had periodically expressed itself in " paroxysms of popular frenzy " which made and unmade political leaders and overturned administrations.   While budget methods and accounting and the machinery of government had no news value, these were made vital through stories of happenings about men in the public eye; and those stories of happenings carried conviction that the methods of administration and the machinery of public business needed overhauling. The rising tax rate became news. Money wasted which was needed to save babies became news; children on the street, while public funds raised to build schoolhouses, playgrounds, and public baths, were being diverted, became news. The uncared-for sick and poor, and padded health rolls were news. The rapid rise in cost of government and some forty thousand obsolete brass fixtures, bought from a friend by a retiring officer in the water department, made news. And above all things else the thought that some one in the public service should be held to account for the abuse of the public trust came to be a subject of daily comment.

And so it was that in the city of New York the people came to talk in terms of administrative reorganization and budgets: a budget as a means of holding officers to account; a budget as a means of telling the people beforehand what money was wanted for; a budget as a means of planning for service needed and locating responsibility for the execution of plans; a budget as a community program to be financed. Thus it was that red tape, unbalanced bids, obsolete fixtures, and wasteful methods of doing business were made the mediums for clothing budgets with flesh and blood; the current happenings incident to efforts to introduce a budget into the management of affairs in New York were made news.

Beginning of a Nation-wide Campaign

This was the beginning of a nation-wide campaign. First it took hold of the people in the cities. Propaganda for budget making was read. The need for a budget spoke through educational, social, and business leaders in every American municipality and through the press; and the people applauded. From the cities it spread to the national government; and from the national government it took hold on the political leadership in the states.

The Inspirational Leadership of President Roosevelt

President Cleveland had been elected in a campaign which had for its slogan: A public office is a public trust. President Roosevelt did much to quicken public conscience — more, perhaps, than any man since the days of Jefferson. He was an outstanding leader, who resorted to methods of direct appeal to the people through the press. And in this he followed in the footsteps of Jefferson, Jackson, and Lincoln. Through the news columns he went before a people conscious of political practices of which they would be rid. Roosevelt had become President at a time of great popular feeling against men and methods through which special interests had gained control of the resources of the nation. This control was being exercised through men not of the people's choice. It had been reduced to a system. The system was in control of an irresponsible boss — the head of an irresponsible party organization. And by operation of the system special privilege had found its way into legislatures and departments of public service. The system worked in defiance of public opinion. Through the system the government had become " irresponsible " and " invisible." The people felt that they had lost control of their institutions of service.

President Roosevelt divined the cause and led the attack. To fight special privilege and to satisfy the demand for more and better service was the task which he set for himself. By his direct appeal and his forcefulness in action, President Roosevelt gained the confidence of a great following. Consideration was also given to methods of administration to prevent waste. Much was done under his leadership to give new direction to national thought. In it all, his strong personality stood out as a public officer, devoted to the cause of better service. But

little legislation had been undertaken which had a direct
bearing on administrative law and none that had to do
with budget making as a method of planning and enforcing executive accountability when his mantle fell on
Mr. Taft.

The Contribution of President Taft

President Taft had been a strong and sympathetic
member of President Roosevelt's cabinet; he had made
an enviable reputation as a constructive administrator in
the Philippines; he was Mr. Roosevelt's choice for suc-
cessor, acceptable to his party and to the people. By his
aggressiveness the President had made many enemies:
Mr. Taft carried with him the full strength of President
Roosevelt's supporters as well as others who distrusted
his political opponent — Mr. Bryan.

In 1909, Mr. Taft became President. During the campaign he had detracted nothing from Mr. Roosevelt's ac-
complishments in fighting against special privilege and in
fighting for the enlargement and betterment of the public
service to meet popular demands. But much was said
by him about a more businesslike handling of public affairs — making a dollar do more and better work.

President Taft began his official term with the largest
popular backing of any chief executive since the Civil
War. He was trusted both by the friends of progress
and reform who had made up President Roosevelt's following and by those who were President Roosevelt's
ardent haters — the representatives of special privilege.
Thus for a time the political sea which had been stirred by
storms of abuse during the Roosevelt administration became quiet. For a period of six months after March 4,
1909, these storms had subsided only to break again
with renewed violence. But the storm center was not
waste of public resources and cost of government, though
Mr. Aldrich and others helped to dramatize the need for

improved methods through interviews in which the senior
senator from Rhode Island was quoted as saying that if
he could run the Federal Government as he would manage a private business, he could save $300,000,000 a year.
The storm center had become " the Payne-Aldrich tariff,"
" standpatism," " the capture of President Taft by the
forces of plutocracy," " the dominance of special privilege."

An Effort to Institutionalize Executive Leadership

Mr. Taft had seemingly gone out of his way to take
personal responsibility for a tariff revision that proved
to be unpopular — a revision which was viewed by Mr.
Roosevelt's progressive and radical following as a surrender to " the interests." This view was also accepted
and advertised by the organized opposition, the Democratic party. And then followed a letter to a congressman which seemed to stamp the President as a reactionary
on matters of patronage. These acts of the President
were unfortunate as viewed by those who were interested
in the development of greater economy and efficiency in
the public service, and the budget idea, for Mr. Taft had
seriously intended to use the great powers and influence
of his office to enlarge on this part of his program.

The news value of a stand taken for any measure by
the President as national leader cannot be estimated.
The novel thing about President Taft's stand was that
he used it to make news of "the need for a national
budget." In the midst of a storm of abuse President
Taft turned from the issues of special privilege to make
news and to stir editorial comment on the waste of resource and the demand for economy by asking Congress
for an appropriation of $100,000 " to enable the President
to inquire into the methods of transacting the public
business — and to recommend to Congress such legisla-

tion as may be necessary to carry into effect changes found to be desirable that cannot be accomplished by executive action alone."

This request in itself gained wide publicity. After several months of waiting, the amount asked for was granted; and again every newspaper advertised the fact as an accomplishment. After the funds became available (June 30), President Taft issued instructions to his secretary, Mr. Charles D. Norton, to make plans for the organization of the work. Later one of the directors of the New York Bureau of Municipal Research in charge of the budget work there was chosen to head a White House staff. These happenings in sequence as news items brought the subject repeatedly to public notice. A meeting at the White House was called in September and a preliminary inquiry was begun, and again the idea had news value. The first task was to organize in each department a committee which would coöperate with the staff of the President in developing a definite plan of work, the announcement of which gave new publicity. The inquiry was immediately got under way, with the result that an analysis had been made of expenditures, and a number of departmental studies were in progress when the President reported to Congress; again the idea was given news value.

A Portrayal of Conditions to be Corrected

This narration has for its purpose to show how it was that news value was given to the subject of methods of doing business in the National Government through the leadership of the President. In his first report to Congress, December, 1910, President Taft said:

"I have been given this fund to enable me to take action and to make specific recommendations with respect to the details of transacting the business of an organization whose activities are almost as varied as those of the entire business world. The operations of the Government affect the interest of every person living within the jurisdiction of the United States. In organization it embraces stations and centers of work located in every city and in many local subdivisions of the country. Its gross expenditures amount to nearly $1,000,000,000 annually. Including the personnel of the military and naval establishments, more than 400,000 persons are required to do the work imposed by law upon the executive branch of the Government.

" This vast organization has never been studied in detail as one piece of administrative mechanism. Never have the foundations been laid for a thorough consideration of the relation of all of its parts. No comprehensive effort has been made to list its multifarious activities or to group them in such a way as to present a clear picture of what the Government is doing. Never has a complete description been given of the agencies through which these activities are performed. At no time has the attempt been made to study all of these activities and agencies with a view to the assignment of each activity to the agency best fitted for its performance, to the avoidance of duplication of plant and work, to the integration of all administrative agencies of the Government, so far as may be practicable, into a unified organization for the most effective and economical dispatch of public business."

In a special message to Congress President Taft asked for the continuation of the first appropriation over another year and for $75,000 additional. This request having been granted March 3d, the work was continued under a commission by order of the President, issued March 8th.

A Definite Program Proposed

One of the conclusions reached as a result of the preliminary inquiry was the following: [1]

" A very conspicuous cause of inefficiency and waste is an inadequate provision of the methods of getting before Congress a definite budget, *i. e.* a concrete and well-considered progress or prospectus of work to be financed."

When the commission was organized sufficiently to permit of collective consideration of work to be done by it, a program of work was formulated which provided for five distinct subjects to be inquired into, as follows:

(1) A budget as an annual financial program.

(2) The organization and activities of the Government, with a view to recommending legislation to prevent overlapping functions and conflicts of jurisdiction.

(3) Problem of personnel;

(4) Financial records and reports;

(5) Business practices and procedures. In pursuit of these inquiries the commission proposed and submitted to the President more than a hundred reports with recommendations, twenty-six of which were sent to Congress as calling for legislation.

Preliminary Staff Inquiry

In the preliminary inquiry one of the first steps taken had been to ask the several departmental committees co-operating with the President to reanalyze the estimates in such manner as to show the different kinds of things that were being purchased by the Government and the amounts spent and estimated for each. As a result of this inquiry the President for the first time had brought before him a summary of such facts as the following: The amounts spent by each bureau, by each department, and the Government as a whole analyzed to show what

[1] See report covering period September 27, 1910, to March 6, 1911, circular 29 of the Commission on Economy and Efficiency.

part was for such things as personal services; services other than personal; materials; supplies; equipment, etc. For the first time it became known that the Government was spending nearly $400,000,000 for salaries and wages (the digest of appropriations made it appear that only $189,000,000 was for this purpose); that the Government was spending $12,500,000 for the transportation of persons; that it was spending $78,000,000 for transportation of things (freight, express, etc.), and, in addition, was spending $18,500,000 for provisions, hotel bills and other subsistence of persons, and $4,500,000 for wearing apparel, etc. These figures now seem small, but at that time they startled men to a new vision.

The President's Commission on Economy and Efficiency

Among the first things undertaken by the Commission after its organization was to continue the analytical work with a view of preparing a report on the need for an annual budget. In July, 1911, forms were drafted. These were discussed with department heads, and on August 1st were submitted to the President for his approval. On August 7th the President sent those forms to the departments and requested that they reclassify the data which were being obtained for the purposes of official estimates then in preparation. The forms asked for information on three subjects: (1) Expenditures for fiscal year ending June 30, 1911; (2) appropriations for the fiscal year ending June 30, 1912; (3) estimates for appropriations for the fiscal year ending June 30, 1913. A different form was prepared for reporting on each of these subjects and a fourth form for a recapitulation. Each of these forms was so drawn as to provide for showing the amounts expended, appropriated, or estimated: (1) By each organization unit; (2) for each class of work to be done; (3) by character of expenditure — such as current expenses, capital outlays, fixed charges, etc.;

and, (4) by the amount which had been expended, appropriated, or estimated under each act or class of acts of appropriation — whether by annual appropriation, permanent legislation, etc. The heads of departments were asked to have these returns in by November 1st, but it was not until after the first of the next year that they were made available to the President. This was due to the fact that the forms required by Congress were along entirely different lines, and it was necessary for the heads of departments to have the official estimate in the hands of the Treasury and before Congress on a prescribed date.

The report of the commission on "The need for a National Budget" was sent by the President to Congress with his approval on June 27, 1912.[1]

Request for Coöperation of Congress in a Budget Procedure

In his letter of transmittal President Taft pointed to the fact that the executive is charged by the Constitution with the duty of publishing "a regular statement of receipts and expenditures" and "that he is also enjoined

[1] This was printed as House document No. 854 of the Sixty-second Congress, second session (568 pages). The members of the commission who participated in the preparation and signed the report, were: Frederick A. Cleveland, chairman; Frank J. Goodnow, for twenty-six years professor of administrative law in Columbia University, now President of Johns Hopkins University; William F. Willoughby, for more than twenty years connected with the government service in various capacities, now Director of the Institute of Government Research; Walter W. Warwick, for many years connected with the comptroller's office and auditing service of the Federal Government, now the Comptroller of the Treasury; and Merritt O. Chance, for twenty-six years connected with various departments of the Government, now postmaster at Washington. From June, 1911, to January, 1912, Mr. Harvey S. Chase was also a member of the commission, but due to illness, he was not able to be in Washington during the time that the budget report was being prepared and therefore did not share in authorship or join in signing the report. The subsequent use which Mr. Chase has made of the report, however, indicates that he is in general accord with the recommendations of the commission.

from time to time to give Congress information on the
state of the Union and to recommend for consideration
such measures as may be deemed expedient." With these
constitutional prescriptions, President Taft held that the
President had the power to prepare and submit to Congress each year " a definite, well-considered budget with
a message calling attention to subjects of immediate importance." The President stated, however, in his message that he did not assume to exercise this power except
in coöperation with Congress; and he urged the necessity
of repealing certain laws which were in conflict with the
proposed practice.

Among the purposes of sending the report to Congress
as described by the President were:

To suggest a method whereby the President, as the
constitutional head of the administration, and Congress
may consider and act on a definite business and financial
program.

To have the expenditures, appropriations, and estimates
so classified and summarized that their broad significance
may be readily understood;

To provide each member of Congress, as well as each
citizen who is interested, with such data concerning each
subject of interest as may be considered in relation to
questions of public policy;

To have these general summaries supported by such
detailed information as is necessary to consider the
economy and efficiency with which business has been
transacted;

In short, to suggest a plan whereby the President and
Congress may coöperate, the one in laying before Congress and the country a clearly expressed administrative
program to be acted on — the other in laying before the
President a definite enactment for his judgment.

Order of the President to Prepare a Budget

This was the first time that any chief executive of the National Government had advocated the "budget idea"; it was the first time that responsible leadership had been urged as an essential to responsible government by one high in authority. This report not only contained a descriptive and critical report on the past practices of the National Government with constructive recommendations, but supported these recommendations with an appendix of forms and a digest of the practices of thirty-eight other countries, in most of which the budget idea had already been incorporated and made a part of the public law.

After a few days of waiting for congressional action following the submission of this report to Congress, President Taft on July 10th issued an order to each head of department to depute some officer with the duty to see that estimates and summaries of estimates for the next fiscal year be prepared in accordance with the recommendations contained in his message of June 27th. And in a letter the President directed the Secretary and Treasurer to print and send without delay to Congress the forms of estimates required by it; also to have sent to him (the President) the information asked for. Explaining the purpose of the executive estimates he said: "This will be made the subject of review and revision and a summary statement in the form of a budget with documents will be sent to Congress by a special message as the proposal of the administration."

Attempt of Opposition Leaders to Prevent Action

At the time that this order was issued, Congress had not yet passed all of the annual appropriation bills — some of the bills as passed having been vetoed by the President. When on August 24th the sundry civil bill became law it contained one clause modifying the form of estimates to incorporate some of the suggestions of the commission, and another clause requiring the heads of departments to submit the estimates in the form and at the time required by law to be submitted and at no other time and in no other form.   Following this, when it came to the attention of President Taft that heads of departments expressed some doubt as to what were their duties in the matter, on September 9th the President sent a letter to each member of the cabinet, in which each was instructed to follow the orders both of the President and of Congress.   Both houses of the legislative branch were organized against the President, who after the November election was a politically defeated executive.   The majority leaders let it be known that they were opposed to the enterprise; and the estimates asked for were much delayed.   About February 1st, however, all the data had been brought together and, on February 26th, President Taft, after conferences with his cabinet, submitted to Congress a budget with a message, which was referred to the Committee on Appropriations and ordered to be printed with accompanying papers.   And there it has since laid without consideration, action, or report.

Favorable Reception Given by the Public

Although the budget proposals of President Taft were pigeonholed by an opposition majority in Congress, they were not pigeonholed by the public.   They were taken up by the press throughout the country.   Almost unanimously they had the support of editorial writers.   Opinion was further registered in a referendum which was taken on the subject by the Chambers of Commerce of the United States.   Furthermore, many leading men, and even some of the members of Congress who, at the time, expressed themselves as being opposed to an executive budget, from time to time since then have come out strongly for the budget idea.

As has been said, the circumstances attending the efforts of President Taft could not have been more unfavorable to successful leadership in so far as his ability to obtain legislation was concerned. Not only had he lost much of his popularity because of the stand he had taken on the tariff and in other legislative and official acts offensive to the progressives, as they later came to be known, but the by-election of 1911 returned a large majority against him in Congress. Hostility to his constructive proposals in Congress and its committee was a matter of course. He had sacrificed public opinion on the altar of " party " fealty. Thereby he had surrendered his " big stick "— the power of direct appeal as a means of enforcing action. When the militant progressive public lost confidence in him, he had no means of compelling action, except through party organization, and half of his " party " as it turned out was hostile to his leadership. Not only his budget proposals but his recommendations for legislation looking toward certain needed departmental reorganization met with like fate. Even his executive orders met with obstructions and delays on the part of officials urging statutes, rules, and practices which had grown up in the course of a hundred years of congressional committee control. Many administrative changes were made reducing the amount of red tape with an annual saving which far outreached the total cost of the staff inquiry; but the constructive recommendations of the President which required congressional coöperation were not given respectful hearing by the controlling majority of the legislative branch of the National Government.

Concrete Results which Followed

Ample rewards were found for effort, however: (1)

in the renewed vigor given to administrative reorganization and budget procedures introduced into the hundreds of American municipalities; (2) in the appointment of numerous state commissions to inquire into and report what changes were necessary to enable these states to conduct their enterprises with greater economy and efficiency; (3) in the many legal enactments in the states reorganizing administrative departments, boards and commissions, and providing for a budget procedure, and (4) in the national issue finally being taken before the people in the platforms of all the principal national parties pledging candidates for election to Congress to the adoption of a national budget procedure.

CHAPTER VI

*Investigations of Need for Economy and Efficiency as
Old as Our Government*

As has been pointed out, one of the first results of the
publicity given by President Taft to the need for administrative reform was the appointment of committees
and commissions of inquiry to report on administrative
reorganization of the state governments. The use of
such bodies, however, is not confined to the last ten years.
As a recognition of a need for better administrative organization and methods, many commissions of inquiry
have been appointed since the beginning of our Government. For example, in the Federal Government a committee was appointed, during the administration of President John Adams, to inquire into and report on possible
necessary changes in methods of distributing public
moneys appropriated to each department, whose findings
and recommendations were published in 1798; following
this, three other committees were appointed and reported
on retrenchment and expenses of government, in 1818,
1822, and 1828. In 1830 a select committee of Congress
was created to whom was referred a section of President
Jackson's message respecting the need for reorganization
of the executive departments; other reports were made on
the retrenchment, public expenditures, and the civil service
in 1842, 1876, and 1882. In 1888 the select committee
headed by Mr. Cockrell was appointed to inquire into the

methods of business of executive departments; this was followed by the Dockery Commission in 1893, which employed experts and made voluminous reports on the subject of administration, organization and methods.   In the second year of Cleveland's second administration, 1894, the members of the cabinet made a joint report.   Besides these general inquiries, many reports, largely by committees on expenditures of Congress, were made on departments.[1]

Similar reports by committees of state legislatures have been made for many years.   Such reports might be counted by the hundreds.   But the significant fact is that only within the last few years has the need for administrative reorganization and an effective procedure for budget-making impressed itself on the public.   This was due to several influences and conditions; namely, the background work that had been going on in the cities; the dramatic interest given by President Roosevelt through his vigorous and appealing leadership; the fact that the national and state governments were threatened with deficits; and the breadth of vision, the magnitude of the inquiry, and the frequent publicity given to the need for administrative reorganization by President Taft.   Thus there came to be a changed attitude on the part of the public that could not be ignored by legislators and public officers seeking electoral support.

[1] In addition to the general inquiries the following dealt with subjects of department administration: Department of State, 1838, 1846, 1881, 1895, 1901, 1909; Department of Treasury, 1794, 1801, 1816, 1837, 1864, 1869, 1871, 1876, 1880, 1890, 1891, 1909; Department of War, 1824, 1843, 1854, 1873, 1876, 1878, 1881, 1904; Department of Justice, 1880; Department of Post Office, 1821, 1822, 1831, 1835, 1836, 1881, 1884, 1901, 1902, 1908; Department of Navy, 1796, 1821, 1839, 1842, 1865, 1872, 1875, 1876, 1878, 1879, 1886, 1893, 1899, 1901, 1902, 1905, 1909; Department of Interior, 1882, 1886, 1892, 1901, 1907; Department of Agriculture, 1868, 1875, 1888, 1899, 1901, 1906, 1907; Department of Commerce and Labor, 1891, 1893, 1905, 1906; Government Office, 17 reports between 1819 and 1909.

The Rôle of Civic Agencies and Bureaus of Municipal Research

In preparing the way for national leadership, too much weight cannot be given to the work of the many unofficial civic agencies which have urged the need for better public service, or to voluntary and unofficial committees which have conducted staff inquiries and coöperated with officers in obtaining intelligent consideration for questions of municipal and state administration. These latter began their work during the Roosevelt administration. The interest manifested at this time in the methods and results of municipal administration is shown by the sudden development of unofficial "Bureaus of Municipal Research." In 1906 a special committee was organized by the Citizen's Union of New York, of which Mr. Fulton Cutting was the head. Through this committee and its staff such results were obtained that in 1907 it was incorporated as an independent, nonpartisan "Bureau of Municipal Research," with a board of trustees of nation-wide reputation, based on their interest in municipal administration. Its point of view was that the conditions found and described in the large cities were quite as much a matter of citizen neglect as they were matters of official wrong-mindedness and boss rule. New emphasis and vigor was given to unofficial civic enterprise by the employment of a staff which approached the problem by the research method. During the next ten years no less than thirty bureaus of similar character were organized which employed trained staffs to study administration conditions and results in as many cities. In many other cities special committees of Chambers of Commerce or other existing agencies were organized; or existing agencies, public or private, employed the staff of the New York Bureau of Municipal Research and other research bureaus, with a view to making more effective coöperation between citizen bodies and officers who sought to bring about efficient administration. The New York Bureau alone lent staff aid in making about fifty surveys and reports to official and unofficial bodies in cities scattered over the length and breadth of the United States; and wherever these inquiries were conducted wide publicity was given to findings and recommendations by the daily press. A number of studies of state administration have also been made by the New York Bureau. These various civic activities and the concrete information given to the public, the new sense of civic duty, the larger appreciation of the need for increased efficiency in public administration in order to meet the larger social demands made by a rapidly growing population, the correspondingly rapid rise in the cost of government, threatened deficits, and increasing tax rates — these are the facts which were brought to the minds of the people and which gave a new emphasis to every appeal for support by new leaders who urged administrative reorganization.

Commissions to Recommend Administrative Reorganization in the State Governments

" The state movement for efficiency and economy" following the inquiry begun by President Taft has been described in a monograph bearing this title prepared by Raymond Moley.[1] In his first chapter the author says: " The formation of commissions, boards, and departments having for their purpose the reorganization of government in the interest of efficiency and economy dates back to the year following the appointment of the Taft Economy and Efficiency Commission for the investigation of the Federal administration. The first state agency created for this purpose was the board of public affairs of Wisconsin in 1911. The New Jersey and

[1] Published by the New York Bureau of Municipal Research as " Bulletin No. 90," containing 163 pages.

Massachusetts commissions were created in 1912, while the following year agencies were established by legislative acts in four more states." The list of commissions which are described in this study, with dates of establishment, follows:

The State Board of Public Affairs, Wisconsin, July 6, 1911; the Economy and Efficiency Commission, New Jersey, April 1, 1912; the Commission on Economy and Efficiency, Massachusetts, June 6, 1912; the Committee of Inquiry, New York, January 6, 1913; the Department of Efficiency and Economy, New York, April 14, 1913; the Joint Committee on Retrenchment and Reform, Iowa, February 6, 1913; the Efficiency and Economy Commission, Illinois, April, 1913; the Economy and Efficiency Commission, Pennsylvania, July 25, 1913; the Economy and Efficiency Commission, Minnesota, October, 1913; the Commission to Investigate the Advisability of Consolidating Certain State Boards and Commissions and to Investigate the Public Health Laws, Connecticut, February 9, 1915; the Legislative Investigating Committee, Alabama, February 13, 1915; the Survey Committee of State Affairs, Colorado, February, 1915; the Efficiency and Economy Committee, Kansas, March 20, 1915; the Committee on Economy and Efficiency, Virginia, March 16, 1916; the Commission of Seven Business Men, Oregon, February, 1917; the Efficiency Commission of West Virginia, March, 1917.

"It should be understood," says Mr. Moley, "that the commissions considered in this bulletin constitute only a portion of the agencies recently created in the states, which have had as their function the improvement of state administration. A number of states created commissions to study state expenditures and budgetary procedure while innumerable attempts have been made by the formation of commissions to hunt graft and corruption. We shall consider only those commissions which have actually made investigations and recommendations covering the structure and methods of administration."

It is of interest to note the reasons assigned and subject of inquiries named in the laws of states providing for these commissions, and the unanimity of opinion in finding that the administrative machinery of the several states should be radically changed.

Among the duties assigned to the State Board of Public Affairs of Wisconsin were the following:

" To coördinate, by mutual agreement with the several public bodies, their investigations, and to provide for such additional investigations as may be necessary to carry out the purposes of the law.

" To investigate duplication of work of public bodies and the efficiency of the organization and administration of such public bodies; formulate plans for the greater co-ordination of such public bodies and the improvement of the state administration in general.

" To prepare a budget report.

" To publish reports and make recommendations to the legislature."

The powers and duties assigned to the commissioner of efficiency and economy of New York were these:

" Make a careful and thorough study of each office, institution, and department maintained by the state and . . . make recommendations to the governor, and to the officer, board, or commission in charge of said office, institution, or department touching the efficiency and economy of the work, business, and service therein."

The Committee on Retrenchment and Reform of Iowa was authorized to:

" Institute such changes in the administration of public affairs as will promote efficiency engineers to assist in the investigation."

The Efficiency and Economy Committee of Illinois was given:

" Full power and authority to investigate all departments of the state government, including all boards, bureaus, and commissions which have been created by the general assembly, such investigations to be made with a view to securing a more perfect system of accounting, combining and centralizing the duties of the various departments, abolishing such as are useless and securing for the state of Illinois such reorganization that will promote greater efficiency and greater economy in her various branches of government."

The Commission on the Consolidation of State Commissions of Connecticut was appointed to investigate and report on:

" The reorganization and consolidation of the various state and county boards with a view to greater economy and efficiency."

These are fairly typical of the views expressed by the legislature of the need for reorganization and especially the need for coördinating the work of the many independent or semi-independent offices and boards. The commissions almost invariably confirmed this view and several of them reported specific plans of consolidation. All agreed that the administration should be more centralized; i. e. that related functions and activities should be grouped and administered together. But there was a difference of opinion with respect to the place and power of the governor. For example, the commissions appointed in New Jersey and Wisconsin adhered to the board idea of administration, recommending the retention of the governor as a negative force and advisory to the legislature. On the other hand, the commissions of Iowa and Minnesota were convinced that the governor should be made a chief executive with heads of departments under and responsible to him.

Recommendations for Government by Commissions

In proposing consolidation, the New Jersey commission recommended the reorganization of the public-service functions under eight departments, each of which would be headed by a board and a commissioner responsible to the board.   The reasons given were these:

"We . . . find that all modern enterprises are conducted by corporations . . . guided by a board of directors; in fact, the law in this state — as in others — provides that business of any corporation shall be managed by its directors, and that each shall have a chief executive called its president. . . . It has, therefore, been our aim to group together commissions and officials engaged in the same kind of work, and to consolidate such work in one department, with a board of directors, and a chief, corresponding to the president of the corporation.   The powers of the consolidated departments we believe should be conferred upon the board of directors, so that it may define the policy to be pursued by the department, and to enact rules and regulations to be observed by the chief and all employees."

The argument for the separate incorporation of each important service has been carried to the point of giving to each board financial independence.   In Wisconsin, as is pointed out later, this is defended as an element of strength in the organization.   The New Jersey commission was more frank than most of the advocates of administration by commissions.   It boldly asserted that the government could best be run by an aristocracy of intelligence with little or no regard for the electorate.   This view is brought out by the further reasoning of the report:

"We believe that the best class of men will be secured to act on such boards if no salary is paid, and if they are allowed only their necessary expenses.   We have seriously considered the advisability of paying some small salary, but experience has shown that for every salary offered there are numerous office seekers, the majority of whom scarcely measure up to the salaries to be paid. We believe that there are many public-spirited men in the state who cannot be induced to enter the employ of the state on a salary basis, but who would cheerfully give their services if they are afforded fair opportunity to have a voice in shaping the policies of the state and improving general conditions."

Such was the plan proposed in New Jersey, for getting trained men as department executives. The single head responsible to the board could then be chosen to execute policies, could then be selected because of his training and fitness; and an inducement could be held out to men who would make public service a career. If politics were allowed to come in there was in their opinion little hope of securing efficiency and economy in the service. This is also one of the accepted doctrines in Wisconsin.

All of the commissions except that of Wisconsin devoted their inquiries and reports largely to questions of reorganization and budget-making procedure. The State Board of Public Affairs of Wisconsin was controlled by men who had taken leading parts in the development of the board idea in that state and had advocated its adoption elsewhere — men interested in specialized services of government rather than in questions of coördination of functions and giving balance and proportion to administrative plans and state finances. This is clearly shown by the list of inquiries made and reports rendered, some of which were conducted by the board itself and others in coöperation with departments and institutions. Twelve of the eighteen subjects reported were:

Farm tenancy in Wisconsin.
Rural credit conditions in portions of Wisconsin.
State loans to farmers.
Distribution of Wisconsin potatoes.

Distribution of Wisconsin cheese.

Distribution of Sheboygan County cheese.

Feasibility of adopting a state brand to standardize Wisconsin products.

Agricultural coöperation and coöperative methods.

Survey of Wisconsin rural schools.

Survey of Wisconsin high schools.

Survey of Wisconsin normal schools.

Survey of Wisconsin State University.

The reports bearing on questions of administration and finance included:

Budget practices of various states and nations.

Feasibility of a central board of control for all public educational institutions.

Departmental reorganization and efficiency of state employees.

In these reports the " government by commission " idea was taken for granted or staunchly defended. The independent, specialized board idea prevailed; and the recommendations for budget procedure were an adaptation to the existing establishments which had been put under board control.

Recommendations for Single-Headed Administration

The most complete plans of the early proposals for administrative reorganization were those of Minnesota, Iowa, and New York. The Iowa and Minnesota plans excluded the constitutional officers, while the New York plan contemplated a revision of the constitution and the inclusion of all administrative agencies in the reorganization. Each of these plans proposed to divide the administrative branch into a few departments which were to be under the control of single heads appointed by the governor and responsible to him, the only exceptions being under the New York plan in the case of departments performing quasi-judicial or quasi-legislative functions.

The opinion of Mr. E. Dana Durand, chief of staff of the Minnesota commission, is of special interest when considered in relation to the conclusions of the New Jersey commission quoted above. He said: " Minnesota, like most other states, is commissioned to death. Some of these boards are paid, but most of them are unsalaried or made up of groups of state officials serving *ex officio*. Boards are all right in their place . . . but that place is not in the administration of government, the execution of the law. The board system tends to delay, to dissipate responsibility, to inefficiency generally. You cannot put your finger on the man who is to blame if anything goes wrong. Several or many minds for counsel; one mind for action — that is a principle long ago enunciated but strangely departed from."

The plans of administrative reorganization and consolidation now in operation in Illinois, Idaho, and Nebraska provide for single-headed departments under the direct control of the governor. These, as well as the several proposed plans for administrative reorganization, are described in detail under Part II.

CHAPTER VII

GENERAL DISCUSSION OF ADMINISTRATIVE REORGANIZA-
TION PLANS TO PROVIDE FOR RESPONSIBLE LEADERSHIP

THE fight in England in the reign of King John, to
make the executive responsible through control over the
purse, was the beginning of a long series of conflicts
between the forces for self-government and a legalized
autocratic ruling class. In America the fight to make the
executive responsible through control over the purse has
been long delayed — expedient finally resorted to as a
means of making popular control effective. It comes at
the end of a century-old contest between the forces of
popular self-government and those which stand for class
rule; latterly this has meant war on the irresponsible
"party" organizations that in turn have profited from
class rule. In this conflict the battle has been waged
around the stronghold of the irresponsible boss, the head
of an irresponsible party system. The forces of the boss
were always well organized, and under capable leaders;
when not occupied in self-defense, they planned and executed forays for spoils. This was made possible because
of lack of responsible leadership — a thing that the
American people had been taught was dangerous.

As has been pointed out many times, the whole history
of American politics has been the history of a struggle
not *for* something, but *against* something; ours was a
negative political philosophy; first we fought *against*
an irresponsible foreign autocracy, which was forced to
acknowledge defeat after an eight years' war for independence; then the electorate asserted itself *against* an

irresponsible American commercial and landed aristocracy which was first defeated under the leadership of Jefferson and was finally overthrown by the old warrior, Jackson; then began the struggle of American democracy *against* the domination of an unaristocratic, and still more irresponsible, "party" organization, the leadership of which was entirely outside the government and beyond the reach of what had come to be a broadly democratic electorate.

Boss Rule vs. Responsible Leadership

For nearly a hundred years the struggle *against* this last form of autocracy, bred in and of a desire for power and thriving on a fat and privileged plutocracy, has been going on with indifferent success. Under these conditions the wellsprings of democracy, impregnated with ideals of human liberty, equality, and brotherhood, have become turbid with passion. Popular resentment has increased, until it has threatened disorder; and by this fact the future of our institutions has been made more uncertain. From frontal attack, special privilege, thus organized, proved to be fully protected, its intrenchment invulnerable. The overthrow of one irresponsible boss or party resulted only in the enthronement of another. Finally, thoughtful men interested in the cause of democracy began to point out the fundamental weakness, not of our Constitution, but of the institutions which the people have permitted to grow up under them. They began to point to the fact that what we needed was a positive philosophy which might speak in terms of human service. We needed to organize to do something good and not simply to prevent something bad. To accomplish what the people desired, it was necessary to provide for an able, effective leadership within the government. And no one did more to emphasize the need for calling the electorate to the support of responsible leadership than Mr. Roosevelt.   In his efforts to build up and maintain a following, he, as chief executive of the nation, held that he was responsible to the whole people.   Public opinion was the "big stick" grasped and used by him to command respect for his leadership and to enforce a discipline within both the service and deliberative branches of the Government through which he sought to get things done.   He said to the people: "I am your chosen leader; come to me; let me know what you want and I'll see to it that you get service; I will see to it that we have the conditions provided for rendering service if I have to go out with the hosts of Armageddon and fight every plutocrat in the country and every congressman in his own district."   And the people believed in him.   They were ready to follow his leadership because they believed in him.

This was the beginning of a new, a constructive, a positive philosophy of citizenship, a constructive purpose for a nation-wide electorate.   And though President Roosevelt did little to institutionalize executive leadership, a new drift was given to public thought which ultimately carried with it the conviction that the way to defeat an outside, irresponsible leadership was to give to the people a responsible leadership.   The way to provide pure air in the house of the people is not to try to create a vacuum, but to provide a means for drawing in that which is unpolluted and serviceable.   The atmosphere of democracy must be filtered and made to flow into useful channels by the power of leadership which may be made accountable.   It was in the quest for a means of developing responsible government, a means for making the public service responsive to public opinion, through a leadership that could interpret and at the same time was accountable to the people, that those who sought popular support turned to administrative reorganization and budget making.

The new background given to political thought, the changed condition which brought to the front the demand for responsible leadership was a recognition of new social need. This first impressed itself on the agencies of service, through the efforts of various humanitarian civic societies and committees. These efforts were independent and decentralized; they led to administrative decentralization. The method used was a further application of past negative philosophy in the effort to dethrone the boss, but it carried with it a positive principle of service, and following this enlarged service demand came the present movement. The effort to overcome this negative philosophy resulted in a positive demand for responsible leadership.

Reorganization and Financial Responsibility in the large Cities

Increasing demands for service were first felt in the cities — the great centers of population. Here was first felt the need for administrative reorganization as a means of giving balance and proportion to plans for service and the apportionment of public funds. The demand for administrative reorganization and centralized financial control became most acute in the national metropolis. When in 1894 the five boroughs,— Manhattan, Brooklyn, Queens, Kings, and Richmond — were about to be consolidated into the Greater City of New York a commission was appointed to frame a new charter. Their aim was to negative the results of decentralization and thereby to prevent boss rule. In the charter which was adopted the old machinery of decentralization through control by standing committees of the legislative body was abandoned. Control by a Board of Estimate and Apportionment composed in the main of independently elected executive officers was substituted in its stead. This central-governing agency was charged with the duty both of

making plans and of executing them.   The institutional
means adopted for planning was a charter requirement
that the Board of Estimate and Apportionment should
make a budget.   The Board of Aldermen, the old legislative body with its standing committees, was retained.
But for purposes of control over the purse it was shorn
of all but its reviewing and approving power.   It could
not initiate finance measures.   The leadership of the committee chairmen was gone.   The leadership became executive.   The legislative body as a whole could reduce
but could not increase items of the appropriation bill proposed by the Board of Estimate and Apportionment.

Thus it was that in New York City the principle of
centralization was introduced.   And an effort was made
to provide for responsible executive leadership by giving
the mayor a seat in the Board of Aldermen.   But no
procedure was enacted to enforce this responsibility.   The
mayor was not made responsible for the administration.
He was only one of four executives elected by the city at
large.   He was not the budget maker.   He was not required to go before the appropriating body; he was only
permitted.   Attempt was made to give publicity by permitting " nobodies " to appear before the Board of Estimate and Apportionment.   But nothing was done to make
the duly constituted forum effective.   The Board of Aldermen could not change the terms and conditions attached to the budget, and no provision was made for
appeal to the electorate by an opposing majority in the
appropriating body.   The members of the central executive council, the Board of Estimate and Apportionment, were elected for a fixed term of years, and when
they came to an agreement on a budget that was, in effect,
the end of it.   The Board of Aldermen might refuse
to pass the measure, but the body was not in good standing and there was no way to make a popular appeal, therefore they approved.   The budget and all matters of

finance came to be largely a matter of secret compromise between independently elected executives. Here was centralization without the means of locating or enforcing accountability.

The Program of the National Municipal League — Federal Plan; Commission Plan; Commission Manager Plan

Soon after this experiment had been launched a civic organization, the National Municipal League, began a nation-wide propaganda for the administrative and legislative reorganization of American municipalities. In 1899 the league published a " municipal program," which was based on the idea of a small council and a chief executive with power to appoint and remove departmental heads. Because a highly centralized administrative organization was proposed, the program of the League came to be known as the " Federal plan," a designation suggested by analogy to the plan of the Federal government. This was part of an underlying movement based on lack of confidence in the legislative branch. Many municipalities adopted the plan of centralization proposed.

The " Federal plan " proving unsatisfactory, a new propaganda sprang up and the League shifted its advocacy to " commission government." This differed from the " government by commission " propaganda in the states in that the " commission government " idea of the cities was a centralization scheme, while the state movement was for decentralization. Again a large number of municipalities followed the leadership and proposals of the League and the " commission government " advocates. Reorganizations followed which did away with the legislative council made up of the many representatives of wards. They went still farther than the New York charter had gone by combining both the legislative and executive functions in a small council elected " at large." The many decentralized administrative departments were centralized, executive leadership being allotted to members of the council.

For several years the " commission government " idea held sway, and much good came from centering public interest in the acts of a few elected officers who could not shift responsibility either for administrative or legislative acts. The weakness of the plan, however, soon became apparent. In doing away with an independent reviewing body the people had deprived themselves of the most effective means of publicity.

The people, seeking for visible government, were again disappointed; and a new propaganda was launched. The efforts of many unofficial civic agencies now turned to the " commission manager plan "; and the program of the National Municipal League was modified accordingly. This plan preserved the small council; it preserved the principle of centralization of executive responsibility, and aimed to increase the efficiency of the service by providing for the appointment of a trained executive accountable to the council.

The Propaganda of the Short Ballot Association

The commission-manager plan was in the nature of a reversion, in that it set up an administrative branch under a chief executive, the manager, and gave to the representative council powers of inquest, criticism, discussion, and decision on matters of public policy. It went farther than the " Federal plan " in that it gave to the reviewing appropriating body the power to appoint and remove the manager. The new form of organization had the support of the Short Ballot Association, an unofficial propagandist civic agency which sought to make popular control more effective by reducing the number of elected officers. Its mission was to undo the work of the " back to the people " propagandists of the first part of the nine-

teenth century when the effort was first made to prevent
autocracy, then later to defeat the boss by " electing every-
body." The Short Ballot Association would center all executive responsibility in a single person whose acts could
be reviewed and who could be held accountable to the
people for leadership. Although it supported the commission-manager plan, this was inconsistent with the short-
ballot propaganda in that the manager was not to be
elected. The commission-manager idea was in fact another device to keep the leadership of the public service out
of politics and free from electoral control; it was another
form of " council of the wise," without provision for political leadership and without definite procedure for inquest
and determination of issues in a public forum from whose
decisions appeal could be made to the people when the proposals of the head of the public service were not supported
by a majority of the representative body. In fact, one
of its claims to popular support was that the manager, as
chief executive, would not be in politics.

Beginning of Administrative Reorganization Movement in State Governments

The movement to institutionalize leadership by reorganization of the public service in a manner to make the
chief executive the outstanding person in politics got its
initial impetus from President Taft's inquiry into the
methods of administration of the Federal Government and
his recommendations which fell on the deaf ears of an
opposition " party " in Congress. The motive for the appointment of the special executive staff in 1910, and of
the Economy and Efficiency Commission in 1911 by
President Taft, had been to reduce the waste and increase
the effectiveness of the administrative branch of the
Federal Government. Of the one hundred and eight reports prepared and submitted by the commission to the
President and the twenty-six reports sent by the President

to Congress with special messages requesting legislative action, only two dealt with the subject of budget making; all of the others dealt with questions of administrative reorganization and procedure. The same dominant motive was present in executive requests and legislative acts leading to the appointment of state committees and commissions on economy and efficiency from 1911 to 1918, as well as in the resolutions calling constitutional conventions and proposing amendments in administrative law.

The reports and recommendations of these many state committees and commissions, as well as the statutory and constitutional enactments which speak in terms of administrative reorganization, are of two general types:

(1) Those designed to locate responsibility through providing for a strong, sole, executive leadership — a leadership within the government which could be effective for directing and improving the public service and at the same time could be reached and controlled by the electorate and their representatives through their constitutional power to control the purse, and

(2) Those designed to protect and continue " government by commission "— the many independent boards, to which had been turned over to the service functions of government to get them beyond the reach of irresponsible party leadership and control, created to prevent the building up of a strong executive.

In most cases the economy and efficiency commissions have reported favoring the first plan. In some instances, however, these commissions were dominated by the civic forces which had sought to defeat the boss through decentralization. In most cases statutory and constitutional proposals and enactments looking toward administrative reorganization followed the recommendations of the economy commissions. In some instances the forces favoring continued decentralization controlled. A third group is made up of states in which the two forces found agreement in compromise with no consistent policy of reorganization dominating, the enactments only partially satisfying the demands of the opposing force.

Reorganization Plans Providing for Centralization of Executive Authority

Among the state plans actually enacted as measures for reorganizing the administration around a responsible executive, Illinois, Idaho, and Nebraska are the most thoroughgoing and consistent in design. Of those which have adhered to the principle of decentralization most closely Wisconsin deserves special mention. New Jersey is an outstanding example of the mixed type.

The Proposed New York Plan of 1915

The Constitutional Convention of New York, in 1915, adopted a plan of state reorganization which for thoroughness of consideration and discussion of the advantages of the executive type stands as a monument to statesmanship. This was bitterly opposed by persons who combined to preserve the old legislative practices on the one hand, and by the advocates of commission government on the other. The proposed new constitution was defeated at the polls, but it has had a marked influence on the political thinking of the whole country. The chief weakness of the plan as worked out was that, while it provided for leadership, it did not adequately provide the means for enforcing accountability through inquest and appeal — it did not provide adequately for popular control.

Illinois Plan

The first state to carry into execution the principles advocated was Illinois. Here the opposition of the several elected constitutional officers was largely avoided by making administrative reorganization a matter of legislative enactment instead of constitutional reform. For this achievement the way had been prepared: first by the report of the economy commission; and later by a campaign before the people, when Governor Lowden and a legislature were elected on the issue. As soon as Governor Lowden was inaugurated he set all the machinery of the government to work to accomplish the purpose. He was elected as a Republican following a Democratic predecessor in office. He found the state offices filled with Democrats. This was a tactical advantage, for it gave him opportunity to refuse to make appointments until the new administrative code had become law. And with very good reason, too! Had not the party given its pledge? How could he make intelligent appointments before he knew what the organization would be? By taking this stand he not only had public opinion back of him, but the pressure of office seekers was also put behind an early passage of the act. And after a complete reorganization had been consummated so far as this could be effected by the legislature a resolution was passed providing for a constitutional convention to complete the work. Fortunately, duties of the independently elected officers of the state did not seriously interfere with the reorganization. The auditor of the state retained an independent check on the administration, but control over requisitions, accounting, and preaudit of bills was placed in the department of finance under the governor. The state treasurer remained the custodian of funds, but all preparation of financial plans and supervision of authorized expenditures came under executive control. The secretary of state still administered a few functions like the collection of the automobile tax, but this did not seriously impair the executive function. The state superintendent of education was independently elected, but this did not stand in the way of the creation of an executive department dealing with education. Through the whole reorganization Governor Lowden's leadership and responsibility to the people stands out.

The most serious obstacle to an effective electoral control over the executive is found not in the independent constitutional offices, but in the old type of legislative procedure which does not admit of leadership by the governor. Because the organization and rules of the legislature did not admit of leadership by the governor, openly, there was no clear definition of issues in shaping matters of policy, in case of controversy, on which sides could be taken in discussion in the deliberative body. For the same reason there was no issue developed which could be taken before the voters either at the by-election or at the end of the fixed term of four years when the governor must justify himself. The cabinet was responsible to the governor but there was no way of making either the government or the cabinet responsible to the electorate or to their representatives.

Plans of Idaho and Nebraska

In 1919 two states followed the Illinois example — Idaho and Nebraska. Of these Idaho adopted a code much in the same form as that enacted under the leadership of Governor Lowden, by transfer of function and general provisions for adjustment of conflicts of existing statutes and jurisdictions. Nebraska sought to avoid conflict by rewriting and codifying all of the existing organic laws.

This work was begun in Nebraska, under authority of the legislature of 1913, by a committee of the House and Senate to study the administrative organization of the state. The committee reported May 15, 1914. In Illinois the recommendations of its commission were made a political issue on 1916. In Nebraska the recommendations of its committee were made a political issue, and in 1918 Governor McKelvie was elected on a platform which

pledged him and the legislature to the enactment of a
civil administrative code "providing for the consolidation of boards, institutions, commissions, and different
departments and agencies of government." In the spring
of 1919 the legislature passed a bill grouping all of the
activities, not assigned to officers and board of the constitution, into six departments. Each of these departments was given a single head appointed by the governor,
with the approval of the Senate but for fixed terms to end
with the governor's tenure. There is in this a limitation
of executive power not consistent with the responsibilities
of the office. Besides, the old legislative procedure remains unchanged, thereby depriving the people of open
discussion of measures initialed by the executive with
responsible officers present to explain and defend.

The Idaho reorganization code was passed in February,
1919. It provides for the consolidation of all functions,
not assigned to officers and boards by the constitution, in
nine departments as in Illinois, with slight differences in
the distribution of duties. Each department has a single
head appointed by the governor and with the exception
of one is removable by him at will. The commissioner of
immigration, labor, and statistics is a constitutional
officer appointed by the governor with the advice and consent of the Senate for a term of two years. Idaho's governor, as in the case of Illinois and Nebraska, is deprived
of the opportunity of personally appearing before the
legislature in committee of the whole or otherwise as a
matter of regular procedure, for giving publicity to
measures advocated and clearly defining issues through
open question and discussion of issues; and there is no
provision for appeal in case of a deadlock, or an opposition majority.

" The Wisconsin Idea "

Wisconsin has been foremost among the states in its advocacy of " government of commission." In fact, its civic leaders have been so conspicuous in the propagation of this system of administration that the government-by-commission plan is frequently referred to as " The Wisconsin Idea "— a designation taken from a volume written by Dr. Charles McCarthy which bears that title. Under the influence of a group of University of Wisconsin men, who interested themselves in making different branches of state administration more serviceable to the people, their government has been broken up into a large number of independent offices and boards.

While all of the states drifted strongly to this method of dealing with the boss in seeking to make the public administration more efficient many of them, in recent years, have abandoned the method — in theory at least. Wisconsin, however, has held consistently to the government-by-commission theory. And during the last few years while consolidations have taken place the decentralized " commission " type of administration is still retained.

The type has already been described. Each main service branch, by act of the legislature, is made independent by being placed under the management of a board or commission — we may say, has been separately incorporated as an eleemosynary institution. The members of each public-service board are appointed for long and overlapping tenures. The public functions administered by each board are supported by continuing appropriations, thereby giving to them what amounts to a state endowment. Thus established, each board undertakes to develop a more efficient service by employment of staff experts.

But the various independencies did not have the machinery for giving balance and proportion to the state administration as a whole — it lacked the means of developing a state program except as this came about in an informal and uninstitutional way through personal contact and understandings between propagandists — leaders who were in no way connected with the processes of popular control. In developing an official means for giving balance and proportion to a state program a central commission was created — the state board of public affairs, to which was assigned among other things the duty of preparing a budget. Thus the supervisory and inquisitorial function was performed by a super-board of which the governor and certain members of the legislature were members.

The weakness of this administrative system, lack of responsibility to the electorate and their representatives, has been recognized. And in the last legislature an effort was made to cure the defect in a way that points to a method of control which may be made consistent with the ideals of democracy by establishing a legislative premiership — a legislative majority leadership with power to control the administration. A bill was introduced which, had it become law, would have given to the representative branch of the government the right to dismiss the administrative heads by what would have amounted to a vote of " lack of confidence." This bill passed both houses and was prevented from becoming law only by executive veto. The implications of the enactment are deserving of special consideration, since it is the first attempt in our national political history whereby government by commission has attempted to face the question of popular control by providing procedure through which responsible leadership might be developed under conditions such that issues might be clearly drawn, reviewed, criticized, and approved or disapproved in the established forum of the people. The virtue of the measure lies, not in its provisions, but in the necessary implication of its outworkings. Assuming that the measure passed by the Wisconsin legislature had not been vetoed by the governor, its necessary operation would be to develop an administrative cabinet responsible to the representative body — and this body necessarily would have developed a responsible majority and minority leadership. Any effort to dismiss an administrative officer would have aligned the forces for and against such action. No such action could be initiated without leadership, and the leadership would cause the members of the representative body to take sides. The procedure of inquest into the office or acts or proposals of the officer would be given a dramatic setting that would give publicity to the issue involved. The continued operation of such a law would in the end develop a system of control much after the plan which has grown up in France — legislative leadership itself under such circumstances would carry with it political issues. This would accomplish the desired purpose of taking control out of the hands of an irresponsible political boss. The only leadership possible would be one which would be in the first instance responsible to the representative body, ultimate control being in the state electorate by making administrative leadership amenable to the representative body — the " parties " developed in the process of inquest and determination of issues would necessarily be made up of those who took sides. Thus the party management would be made up of the leaders who represented a majority on the one hand and a responsible opposition. The necessary result would be a legislative prime minister. In the evolution of such a system, whether the departments were managed by boards or by single heads, it would produce responsible government; a government made responsible through a leadership that would be under electoral control.

Wisconsin Idea vs. Illinois Plan

The measure, however, did not become law, and Wisconsin still has an administration which in type lacks the processes of popular control.   Accepting the measure which was defeated as a declaration of intent and purpose and the contrast is striking by which the two neighbor states, Illinois and Wisconsin, are seeking to develop responsible government.   The one, Illinois, has sought to square its institutions with the underlying principle of democracy through an elected executive prime minister; the other, Wisconsin, has sought to accomplish this end through a legislative prime minister.   Neither method has been fully elaborated.   Each is lacking in essential points. The Illinois plan still lacks a procedure by which the representative body may perform the function of inquest, discussion of issues raised by a responsible leadership with a right of appeal to the people.   The Wisconsin plan for the establishment of a responsible leadership has not yet got beyond the academic stage.   But in case the theory of legislative control comes to be established it must necessarily carry with it a procedure which, through the definition and discussion of issues that arise in the contest between leaders, will reach to the electorate.

The New York Standing Committee System

These two states are taken as types because they have gone farthest in the development of two methods of control over the administration which hold out promise to the electorate.   New York is the most conspicuous adherent of the old type of control through standing legislative committees, the system which has contributed most to the persistent domination of the irresponsible boss and his machine.   The Constitutional Convention of 1915 undertook to reorganize the state along the lines later followed by Illinois, but the plan was opposed both by the old-time irresponsible party organizations and by the reform element who had won their successes through decentralization. The result was that the standing-committee system and the irresponsible boss became the more firmly intrenched.

In these states (Illinois, Wisconsin, and New York) are found the highest development of the three distinct types of leadership — the elected executive type, the commission type, and the legislative standing committee type. Many other states have passed measures of reorganization, but, generally speaking, they are the result of mixed political emotion, with lack of definition of institutional program. In each state the people have been reaching out for responsible government. In no states, however, has the question of popular control been squarely faced.

CHAPTER VIII

GENERAL DESCRIPTION AND CLASSIFICATION OF RECENT
STATE BUDGET ENACTMENTS

ALTHOUGH an opposition party in power prevented the consideration of President Taft's proposed budget by Congress, it made a very strong appeal to the country. The good opinion gained for it is reflected in many ways, but in no way more convincing than in the action taken by the several states. Forty-four of the forty-eight States have enacted, or have pending, constitutional or statutory measures on the subject.

Budget Legislation in California and Wisconsin

Wisconsin and California were the first to obtain legislative action. California had been a boss-ridden state for years, and its finances were in a condition to call for leadership. This was found in Hiram Johnson who, after a vigorous campaign, was installed in office in January, 1911, with a sympathetic legislature back of him. The appropriations were handled in the usual way, and in March they began to flood the desk of the governor. Thereupon he called for the information supporting each grant, but much of the desired data was wanting. He signed such bills as commended themselves, but characterized the proceeding as "a disgrace to the people of an intelligent commonwealth." A state board of control was created with large powers both of audit and approval and the next year, 1912, a budget was prepared for submission to the 1913 legislature.

During the same year, 1911, the Wisconsin legislature passed a law which created a state board of public affairs to conduct investigations into state administration and to introduce methods which would promote economy and efficiency. Wisconsin has been one of the foremost of the states in its effort to overthrow the rule of the irresponsible party boss. In the case of state reorganization, what gave body and vitality to the movement was the increasing demands for service. In the case of the budget movement, it was the lack of balance and proportion given to state development and the rapid rise of expenditures that led thinking men to see the need for more effective control over the finances. So long as the various specialized civic agencies and local constituencies were each left to promote the subject of its special interest through a multitude of boards and commissions on the one hand, and a multitude of standing legislative committees by logrolling methods on the other, there must necessarily be lack of balance and proportion in the development of the public service; there must be dissatisfaction shown at the mounting cost of government. Although Wisconsin was more fortunate than most states in the public spirit shown by a group of progressive civic leaders who were in virtual control in and about the state University located at the capital city, the need for some means of thinking about the whole state enterprise was no less apparent.

While the "Wisconsin idea" had done much to make the state government effective a strong opposition campaign was started. In 1909 the tax commission was asked to inquire into the state of the finances, and their report was submitted in 1911, following which the legislature put the finances also under a central commission, the "State Board of Public Affairs," and in 1913 a definite budget procedure was adopted.

Massachusetts had gone even further than Wisconsin in the work of administrative decentralization. It had more than two hundred independent or quasi-independent agencies, over forty of which were boards and commissions. In 1912 the legislature provided for a state finance board, known as the commission on economy and efficiency, but it did not undertake seriously to establish a budget until 1918.

Budget Legislation in Other States

What had been found true in California, Wisconsin, and Massachusetts was found true in other states. In 1913 the budget movement spread to six states: Arkansas, Illinois, New York, North Dakota, Ohio, and Oregon. Louisiana followed in 1914 and Massachusetts took further action, enlarging the powers of its economy and efficiency commission. In 1915, Connecticut, Iowa, Minnesota, Nebraska, Vermont, and Washington passed budget laws and North Dakota and Wisconsin further developed their plans; and New York submitted to the people a proposed new constitution which had in it a budget provision. In 1916 Louisiana and Maryland amended their constitutions to make a budget mandatory. New Jersey provided for a budget by statute and New York passed the Sage-Maier law.

In 1917 statutory budget provisions were passed by Illinois, South Dakota, Tennessee, Kansas, New Mexico and Utah. Besides these, Delaware and Mississippi provided for a trial procedure for the next legislative session, and North Carolina imposed on the Legislative Reference Bureau the duty of collecting, preparing, and submitting estimates. Vermont also revised the procedure enacted in 1914.

In 1918, two states, Massachusetts and West Virginia, provided for a budget procedure by constitutional amendment, and Georgia, Kentucky, Mississippi, and Virginia set up a regular budget procedure by statutory enactment.

In the spring sessions of 1919, Indiana enacted a proposed constitutional amendment, and fourteen states passed budget laws; namely, Alabama, Arizona, Colorado, Idaho, Maine, Michigan, Montana, Nevada, New Hamshire, North Carolina, Oklahoma, South Carolina, Texas, and Wyoming. South Dakota and Connecticut amended their laws and Nebraska and New Mexico repealed their old laws by the passage of the new ones.

Of the remaining four states all of the legislatures have had the subject before them. The Pennsylvania legislature passed a budget law in 1917 which was vetoed by the governor. In Florida, Missouri, and Rhode Island the subject was brought before the legislature by executive message.

Budget Movement, a Quest for Responsible Leadership

In considering the recent movement for a budget procedure, this fact cannot be given too great weight: that the quest for responsible government is the quest for a means of making effective popular control over public servants — both administrative and deliberative. A form of organization adapted to getting things done is as necessary to the development of ideals and a dominant popular will as it is to rendering service demanded. Having provided an organization effective for purposes of ministering to public wants, it is quite as important to provide an organization and procedure which will be effective as a means of popular control. In fact, these two things must go hand in hand. If adequate means of popular control are not provided for, the people themselves in defense of their liberties will insist on a weak organization for rendering service. This is the normal and usual reaction against irresponsible leadership to prevent it from being so strong as to become dangerous. The overthrow of autocratic power is always considered more important in a democracy than efficient service. And when the service organization becomes impaired in order to overthrow executive autocracy, executive leadership remains weak until the demands for service reestablishes it on a responsible basis. Our whole history, our negative political philosophy, our constantly recurring upsets of administrative organization, bear witness to truth of this conclusion.

Strong, able leadership is as necessary to the effective administration of public service as it is to the administration of private business. But the leadership must be made responsible and responsive to public opinion, otherwise it will be inhibited. A democratic electorate is the organ or agency of the state for sounding public opinion. A representative body is the only practical means of inquest, criticism, and discussion of the acts and proposals of the administration in aid of the electorate. To connect this organ of inquiry and discussion with the people, its deliberations must be conducted in the open — must be made public knowledge.

It is with a view of making the representative branch of the government effective for purposes of inquest, criticism, and discussion, effective for impressing the will of the people on the administration through its leadership, that control over the purse has been given to them.

A budget procedure is the only effective means which has ever been devised for forcing administrative leadership, the responsible executives, to come before the representative body not alone to give an account of past acts, but to require them to make known their plans for the future before further support is given. To make such a procedure effective as a means of popular control, however, it is not enough to provide a means whereby a few representatives, or all of them, may become informed before they are called on to vote supplies; this is necessary, but it is quite as necessary that the information developed shall reach the people. Any procedure for the consideration of the acts and proposals of the public service, and the determination of questions of policy and public law, must be the procedure of a public forum. The inquiries, discussion and determination of the forum must be so cast as to give them news value. Otherwise they cannot be generally known. This is the only way that the forum of the people can be made public. The conduct of all proceedings in such a manner as to give them current news value is of special importance in the consideration of a budget, since the budget is at once the means of enforcing accountability and of promoting and protecting the public service. For either result it should be prepared, explained, and openly discussed by officers directly or indirectly responsible to the people. The procedure governing the presentation of the budget must provide the occasion and the means of publicly reviewing every question and criticism raised by representatives before public moneys are voted; and finally the procedure developed should make known how each representative stands with respect to each service for which support requested is given or denied.

It is by this standard for judgment that the recent proposals and enactments for the development of a budget proposal in the states and in Congress should be appraised.

Three General Types of State Budgets

The recent enactments for a budget procedure in the forty-four states mentioned above are of three general types, as shown by the table on page 124, the executive type, the commission type, and the legislative type. The commission type is of two kinds: one, the membership of which is appointed by the executive or made up of executive and administrative agents; another, the membership of which is in part *ex officio* or by appointment executive, and in part *ex officio* or by appointment legislative.

The executive type, as the term is here used, is a form of procedure which looks to a popularly elected chief

executive as the person responsible for giving an account
of acts of the administration, involving the raising and
spending of public money, and for the preparation of a

TABLE SHOWING STATES WHICH HAVE PASSED BUDGET LAWS

Year	Executive Type	Board or Commission Type		Legis-lative Type	No. by Yrs.
		Executive	Mixed Ex-Leg.		
1911		Calif.	Wisc.		2
1913	Ore. Ohio			Ark.	3
1915	Iowa Minn. Neb. (a)	Conn. (a) Wash.	N. Dak. Vt.		7
1916	Md. (b) N. J.	La.		N. Y.	4
1917	Del. (c) Ill. Kan. N. Mex. (a) Utah	Tenn.	S. Dak. (a)		7
1918	Mass. (b) Miss. Va.	Ky. W.Va.(b)	Ga.		6
1919	Ariz. Colo. Idaho Ind. (d) Nev. N. H. Okla. S. C. Wyo.	Ala. Mont. Mich. Texas	Me. N. C.		15
Totals.	24	11	7	2	44

(a) Provisions changed and revised in 1919.
(b) Adopted constitutional amendment.
(c) Experimentally, for one session only.
(d) Constitutional amendment to be submitted to people.

plan or program of administration for the future period for which appropriations are asked — this account of past acts and program for the future to be made the subject of inquiry, discussion, and action in the representative, deliberative branch of the government.

The commission type, as the term is here used, is a form of procedure which looks to a board as the agency through which the account of acts of the administration involving the raising and spending of public money is to be presented; and which is also to prepare the estimates for the future period to be financed that come before the representative, deliberative branch of the government for inquiry, discussion, and action.

The legislative type, as the term is here used, is a procedure which looks to the legislature for the preparation of a plan or program for administration during a future period to be financed — receiving and treating all accounts of past acts and all estimates for the future period to be financed as advices or information to be considered by them or by a staff or committee acting for them — for which purpose the executive and the administrative officers, in so far as they have duties to perform, act in a ministerial or advisory capacity.

Whatever the type, if the budget is to operate effectively as an agency of control, the authority charged with the duty of making it must be possessed of these essentials and powers:

1. It must be provided with an adequate staff, competent to study the needs of the administration in order that an informing exhibit may be prepared, showing the cost of operation of the existing establishment, and accurately showing present financial conditions, so as to enable the sponsors for the future program to be financed to explain and defend their recommendations or requests.

2. It must be provided with the means necessary to supervise carefully current expenditures, and inhibit ac-

tion contrary to the spirit and intent of the grants made by the appropriating branch.

And if the budget is to be the means of making popular control effective there must be a procedure developed in the appropriating body which locates responsibility for leadership — bringing into relief the men and measures which are to be made the subjects of electoral choice. Our whole electoral system is based on recognition of the fact that institutions must be operated by men. Democracy insists on a leadership which is trusted. The budget system to be effective for purposes of popular control must carry with it a means of determining what measures or policies are to be adopted and what men are to be trusted to execute them. Any system of budget making which fails in this is not consistent with the ideals of democracy.

Appraisement of Types of State Budgets

The first, the " executive type," assumes that the government can best be made responsible by requiring the governor, as the elected head of the administration, not only to assume responsibility for past administrative acts, but also for all administrative plans looking toward the improvement of the service. Thus the budget procedure is one of establishing and enforcing accountability to the people and their representatives.

The second, the " commission type," assumes that both the financial statement and the administrative program for a future period can best be prepared by a group which is neither responsible for executing policies previously determined on or for determining policies for the future.

The third, the " legislative type," assumes that the policy determining body itself, from information called for and developed through inquiry, can best formulate the administrative policies which it is to pass on, thereby relieving the executive from all responsibility for leadership. This third type is a continuation of the principle of legislative domination established during the revolutionary period and continued for more than a century — a principle in the operation of which the government by standing committees, boss rule, logrolling methods, and pork-barrel politics in its worst form has developed. Only two states frankly adopted a budget system of this type — New York and Arkansas. In New York a strong staff agency has been created to assist the legislature in its work. In the outworking of the plan in that state the demand for a more orderly handling of the finances have been met; but in both states the government is just as invisible to the people, and just as irresponsible, as before.

The second type is an outgrowth of that school of American political thought which had for its purpose to defeat the boss, and prevent the building up of "parties" by distribution of patronage and spoils, thereby weakening both the executive and the legislative branches of the government and placing the administration in the hands of boards. The budget commission is simply another board imposed through which the activities of the various independent administrative bodies are to be coördinated. In Wisconsin, North Dakota, South Dakota, Maine, North Carolina, Vermont, and Georgia this is a mixed commission, made up largely of *ex officio* members in part taken from the administration and in part taken from the two houses of the legislature, the idea being that by such means an agreement may be reached through conference. This, however, confuses responsibility and does not make for publicity. In fact, it is an abandonment of the underlying principles of responsible government. In California, Washington, Montana, Michigan, Connecticut, West Virginia, and the five Southern states, Louisiana, Texas, Tennessee, Kentucky, and Alabama, the budget commission is made up of executive and administrative officers.   These continue to accept the idea that the executive is not competent to take leadership or is not to be trusted.   California, perhaps, is to be excepted, since the commission under the strong leadership of Governor Johnson in practice operated as his staff agency.   There a procedure of monthly or periodical allotments was adopted by which the commission was put into constant and effective supervisory relation over expenditures.   But, generally speaking, the plan itself is one which is intended to relieve the governor of responsibility, and it does not contribute to making popular control effective.

The first, the executive type, has been accepted by twenty-three states.   This has been the direct outgrowth of an effort to locate and enforce responsibility.   But in no case has an organization and procedure been effected which fully meets the requirement.   The old legislative procedure has been retained.   Several of these states have provided the governor with the staff means for keeping in touch with the administration, and of preparing well-considered estimates of expenditures as a basis for his requests for funds.   Under the leadership of Governor Lowden Illinois has gone further than any other state in the organization of a department of finance, the head of which is appointed (with the Senate's approval) and removable by the governor at will.   This department is responsible for all departmental accounting, the preparation of specifications to be used in making purchases, the review and approval of contracts.   Monthly requisitions for authorization to spend departmental appropriations are required, thereby giving to the governor through his director of finance the means of administering expenditures currently; and a special officer and staff is charged with the duty of compiling the data and at the end of the year of preparing the estimates to be reviewed by the governor.   Governor Lowden also went before the legislature personally to present the budget, and strict orders were given to all the governor's departments that no one should ask for appropriations or increases except through the department of finance. In a number of the states adopting this type of budget practically nothing has been done by way of administrative reorganization either to provide adequate staff facilities to enable the governor to act intelligently, or to locate responsibility. And in all of them the old legislative procedure still remains — a procedure which is not designed either for informing the members of the legislature or for giving publicity to inquiry, criticism, and discussion of the acts and proposals of the executive and spending officers.

Finally, it may be said that in no state has provision been made whereby responsible leaders may appeal directly to the people on issues in controversy in case of a deadlock.

In conclusion it may be said, therefore, that the " legislative type " is not and cannot be made to serve the purposes of a democracy; that the other two types, while they may be made consistent with democratic ideals, to do so each must work out an entirely different procedure for locating and enforcing responsibility. Neither the " executive type " or the " commission type " has so far developed a procedure which makes for publicity; and neither has provided or attempted to provide for an effective means of appeal to the people on vital issues.

PART II. DETAILED ACCOUNTS OF PROPOSED
PLANS AND RECENT LEGAL ENACTMENTS
FOR ADMINISTRATIVE REORGANIZA-
TION IN STATE GOVERNMENTS

CHAPTER IX [1]

EARLIER PROPOSED PLANS FOR CENTRALIZATION OF
EXECUTIVE AUTHORITY

MINNESOTA, Iowa, and New York were the first states
to conduct comprehensive and scientific studies of their
administrative agencies. Although the plans of reorganization which were proposed in these states were never
adopted, they are still of sufficient interest because of their
influence on subsequent plans of centralization in other
states to warrant a brief description. Minnesota and
Iowa began their investigations with reference to administrative reorganization in 1913. The Minnesota plan
for consolidation was worked out with greater care and
in greater detail than the Iowa plan. For this reason
it has probably been more generally known outside of the
state than any other similar scheme, with the possible
exception of the plans of New York and Illinois. The
former was worked out in great detail and at the same
time was subjected to a searching discussion during the
Constitutional Convention of 1915. These have all had
definite influence upon the reorganization plans which
have since been developed.

THE MINNESOTA PLAN

In 1913 the governor of Minnesota appointed an efficiency and economy commission. This commission was
composed of thirty members appointed by the governor

---

[1] A considerable part of the material contained in this and the
three subsequent chapters has appeared in a supplement of the
National Municipal Review, for November, 1919.

and represented the political and industrial interests of all sections of the state. The commission began its work in the fall of 1913. It received its support from private sources, since the legislature provided no appropriation for the work. The commission employed a staff consisting of a consulting statistician, Dr. E. Dana Durand, former director of the United States census, a secretary, and a clerk.

Two Reports and Findings of Commission

The commission published two reports, one a preliminary report in May, 1914, the other a final report in November, 1914. The main features of the commission's consolidation plan were outlined in the preliminary report. The final report contained bills drawn by the commission for carrying into effect the recommendations of the first report with regard to reorganization and the establishment of a budget system. Each of the reports contained a rather crude chart showing the existing organization of state government and the proposed plan of the commission.

The recommendations of the commission, as embodied in the preliminary report, related to three subjects; namely, centralization of administrative authority, the merit system of civil service, and the adoption of a budget system. Under the subject of administrative reorganization, the principal defects of the existing system were pointed out as:

(1) Multiplicity of independent branches; (2) diversity in form; and (3) predominance of the board system. The report showed that there were about seventy-five independent administrative agencies, that a great number of these agencies were administered by *ex officio* boards, and that there were certain essential state functions performed by private associations. This variety in the form of organization, the commission asserted, had no logical

basis and only tended to confuse the public and destroy responsibility. The board system, it declared, tended to delay, inefficiency and dissipated responsibility. Furthermore, it found that the necessity for boards was limited to quasi-legislative and quasi-judicial work, and that boards were not useful for administrative work. Finally, it asserted that since board members usually have overlapping terms, and each governor may appoint only a minority, each board is a government by itself.

Recommendations of Preliminary Report

The commission proposed to set up six executive departments; namely finance, public domain, public welfare, education, labor and commerce, and agriculture. A few special functions were to be performed by the administrative agencies outside these departments, such as the civil service commission and the tax commission. The constitutional officers were not to be affected by the proposed reorganization. The heads of the proposed departments were to be as follows: (1) Treasurer, constitutional officer, elected by the people, acting as director of finance; (2) director of public domain, appointed by the governor with the consent of the Senate; (3) director of public welfare, appointed by the governor with the consent of the Senate; (4) education; (a) board of education appointed by the governor; director of education appointed by the board; (b) board of regents appointed by the governor; president of university appointed by the regents; (5) director of labor and commerce appointed by the governor with the consent of the Senate; and (6) director of agriculture, appointed by the governor with the consent of the Senate.

Executive Heads of Departments

It will be seen that the plan of the commission contemplated two exceptions to the general rule that there shall be a single head appointed by the governor for each department. These exceptions were the department of finance and the department of education. In the former case the treasurer, who is a constitutional officer elected by the people, was to be made head of the department. In the latter case the commission recommended two boards, the regents of the university and the new board of education having charge of all other state educational work. This, it appears, was a concession, as the commission said that in recommending this form of organization it was following the general practice or custom to treat education as independent of other functions of government.

The directors, were to be appointed by the governor, were to hold office at his pleasure and be responsible to him for the conduct of their departments. They were to be the assistants of the governor in the conduct of the administration. Furthermore, they were to constitute the governor's cabinet, similar to the cabinet of the President of the United States, thus making the administration a unit. The governor's term being only two years, the terms of the cabinet members were similarly limited.

In each of the departments proposed by the commission, bureaus were to be set up as outlined and described. The bureau chiefs under the directors were to be trained experts. They were to constitute the permanent departmental staff and were to come under the merit system of civil service, and consequently were not to be changed · when a new governor came into office.

Advisory Boards

While the commission recommended the placing of all executive functions in the hands of individuals, it saw the need for certain boards with advisory, quasi-legislative, and quasi-judicial powers. To the department of finance the commission recommended the attachment in an advisory capacity of the existing board of investment, a constitutional and *ex officio* body charged with the investment of state trust funds. It was proposed to attach to the department of labor and commerce the existing board of railroad commissioners, a body of three members elected by the people. For the departments of public domain, welfare, and agriculture, special advisory boards appointed by the governor with overlapping terms, were recommended.

Recommendations of Final Report

The final report of the commission differed from the preliminary report in that it recommended five instead of six departments — the department of finance being eliminated and placed among the general offices not included in the recommendations of the commission.

Results Achieved

The net gain for the State of Minnesota from the work of this commission was very small so far as administrative reorganization was concerned. Only one piece of legislation may be ascribed to the influence of the work of the commission and that was the budget law enacted in 1915. The particular value of this commission's work lies in the influence that it has had upon subsequent plans of reorganization in other states.

THE IOWA PLAN

The Iowa legislature of 1913 authorized the joint committee on retrenchment and reform to employ expert accountants and efficiency engineers who were to make a survey of the administrative organization of the state. The committee, in March of 1913, engaged a firm of efficiency engineers to make the survey. The sum of $10,000 was appropriated to meet the expenses of the proposed investigations.   The efficiency engineers finished their investigation and submitted their final report in type-written form in December, 1913.

Report of Efficiency Engineers

In preparation, the efficiency engineers made examinations of all offices and departments located at the state capitol, including both constitutional and statutory offices. Besides suggesting changes in methods and pointing to possible economies in the work of the several offices and departments, the report recommended a general regrouping of the administrative functions of the state government.   The reorganization program did not, according to the statement of the engineers, propose changes thought to be desirable in the constitution of the state, but confined its recommendations to changes that could be brought about by legislative action and to consolidation by grouping some of the elected offices.

The plan proposed the union of the offices of the state auditor and the state treasurer through the establishment of a finance department.   Under the direction of this department was to be placed the control of the whole accounting system of the state and also the preparation of a budget.   The plan also proposed the establishment of a legal department through the union of the offices of the secretary of state and the attorney general.   This new department was to handle all matters of legal records and justice.   The creation of both these departments was to be effected by a union or rearrangement of the functions and duties, thus leaving to each officer his constitutional status.

The plan also proposed to create the office of the state purchasing agent, an official to be known as the chief accountant, and a civil service commission or bureau to be organized to administer the merit system which was to be used in filling all administrative positions except the constitutional offices and the heads of the seven proposed departments.

The proposed departments other than the general administrative offices mentioned above were to be as follows: (1) agriculture; (2) commerce and industries; (3) public works; (4) public safety; (5) public health; (6) education; (7) charities and corrections.

All the existing divisions and agencies of the executive branch of the government other than the constitutional offices and certain general administrative offices already noted were assigned to some one of the seven proposed departments. Each of these departments was to be under the immediate control of a director general. The governor himself was to assume the portfolio of director general of the department of public safety. The heads of the remaining six departments were to be appointed by the governor with the consent of the Senate.

It was also proposed that the existing executive council should be abolished and a new executive council, consisting of the director generals of the seven departments, should be created. This executive council was to perform the function of cabinet to the governor, who was to be its chairman.

Report of Committee

Almost a year after the report of the efficiency engineers was submitted to the committee, the committee in turn prepared a report which it submitted to the General Assembly of 1915. This report contained a brief outline of quite a different plan of reorganization supported by a few general statements as to the need for grouping together the administrative agencies of the state.

One essential difference in the scheme of reorganization proposed by the report of the joint committee appears in that it proposed the grouping of all executive functions of the state, except a few which were placed under " general administration," into three great divisions designated under the heads of : (1) department of social progress; (2) department of industries; (3) department of public safety. The department of social progress was to include and have supervision over educational and allied functions, such as libraries and archives, and in addition the prison-parole functions. The department of industries was to include and have supervision over agricultural functions, also all regulatory functions in connection with labor, commerce, insurance, and banking. The department of public safety was to include and supervise the law enforcing functions, the conservational and custodial functions, the functions of registration and inspection, and in addition the work of the state highway commission. Each of these departments was to be under the direction of a head appointed by the governor. The report contained no statement of the functions of the numerous subdivisions under each of the three proposed departments.

Results

No legislation resulted directly either from the recommendations of the efficiency engineers or from the recommendations of the committee on retrenchment and reform. A budget law, however, was enacted by the 1915 legislature.

THE NEW YORK PLAN OF 1915

As early as 1910 Governor Hughes in his annual message to the legislature of New York State recommended administrative reorganization and consolidation, which he said would " tend to promote efficiency in public office by increasing the effectiveness of the voter and by diminishing the opportunities of the political manipulators who take advantage of the multiplicity of elective offices to perfect their scheme at the public expense." Furthermore, he expressed the belief that responsibility should be "centered in the governor, who should appoint a cabinet of administrative heads accountable to him and charged with the duties now devolved upon elective state officers."

Recognition of Need for Reorganization

Following this message of Governor Hughes, a resolution to amend the constitution was introduced in the Assembly of 1910 providing for the appointment of all state officers except the governor and the lieutenant governor. A heated discussion ensued, with the result that the resolution failed to pass.

The movement for centralization of responsibility was again revived in the election campaigns of 1912. In 1913 the legislature passed a bill establishing a department of efficiency and economy under a commissioner appointed by Governor Sulzer and confirmed by the Senate for a term of five years. In 1914 this department, in coöperation with the Bureau of Municipal Research of New York City, began the preparation of a report on the government and administration of the state for the Constitutional Convention which was to meet the following year. As a result of the combined efforts of these two agencies there was published in January, 1915, a large volume of more than seven hundred pages, entitled "Government of the State of New York: A Survey of its Organization and Functions." This volume gave a minute description of the legislative, judicial, and administrative organization of the state government. It also set forth graphically all the boards, departments, commissions, bureaus, and offices of the state, together with their functions, number of their employees, salaries and other costs, and their organic relations or absence of relations. The report showed that there were one hundred and sixty-nine agencies of the state government, most of which had been created in recent years.   It also pointed out that the entire structure of the state government seemed to have " grown up from year to year, rather than to have been built according to any studied plan of scientific and economic needs." Numerous conflicts of authority and overlappings of jurisdiction were pointed out.   One hundred and eight boards were shown to exist.   " A number of them," said the report, "were created for similar purposes and a number perform functions for which there already existed at the time of their creation fully organized departments of the government.   Some are elected by the legislature, some appointed by the governor, some are of *ex officio* membership, some are paid, others are not paid."

Study of Existing Machinery

Upon the completion of this joint undertaking the Bureau of Municipal Research was requested by the Constitutional Convention Commission to prepare an appraisal of the existing organization of the state government.   In compliance with this request the Bureau issued a volume entitled " The Constitution and Government of the State of New York " (Municipal Research No. 61) in which the existing structure and methods of the state government were subjected to careful and comprehensive appraisal.   The Bureau also worked out a proposed plan of administrative reorganization which it laid before the committees of the Constitutional Convention.

Political Parties Become Interested

In 1914 both great political parties of the state seemed clearly to recognize the failure of the existing administrative system.   The Republican platform of that year, framed especially with a view to constitutional revision, said: " We recommend a substantial reduction in the number of elective officers by the application of the principles of the short ballot to the executive officers of the state. To prevent the multiplication of offices, we recommend that the various administrative functions of the state, so far as practicable, be vested in a limited number of departments. The present duplication of effort and expense in the public institutions of the state should be remedied by the establishment of a simpler and better organized system." The Democratic platform of the same year declared: "There should be no divided authority or responsibility in executing and administering the laws of the state. The time has come to give the people control of their executive government. The responsibility should be centered in the governor. He should have the absolute power of removal. The various boards and commissions should be made subject to the control of the governor."

The Work of the Constitutional Convention

As a result of the agitation for administrative reform and reorganization several plans were prepared and laid before the Constitutional Convention, which met in the summer of 1915. After due consideration of these plans by the committee on the governor and other state officers, a proposed amendment to the constitution was submitted to the Convention for discussion on August 11, 1915. This amendment proposed to establish fifteen departments: namely, justice, audit and control, education, public utilities, conservation, civil service, state, taxation and finance, public works, health, agriculture, charities and corrections, banking, insurance, and labor and industry. The heads of the department of justice and of the department of audit and control were to be the attorney general and comptroller, respectively, elected at the same time and for the same term as the governor. The department of education was to be controlled by the regents of the university, who were to appoint the chief administrative officer of the department. The department of public utilities was to consist of two commissions of five members each, appointed by the governor with the consent of the Senate for terms of five years, and removable by the Senate upon recommendation of the governor. The department of conservation was to be under the direction of a conservation commission of nine members appointed by the governor with the consent of the Senate for overlapping terms of nine years. This commission was to appoint the chief administrative officer of the department. The department of civil service was to be under the direction of a civil service commission consisting of three members appointed by the governor with the consent of the Senate for overlapping terms of six years. The remaining departments were to be administered by single heads appointed by the governor with the consent of the Senate and removable by him in his discretion. After the adoption of this amendment, no new departments were to be created by the legislature, but all new functions were to be assigned to one of the existing departments. The legislature was to provide for the internal organization of the departments.

The general principles set forth in this amendment had been discussed before the committee on finance and the committee on the governor and other state officers by such men as Ex-President Taft, President Lowell of Harvard, and President Goodnow of Johns Hopkins. Following the introduction of the amendment into the Constitutional Convention, there were discussions of various phases of the proposed administrative reorganization. Mr. Elihu Root said that the existing system was an "invisible government" in which the political boss ruled the state in spite of the legislature, the governor, and the other elective officers. He said further that men were appointed to office not for the service they would render to the state but for the service they were to render to promote the power of political organizations. Such a system, he declared, found " its opportunity in the division of powers, in the six-headed executive, in which, by the natural workings of human nature, there shall be opposition and discord in the playing of one force against the other, and so when we refuse to make one governor, elected by the people, the real chief executive, we make inevitable the setting up of a chief executive not selected by the people, not acting for the people's interest, but for the selfish interest of the few who control the party, whichever party it may be." In criticizing the provisions of the proposed amendment Governor Smith, then a member of the Constitutional Convention, said that the governor should have the absolute power of appointment and removal of the heads of departments without hindrance on the part of the Senate. He said that without such provision responsibility could not be fixed and the entire plan might thus be defeated (Revised Record of Constitutional Convention, page 3353).

Plan of Reorganization Proposed by the Convention

The result of the discussions was a considerable modification of the plan presented to the Convention by the committee on the governor and other state officers. The plan of administrative organization as finally adopted by the Constitutional Convention provided for seventeen departments to exercise the civil, executive, and administrative functions of the state, scattered among more than one hundred and fifty boards, offices, commissions,˙ and other agencies. These departments were as follows: (1) law; (2) finance; (3) accounts; (4) treasury; (5) taxation; (6) state; (7) public works; (8) health; (9) agriculture; (10) charities and corrections; (11) banking; (12) insurance, (13) labor and industry; (14) education; (15) public utilities; (16) conservation, and (17) civil service. The heads of the department of law and of the department of finance were to be the attorney general and the comptroller respectively, who were to be elected at the same time and for the same term as the governor. The head of the department of labor and industry was to be an industrial commission or commissioner to be provided by law, appointed by the governor with the advice and consent of the Senate. The department of education was to be administered by the university of the state of New York, the chief administrative officer of which was to be appointed by the regents of the university. The department of public utilities was to consist of two public service commissions, the commissioners to be appointed by the governor, by and with the advice and consent of the Senate. The governor might remove any commissioner for cause after an opportunity to be heard. The department of conservation was to be under the direction of the conservation commission consisting of nine commissioners appointed by the governor, by and with the advice and consent of the Senate with overlapping terms of nine years and serving without compensation. The commission was authorized to appoint and remove a superintendent and also to appoint his subordinates. The department of civil service was to be under the direction of a civil service commission consisting of three members appointed by the governor, by and with the advice and consent of the Senate for overlapping terms of six years. The remaining ten departments were to have single heads who were to be appointed by the governor and removable by him in his discretion. The reason given for the concurrence of the Senate in the appointment of heads of the departments of labor and industry, public utilities, conservation, and civil service was because such departments performed both legislative and administrative functions. After the adoption of this plan no new departments were to be created by the legislature, but all new functions were to be assigned to one of the existing departments. The internal organization of the departments was to be provided for by legislation.

Only very general powers were prescribed for the several departments. In some cases the prescribing of duties was left entirely to subsequent legislative action. In the case of the department of finance it was stated that the comptroller should exercise all powers and duties at that time devolving upon him except the powers of examination and verification of accounts, which duties were vested in the department of accounts.

This plan of reorganization, if adopted, would have reduced the number of elective state officers from seven to four, leaving only the governor, lieutenant governor, comptroller, and attorney general to be chosen by the voters. The secretary of state and the treasurer were to become appointive by the governor, and the office of state engineer and surveyor was to be abolished.

Proposed Reorganization Defeated at the Polls

The plan of administrative reorganization and consolidation proposed by the Constitutional Convention, embodied in the proposed constitution and submitted to the people in November, 1915, was defeated at the polls. Until the present year, when the state reconstruction commission began its work, there has been little thought of reviving the movement in New York for administrative reorganization and consolidation. The work of this commission will be taken up in Chapter XII.

CHAPTER X

THREE states have recently passed and put into operation laws which reorganize their administrative machinery in such a manner as largely to centralize executive responsibility, viz., Illinois in 1917; Idaho and Nebraska in 1919.

ILLINOIS PLAN

The legislature of 1913 provided for the appointment of a committee on efficiency and economy which was composed of four members from each house of the legislature. The committee was given full power to investigate all departments and agencies of the state government. Such investigation was made with the view of combining and centralizing the work of the various state agencies and abolishing those that were found useless. The committee was given the power to employ assistants and was provided with an appropriation of $40,000.

Work of the Committee on Efficiency and Economy

Upon beginning its work in August, 1913, the committee employed a staff of investigators which was placed under the direction of Professor John A. Fairlie of the University of Illinois. The numerous administrative agencies of the state were arranged in twelve groups according to their general functions, and each one of these groups was assigned to a trained investigator who studied closely the conditions and made a report to the committee. Tentative plans for consolidation were drawn up and for several months meetings were held at short intervals. Later, public hearings were held in Chicago and Springfield, at which many state officers and representatives of associations and organizations appeared and discussed the proposed plan of reorganization. As a result, much additional information was secured and some changes were made in the tentative proposals.

Two reports were issued by the committee; a preliminary report in June, 1914, and a general report almost a year later. The latter report, a volume of more than one thousand pages, contained the recommendations of the committee, the reports of the special investigators, a comparative statement of appropriations covering three legislative periods, and charts illustrating both the existing administration and the proposed reorganization.

The defects of the existing arrangement of the Illinois administration, as pointed out by the committee, were lack of correlation, scattered offices, no standards of compensation, overlapping of functions, irregularity of reports, ineffective supervision, no budget system, imperfect accounts, inadequate advice on legislation, and irresponsible government.

Committee's Plan of Administrative Reorganization

The committee's proposed plan of reorganization provided for the consolidation of all the administrative agencies, with the exception of a few general offices, into ten departments as follows: (1) finance; (2) charities and corrections; (3) education; (4) public works and buildings; (5) agriculture; (6) public health; (7) labor and mining; (8) trade and commerce; (9) law, and (10) military affairs. The agencies left outside these departments were the secretary of state, board of elections, civil service commission, and the legislative reference bureau.

The proposed departments of finance, charities and corrections, education, public works and buildings, trade and commerce were to be under the control of commissions. The departments of agriculture, public health, labor and mining were to be administered by single heads appointed by the governor with the approval of the Senate. The department of law was to be under the control of the attorney general, a constitutional officer. The department of military affairs was to continue as previously organized.

The committee accompanied its recommendations to the legislature of 1915 with bills designed to carry into effect its recommendations, but with the exception of a bill revising the law relating to state contracts, none of the bills passed the legislature.

Governor Lowden's Rôle in the Reorganization

Governor Lowden in his primary campaign during the summer of 1916 made numerous speeches in which he pointed out the great need for administrative consolidation and for the establishment of a budget system. In his inaugural message he spoke still more enthusiastically on the subject of administrative reorganization and consolidation. Immediately following his inauguration work was commenced upon the necessary bills to carry out his ideas. The reports of the efficiency and economy committee constituted the basis for the preparation of these bills; however, " the specific form of organization recommended by the committee was, after mature deliberation, rejected as not conducive to either strength, harmony, or unity of administration."

It was apparent that the committee had not only been inconsistent in its recommendations for the overhead organization of the proposed departments, but it had also compromised principles in favor of expediency. Some departments were to be administered by single heads, others were to be under the control of boards. For example, the committee recommended the creation of a de- ·

partment of finance under a state finance commission to consist of a state comptroller, tax commissioner, and revenue commissioner, appointed by the governor with the approval of the Senate, together with the auditor of public accounts and the state treasurer, both serving *ex officio*. Each of these officials was to be in charge of a particular division having specific statutory duties to perform. The finance commission was to act only as a means of bringing together these independent divisions. Responsibility for the work of the department could not, therefore, be definitely located. As another example, the commission recommended the establishment of a department of public works and buildings under a public works commission of three members; namely, a commissioner of highways, a commissioner of waterways, and a fish and game commissioner; with a bureau for each of these services and other bureaus under the superintendent of buildings and grounds, the superintendent of state parks, and state art commission. For all practical purposes the several bureaus and divisions would have been independent of each other. Statutory duties devolved upon subordinate officers and boards within the department. The department had no one responsible head having control of all its activities.

After having carefully considered the committee's plan of reorganization in the light of the facts just pointed out, Governor Lowden came to the conclusion that while the general recommendations of the committee were valid and ought to be incorporated in law, its specific recommendations for the overhead organization were not only "inexpedient, but detrimental to administrative efficiency." He was of the opinion that there should be a consistent and uniform plan of reorganization which would be applicable to all the departments. That is, he did not believe that part of them should be under a single head appointed by the governor and others should be con-

trolled by one or more commissions, which were in some
cases composed of both appointive and *ex officio* officers.
He realized that it was inexpedient for the time being to
attempt a change in the constitution, but he determined
that the plan so far as adopted by statutory means should
be a uniform one and therefore a proper basis upon which
to build up the complete plan of reorganization whenever
the time came to amend the constitution.   He also thought
that a single bill instead of a number of bills, as proposed
by the committee, could be provided which would embody
the necessary legislation to put the plan into effect.   Accordingly, an act was drawn and passed by the legislature of 1917 called the Civil Administrative Code, which
abolished more than one hundred independent and statutory offices, departments, boards, commissions, and other
agencies and consolidated their functions and duties into
nine great departments, each having a responsible head
known as the director.

Organization Under the Civil Administrative Code

The Civil Administrative Code, as it passed the legislature, organized all the civil governmental agencies under
the jurisdiction of the governor, with the exception of a
civil service commission and of certain minor and temporary boards, into nine great administrative departments as
follows: (1) department of finance; (2) department
of agriculture; (3) department of labor; (4) department
of mines and minerals; (5) department of public works;
(6) department of public welfare; (7) department of
public health; (8) department of trade and commerce;
(9) department of registration and education.

These nine departments do not include the military
functions, the general governmental functions of the six
elective constitutional officers: namely, the lieutenant
governor, secretary of state, auditor of public accounts,
state treasurer, attorney general, and superintendent

of public instruction, and the duties of the trustees of
the University of Illinois, an elective body of nine members. The elective state board of equalization was not
at first included, but it has since been abolished by the
1919 legislature and its functions placed in the department of finance under the control of a tax commission of
three members.

Department Heads

Each of the nine departments is under a single head
called a director, who is appointed by the governor with
the approval of the Senate for a term of four years,
beginning on the second Monday in January next after
the election of the governor. The annual salary laid
down in the code for each of these directors is as follows:
Director of finance, $7,000; director of agriculture,
$6,000; director of labor, $5,000; director of mines and
minerals, $5,000; director of public works and buildings,
$7,000; director of public welfare, $7,000; director of
public health, $6,000; director of trade and commerce,
$7,000; director of registration and education, $5,000.

Subordinate Administrative Officers

In addition to the director of the departments certain
subordinate officers are created for each of the departments and their annual salaries designated as follows:

In the department of finance: Assistant director of
finance, $4,200; administrative auditor, $4,800; superintendent of budget, $3,600; superintendent of department
reports, $3,600.

In the department of agriculture: Assistant director
of agriculture, $3,600; general manager of the state fair,
$3,600; superintendent of foods and dairies, $4,800;
superintendent of animal industry, $3,600; superintendent
of plant industry, $3,600; chief veterinarian, $4,200;
chief game and fish warden, $3,600.

In the department of labor: Assistant director of labor, $3,000; chief factory inspector, $3,000; superintendent of free employment offices, $3,000; chief inspector of private employment agencies, $3,000.

In the department of mines and minerals: Assistant director of mines and minerals, $3,000.

In the department of public works: Assistant director of public works and buildings, $4,000; superintendent of highways, $5,000; chief engineer, $5,000; supervising architect, $4,000; supervising engineer, $4,000; superintendent of waterways, $5,000; superintendent of printing, $5,000; superintendent of purchases and supplies, $5,000; superintendent of parks, $2,500.

In the department of public welfare: Assistant director of public welfare, $4,000; alienist, $5,000; criminologist, $5,000; fiscal supervisor, $5,000; superintendent of charities, $5,000; superintendent of prisons, $5,000; superintendent of pardons and paroles, $5,000.

In the department of public health: Assistant director of public health, $3,600; superintendent of lodging house inspection, $3,000.

In the department of trade and commerce: Assistant director of trade and commerce, $4,000; superintendent of insurance, $5,000; fire marshal, $3,000; superintendent of standards, $2,500; chief grain inspector, $5,000.

In the department of registration and education: Assistant director of registration and education, $3,600; superintendent of registration, $4,200.

The above-named subordinate officers are under the control of the directors of their respective departments and perform such duties as the directors prescribe. The manner of their appointment is the same as that of the directors.

While the code makes no specific provisions for divisions or bureaus within the several departments, it would seem to indicate by the titles of the subordinate officers that such divisions or bureaus are to be set up; and in practice they have been established, as may be seen from an examination of the " Report of the Directors Under the Civil Administrative Code, 1918."

Quasi Legislative and Quasi Judicial Boards

The survey of the administrative activities of the state showed that there were certain boards or commissions which discharged quasi-legislative or quasi-judicial functions.   In the framing of the administrative code, the fundamental principle was followed; namely, that one man should have the entire responsibility in the discharge of functions which are purely executive, consequently the single-headed departments.   However, in the discharge of functions which are quasi-legislative or quasi-judicial it was deemed essential that the opinion of a reasonable number of men acting as a group should be procured.   Hence the code provides that all functions which are primarily quasi-legislative or quasi-judicial are to be vested in the proper boards or commissions. These boards or commissions and the annual salaries of the several members are provided for as follows:

(1) The food standards commission in the department of agriculture, composed of the superintendent of foods and dairies and two officers designated as food standard officers, the latter receiving $450 each;

(2) The industrial commission in the department of labor, composed of five persons, each receiving a salary of $5,000.

(3) The mining board in the department of mines and minerals, consisting of the director of the department of mines and minerals and four persons designated as mine officers, at a salary of $500 each.

(4) The miners' examining board in the department of mines and minerals, consisting of four persons receiving a salary of $1,800 each.

(5) The public utilities commission in the department of trade and commerce, composed of five members designated as public utility commissioners at a salary of $7,000 each, and having a secretary at a salary of $4,000.

(6) The normal school board in the department of registration and education, composed of the director of the department, the superintendent of public instruction, and nine other persons.

(7) The tax commission in the department of finance. composed of three members at an annual salary of $6,000 each.

The members of these boards are appointed by the governor with the approval of the Senate. All serve for a term of four years, except the members of the tax commission and the normal school board, which are appointed for overlapping terms of six years. Each of these boards acts as an independent entity. While the director of mines and minerals is a member of the mining board and the director of registration and education is a member of the normal school board, each board, nevertheless, exercises its functions without any supervision or control by the director of the department to which it is attached. However, each of these boards is, from the standpoint of organization and finance, a component part of the department to which it belongs.

Both the executive officers and the members of the quasi-legislative and quasi-judicial boards, excepting the two food standard officers, the members of the mining board, and the members of the normal school board, are required to devote their full time to the duties of their several offices. All employees of the departments are under the civil service regulations of the state. The organization of the work of the departments, as well as the assignment of duties to the subordinate officers, is left to the discretion of the department heads. Subject to the chief executive each director is free within a certain scope to organize the work of his own department.

Advisory Boards

Since questions of policy and expediency are continually being presented for solution in administrative departments, it was deemed wise to make provisions in the code for advisory boards to assist and advise the directors of the departments and the governor in matters of policy and administration. Hence the following advisory boards are created:.

In the Department of Agriculture: A board of agricultural advisers, composed of fifteen persons and a board of state fair advisers, consisting of nine persons, not more than three of whom are to be appointed from any one county.

In the Department of Labor: A board of Illinois free employment office advisers, composed of five persons; a board of local Illinois free employment office advisers for each free employment office, composed of five persons on each local board.

In the Department of Public Works: A board of art advisers, composed of eight persons; a board of water resource advisers, a board of highway advisers, and a board of park and buildings advisers, each composed of five persons.

In the Department of Public Welfare: A board of public welfare commissioners, composed of five persons.

In the Department of Public Health: A board of public health advisers, composed of five persons.

In the Department of Registration and Education: A board of natural resources and conservation advisers, composed of seven persons; a board of state museum advisers, composed of five persons; and an immigrants' commission, consisting of five persons, one of whom is the director of registration and education.

Members of these advisory boards are chosen because

of their experience or professional qualifications in their particular lines of endeavor. While it is not required that they devote their entire time and attention to the business of the state, they are expected as a matter of public duty to put their skill and professional experience at the government's disposal whenever needed. The members of the several advisory boards receive no compensation.

The code vests each advisory board with the power to study the entire field to which it is related, to advise the departmental officers, to recommend to the governor and the legislature, and to investigate the conduct and the work of the department with which it is associated. Such boards are also permitted to adopt rules and regulations not inconsistent with law and are required to hold meetings and keep minutes relating thereto.

Office Tenures

The code gives the governor the power, immediately upon his taking office, to appoint all of his administrative officers with the advice of the Senate for a term of office coterminous with his own; that is, four years. The only exceptions are the tax commission and the normal school board, the members of which, other than the director of registration and education on the normal school board, are appointed for overlapping terms of six years. A possible restriction upon the power of the governor to constitute the personnel of his administration is found in the fact that the Senate may withhold its approval to certain of the appointments which he may wish to make.

Location of Offices

Changes are also made by the provisions of the code with respect to the location of offices. Before the code was adopted some offices were located at Springfield, some in Chicago, and some in a number of smaller cities of the state. Under the code each department is required to maintain a central office at the capital, but for the discharge of certain activities of its office it may maintaiñ branch offices in other parts of the state. This plan not only makes a large saving to the state in office rents, but it enables the citizens of the state to know at once where they can find the department with which they wish to do business.

Functions of Departments

The department of finance is regarded as being not only the most important of the code departments, but as having practically a new field of work. Outside of the function of the governor's auditor and the compilation of budget estimates by the legislative reference bureau it took over no work performed by previously existing administrative agencies. Briefly, the functions of this department are to examine the accuracy and legality of accounts and expenditures of other code departments; to prescribe and install a uniform system of accounting and reporting; to examine, approve, or disapprove all bills, vouchers, and claims against the other departments; to prepare the budget for submission to the governor; and to formulate plans for better coördination of the work of the departments. Under the finance code, enacted by the 1919 legislature, the powers of this department are extended in a large measure over the non-code departments and agencies. Through his power to alter the estimates in the preparation of the ·budget, the director of finance next to the governor becomes the most powerful officer in the code administration.

All agricultural and related activities, as well as food inspection, are included under the department of agriculture. This department promotes horticulture, livestock industry, dairying, poultry raising, bee keeping, forestry, fishing, and wool production. It gathers and disseminates knowledge pertaining to agricultural interests. The inspection of commercial fertilizers and the conduct of state fairs are under its control.

The functions relating to the regulation of labor, the promotion of the welfare of wage earners, and the improvement of working conditions are performed by the department of labor. This department collects, systematizes, and reports information concerning labor and employment conditions throughout the state. The industrial commission under this department administers the laws pertaining to arbitration and conciliation.

The department of mines and minerals controls the inspection of mines, the examination of persons working in mines, and the fire-fighting and mine-rescue stations.

The department of public works and buildings, next to the department of finance, is probably the most important. It has control over the construction of highways and canals, supervision of waterways, erection of public buildings and monuments, upkeep of parks and places of interest, and purchase of supplies for the departments and charitable, educational and penal institutions. The purchasing division of the department amounts practically to a central purchasing agency for the code departments. Leases are made for the several departments by this department.

The department of public welfare has jurisdiction over all charitable, penal, and reformatory institutions of the state. It also performs the functions of the board of pardons.

The department of public health exercises general functions relating to health and sanitation except the examination and registration of physicians and embalmers. It maintains chemical, bacteriological, and biological laboratories, and distributes antitoxines, vaccines, and prophylactics for the prevention and treatment of communicable diseases.

The department of trade and commerce has charge of the regulation of insurance, grain inspection, inspection of railway safety appliances, fire inspection, and the regulation of weights and measures. The public utilities commission operates under this department.

The principal work of the department of registration and education is the examination of applicants for state licenses in the trades and professions. In conducting such examinations the department has the assistance of ten examining boards, one for each trade or profession, the members of which are appointed by the director. The administration of the state normal schools is placed in this department under the direction of the normal school board. The department acts as an investigating agency for a number of the other departments.

Operation of the Reorganization Plan

In his message to the 1919 legislature, Governor Lowden said, concerning the operation of the Illinois consolidation plan:

" The civil administrative code went into effect on July 1, 1917. It amounted to a revolution in government. Under it a reorganization of more than one hundred and twenty-five boards, commissions, and independent agencies was affected. Nine departments, with extensive and real power vested in each head, have taken the place of those bodies which were abolished, and discharge, under the general supervision of the governor, the details of government for which the governor is responsible. At the time the bill was up for consideration it was claimed that it would result in both efficiency and economy.

" It has more than satisfied all the expectations that

were formed concerning it. The functions of the government are discharged at the capitol. The governor is in daily contact with his administration in all its activities. Unity and harmony of administration have been attained, and vigor and energy of administration enhanced.

"It seems to me almost providential that it should have been enacted into law before war actually came. A large number of the state's most expert officials and employees were drawn upon by the government at Washington because of the exigencies of the war. The same difficulties arose in the conduct of public business, which vexed private business so much. There was necessarily much confusion. The cost of all supplies rose rapidly. Unless the more than one hundred scattered agencies, which had existed heretofore, had been welded by the civil administrative code into a compact and coördinate government, anything like efficient state government, during these difficult times, would have been impossible. Illinois, through the greater elasticity and efficiency of her new form of government, was able to meet every emergency of the war without an extraordinary session of her legislature."

Criticisms of the Code Organization

Three objections may be made to the organization under the civil administrative code, one of which may be regarded as a defect in the code itself, and the other two as omissions.

In the first place, the code fails to give the governor full and unhampered authority in the appointment of his chief administrative officers and also of a number of subordinate officers. When the governor's appointments require the approval of the Senate, it may be a very easy matter, in case of political or other disagreement between the governor and the Senate, for the Senate to block his appointments and consequently thwart his desires in the administration of the departments or to insist upon compromises in legislation. However, there is a great deal of public opinion in favor of the confirmation of appointments of the leading officers by the Senate. The argument is made that generally the need for confirmation brings about greater care in nominations and that competent nominees are not likely to fail of confirmation. It is undoubtedly contrary to the principle of responsibility to have a number of subordinate officers appointed by the governor with the approval of the Senate. Such appointments, it seems, should be made by the department heads after consultation, if necessary, with the governor.

In the second place, the code does not attempt to codify the existing laws relating to the administration. The old laws stand as they were before the adoption of the code. Only the agencies through which their provisions are enforced have been changed. If the provisions of the law were followed to the letter, there would be much overlapping and duplication of work. Fortunately, however, the provisions were made in the code requiring cooperation between the new departments whereby much of this duplication may be avoided in the actual administration of the work.

In the third place, the code is not as comprehensive as it should be. As has been pointed out, it does not include all the administrative agencies of the state — the constitutional administrative officers other than the governor; namely, the lieutenant governor, secretary of state, treasurer, auditor of public accounts, attorney general, and superintendent of public instruction, all of which are elective; one statutory and elective board — that is, the trustees of the University of Illinois, the civil service commission and a few minor agencies exist independently of the code departments. It was found impractical and inexpedient to make the code, at the time it was enacted, include these agencies. It is hoped by those who took leadership in the administrative reorganization, however, that the Constitutional Convention which is to be held beginning in January, 1920, will complete the work of consolidation so far as the constitutional administrative agencies are concerned.

Even with these shortcomings, the Illinois civil administrative code constitutes the first comprehensive scheme enacted into law to render our state government stronger and more efficient.

IDAHO PLAN

Without a preliminary survey but with the backing of Governor Davis, the 1919 legislature of Idaho passed as an emergency measure under the constitution an "administration consolidation act," which went into effect on March 31st. This act abolished some forty-six offices, boards, and commissions, and consolidated their functions into nine departments. The state administration, in so far as it is not definitely prescribed by the constitution, was completely reorganized. The state board of education is the only previously existing statutory board that continues.

The purpose and scope of the consolidation act are indicated by section 1, which says: "The supreme executive power of the state is vested by the constitution . . . in the governor, who is expressly charged with the duty of seeing that the laws are faithfully executed. In order that he may exercise the portion of the authority so vested and in addition to the powers now conferred upon him by law, civil administrative departments are hereby created, through the instrumentality of which the governor is authorized to exercise the functions in this chapter assigned to each department respectively."

Organization under the Administration Consolidation Act

As in the case of Illinois, the Administration Consolidation Act of Idaho organizes the administrative agencies of the government, with the exception of the constitutional offices and boards and board of education into nine departments.   These departments are as follows:

(1) Department of agriculture; (2) department of commerce and industry; (3) department of finance; (4) department of immigration, labor and statistics; (5) department of law enforcement; (6) department of public investment; (7) department of public welfare; (8) department of public works; (9) department of reclamation.

The six constitutional elective offices not affected by the reorganization are, lieutenant governor, secretary of state, state auditor, state treasurer, attorney general, and superintendent of public instruction; there are also the five constitutional boards, which are not changed in structure or powers, viz., the state board of equalization; state board of pardons; state board of prison commissioners, state board of land commissioners, and directors of the asylum for the insane.   These boards, however, all have *ex officio* membership except the directors of the asylum for the insane, which directors are appointed by the governor with the approval of the Senate.

Single-headed Departments

Each of the nine departments has a single head, called a commissioner, who is charged with the execution of the powers and duties vested by law in his department. These commissioners, with the exception of the commissioner of immigration, labor and statistics, are appointed by the governor and removable by him in his discretion. The commissioner of immigration, labor, and statistics,

who acts as the head of the department of immigration, labor and statistics, is a constitutional officer, appointed by the governor with the consent of the Senate for a term of two years. He is the only one of the department heads whose tenure of office is fixed. Certain experience requirements are prescribed for certain of the departmental heads as well as their subordinate officers. For example, the commissioner of commerce and industry and any director in his department may not be financially interested in any banking or insurance corporation subject to the supervision of the department, and the commissioner must have had at least five years' practical experience in the banking business. The annual salary of each commissioner is fixed at $3,600. All other salaries under the Administration Consolidation Act are fixed by the commissioner of the department concerned, with the approval of the governor. The salaries, however, are not to exceed the amounts fixed by the legislature.

Administrative Officers

In addition to the commissioners of the departments, the following executive and administrative officers, enumerated after the name of each department respectively, are created:

In the Department of Agriculture: Director of markets; director of animal industry; director of plant industry; director of fairs.

In the Department of Commerce and Industry: Director of insurance; manager of state industrial insurance.

In the Department of Land Investigation: Fish and game warden.

In the Department of Public Welfare: Public health adviser.

In the Department of Public Works: Director of highways.

In the Department of Reclamation: Director of water resources.

The above-named subordinate officers are appointed by the governor and are under the direct supervision and control of the commissioner of the respective departments to which each belongs and are required to perform such duties as the commissioner shall prescribe. The initial organization of each department is, however, left largely to the discretion of the commissioner.

As in the case of the Illinois Administrative Code, the Consolidation Act of Idaho does not lay down specific provisions for bureau divisions under the several departments. However, the titles of the subordinate officers would indicate that such organization into divisions or bureaus is to be made at the discretion of the department heads.

Agricultural Advisory Board

One advisory board is provided for by the Consolidation Act. This is the board of agricultural advisers, a non-executive board, created in the department of agriculture. It is composed of nine persons appointed and removable by the governor. The members of this board receive no compensation. They are required to be representative citizens of the state, engaged in agricultural pursuits, not excluding representatives of the agricultural press and of the state agricultural experiment station. This board is given the power to consider and study the entire field of agriculture and advise the executive officers of the department upon their request; recommend on its own initiative policies and practices, which recommendations the executive officers of the department shall duly consider, and give advice or make recommendations to the governor and legislature if so requested, or on its own initiative. This board may examine the books and the records of the department at any time. It is required

who acts as the head of the department of immigration, labor and statistics, is a constitutional officer, appointed by the governor with the consent of the Senate for a term of two years. He is the only one of the department heads whose tenure of office is fixed. Certain experience requirements are prescribed for certain of the departmental heads as well as their subordinate officers. For example, the commissioner of commerce and industry and any director in his department may not be financially interested in any banking or insurance corporation subject to the supervision of the department, and the commissioner must have had at least five years' practical experience in the banking business. The annual salary of each commissioner is fixed at $3,600. All other salaries under the Administration Consolidation Act are fixed by the commissioner of the department concerned, with the approval of the governor. The salaries, however, are not to exceed the amounts fixed by the legislature.

Administrative Officers

In addition to the commissioners of the departments, the following executive and administrative officers, enumerated after the name of each department respectively, are created:

In the Department of Agriculture: Director of markets; director of animal industry; director of plant industry; director of fairs.

In the Department of Commerce and Industry: Director of insurance; manager of state industrial insurance.

In the Department of Land Investigation: Fish and game warden.

In the Department of Public Welfare: Public health adviser.

In the Department of Public Works: Director of highways.

In the Department of Reclamation: Director of water resources.

The above-named subordinate officers are appointed by the governor and are under the direct supervision and control of the commissioner of the respective departments to which each belongs and are required to perform such duties as the commissioner shall prescribe. The initial organization of each department is, however, left largely to the discretion of the commissioner.

As in the case of the Illinois Administrative Code, the Consolidation Act of Idaho does not lay down specific provisions for bureau divisions under the several departments. However, the titles of the subordinate officers would indicate that such organization into divisions or bureaus is to be made at the discretion of the department heads.

Agricultural Advisory Board

One advisory board is provided for by the Consolidation Act. This is the board of agricultural advisers, a non-executive board, created in the department of agriculture. It is composed of nine persons appointed and removable by the governor. The members of this board receive no compensation. They are required to be representative citizens of the state, engaged in agricultural pursuits, not excluding representatives of the agricultural press and of the state agricultural experiment station. This board is given the power to consider and study the entire field of agriculture and advise the executive officers of the department upon their request; recommend on its own initiative policies and practices, which recommendations the executive officers of the department shall duly consider, and give advice or make recommendations to the governor and legislature if so requested, or on its own initiative. This board may examine the books and the records of the department at any time. It is required

who acts as the head of the department of immigration, labor and statistics, is a constitutional officer, appointed by the governor with the consent of the Senate for a term of two years. He is the only one of the department heads whose tenure of office is fixed. Certain experience requirements are prescribed for certain of the departmental heads as well as their subordinate officers. For example, the commissioner of commerce and industry and any director in his department may not be financially interested in any banking or insurance corporation subject to the supervision of the department, and the commissioner must have had at least five years' practical experience in the banking business. The annual salary of each commissioner is fixed at $3,600. All other salaries under the Administration Consolidation Act are fixed by the commissioner of the department concerned, with the approval of the governor. The salaries, however, are not to exceed the amounts fixed by the legislature.

Administrative Officers

In addition to the commissioners of the departments, the following executive and administrative officers, enumerated after the name of each department respectively, are created:

In the Department of Agriculture: Director of markets; director of animal industry; director of plant industry; director of fairs.

In the Department of Commerce and Industry: Director of insurance; manager of state industrial insurance.

In the Department of Land Investigation: Fish and game warden.

In the Department of Public Welfare: Public health adviser.

In the Department of Public Works: Director of highways.

In the Department of Reclamation: Director of water resources.

The above-named subordinate officers are appointed by the governor and are under the direct supervision and control of the commissioner of the respective departments to which each belongs and are required to perform such duties as the commissioner shall prescribe. The initial organization of each department is, however, left largely to the discretion of the commissioner.

As in the case of the Illinois Administrative Code, the Consolidation Act of Idaho does not lay down specific provisions for bureau divisions under the several departments. However, the titles of the subordinate officers would indicate that such organization into divisions or bureaus is to be made at the discretion of the department heads.

Agricultural Advisory Board

One advisory board is provided for by the Consolidation Act. This is the board of agricultural advisers, a non-executive board, created in the department of agriculture. It is composed of nine persons appointed and removable by the governor. The members of this board receive no compensation. They are required to be representative citizens of the state, engaged in agricultural pursuits, not excluding representatives of the agricultural press and of the state agricultural experiment station. This board is given the power to consider and study the entire field of agriculture and advise the executive officers of the department upon their request; recommend on its own initiative policies and practices, which recommendations the executive officers of the department shall duly consider, and give advice or make recommendations to the governor and legislature if so requested, or on its own initiative. This board may examine the books and the records of the department at any time. It is required

to adopt rules and regulations not inconsistent with law, also to hold meetings, and to keep a record of the minutes of such meetings.

General Powers of Department Heads

The commissioner of each department is empowered to prescribe rules and regulations for his department, not inconsistent with law. Each department must maintain a central office at the capitol and may, with the approval of the governor, establish such branch offices as may be necessary. Each department is empowered to employ necessary employees and to fix the rate of compensation. All employees are required to render not less than seven hours of labor during each regular working day and are allowed fourteen days' leave of absence in each year with full pay.

Inasmuch as the existing laws remain unchanged — the Consolidation Act changing only the agencies through which the laws are enforced — provisions are made in the act under which " the governor shall devise a practical and working basis for coöperation and coördination of work, eliminating duplication and overlapping of functions." The departments are required to coöperate with each other in employment of services and the use of their quarters and equipments. The commissioner of any department may require the employee of any department, subject to the consent of the superior officer of the employee, to perform any duty he may require of his own subordinates.

Functions of Departments

The department of agriculture exercises the power and is charged with the general duty of promoting agriculture throughout the state; and with introducing methods of conducting the agricultural industries in order to increase the production and facilitate the distribution of products. It collects and publishes statistics relating to production and marketing of crops, cattle, and other farm products. It assists, encourages, and promotes the organization of farmer' institutes, horticultural and agricultural societies, and the holding of live-stock shows, fairs, and other exhibits of farm products. It has authority to maintain a market news service, including information as to crops, freight rates, commission rates, and other matters of service to producers and consumers. Home seekers in the state of Idaho are to be assisted and encouraged in every way possible by this department. The department is required to receive applications for farm help, also applications from farm laborers, and to render service in placing employees without expense either to the employer or the employee. The inspection of nursery stock and the prevention of infectious and contagious plant and animal diseases are duties of this department.

The department of commerce and industry is vested with the powers and duties formerly exercised by the state bank department, the state insurance department, the state insurance manager, the board of appeal from the decisions of the banking commissioner, and the mine inspector. This department is required to execute all laws relating to banks and banking and to insurance and insurance companies doing business in the state. It is also required to administer the state industrial insurance fund.

The department of finance exercises the rights, powers, and duties vested by law in the state examiner and the state depository board. This department prescribes forms of vouchers, of accounts and reports, and installs uniform bookkeeping. It supervises and examines state accounts and the accounts of private concerns receiving state money. It also keeps accounts of the state's chattel property and inspects its securities. State depositories are designated by this department and are required by it to furnish proper securities. This department is required to demand and receive reports from the state treasurer, state auditor, state bank examiner, and other officers.   It may inspect any state office or any state depository.   All state laws relating to the assessment of property and the levy, collection, apportionment, and distribution of taxes are supervised and enforced by this department.   The state board of equalization, a constitutional and *ex officio* body, is associated with this department.   The preparation of the budget data for the governor is assigned to this department, as well as the supervision of the duplication of work in the departments.

The department of immigration, labor and statistics is the bureau of immigration, labor and statistics, formerly established by the constitution (article 8, section 1) and laws.   It is empowered to promote the welfare of workers, their commercial, industrial, social condition — and to protect their health.   It collects information upon the subject of labor in its relation to capital, the hours of labor, and the earnings of laboring men and women. The officials of this department are required to visit shops, factories, mercantile establishments, and other places where working people are employed.   The department may determine and prescribe what safety devices, safeguards, and other means or methods of protection are needed to safeguard the employees of factories and workshops.

The department of law enforcement exercises the rights, powers, and duties originally vested in the fish and game warden, secretary of the state highway commission (so far as his duties relate to the registration of motor vehicles), state board of medical examiners, state board of dental examiners, board of osteopathic examination, Idaho state board of examiners in optometry, board of pharmacy, state board of examination and registration of graduate nurses, board of examining surveyors, state engineer, as *ex officio* chairman of the state board of examining surveyors, Idaho state board of veterinary medical examiners, state board of accountancy, state board of examiners of architects, and examining committee of the state board of health for the examination of embalmers. This department establishes and maintains fish hatcheries and game preserves and takes all necessary measures for the preservation, distribution, introduction, and restoration of fish and game. It supervises the registration and licensing of automobiles, motor vehicles, and motor-vehicle manufacturers, dealers, and chauffeurs; also enforces all the penal and regulatory laws of the state in the same manner and with like authority as the sheriffs of the counties.

In order to assist the department of law enforcement in the registration of occupations, the commissioner may name from time to time boards, varying from three to six persons, from the various professions to conduct the examinations and to pass upon the professional attainments of the applicants for state licenses. All professional certificates and licenses are issued by the department of law enforcement.

The department of public investments controls, loans, and invests all the permanent funds of the state in such securities as are designated in the state constitution. It fixes the rate of interest to be charged upon all loans upon real estate; has the care and custody of all certificates and contracts for the sale of state lands and timbers, all leases of state lands, all mortgages, bonds, and other securities in which the permanent funds of the state are invested, and collects all moneys due the state on the same.

The department of public welfare is charged with the exercise of the powers and duties vested in the board of directors of the Northern Idaho Sanitarium, the board of directors of the Idaho State Sanitarium, the board of trustees of the soldiers' home, the state board of health, the bureau of vital statistics, the dairy, food, and sanitary inspector, and the state chemist.

The department of public works exercises the powers and duties formerly vested in the state highway commission, the state highway engineer, the board of trustees of the capitol building, and the Heyburn Park board of control. This department is required to lay out, construct, and maintain state highways; to improve, alter, or extend such highways; and to purchase, condemn, or otherwise supervise the necessary lands for highway rights of way. It is also required to coöperate with, and receive aid from, the Federal Government for the construction and improvement of any state highway. Coöperation is established between the county and highway district commissions and this department. The purchase of supplies and materials for the various state agencies is also placed under this department.

The department of reclamation exercises the powers and duties vested in the state engineer and the state board of land commissioners, a constitutional body, in the administration of the Carey Act and chapter 241 of the compiled laws.

What the Reorganization Accomplishes

While the organization under the Administration Consolidation Act does not include the functions performed by six constitutional administrative officers other than the governor, and by five constitutional boards, the functions of two of these boards are amalgamated with the work of the new departments. The functions performed by the state board of equalization, a constitutional board of *ex officio* membership, are merged into the department of finance. Likewise, the functions of the state board of land commissioners, an *ex officio* and constitutional body, are taken over largely by the department of reclamation. In the case of the other constitutional boards; namely, the state board of pardons, the state board of prison commissioners, and the directors of asylums for the insane, no definite provisions are made in the Consolidation Act for their association with the new departments. One statutory board performing educational functions still exists, since the code does not take into account the educational activities of the state.

The Idaho Act does not attempt to codify the existing laws relating to administration, but it makes provisions, as does the Illinois code, to avoid overlapping and duplication of work by requiring coöperation between the new departments.

The Idaho Consolidation Act has accomplished as thorough a reorganization of the state administration as is possible without changing the constitution. It contains the basis of a well-ordered and consistent plan. However, as in the case of Illinois, constitutional changes are necessary in order to make the plan complete.

NEBRASKA PLAN

The 1913 legislature of Nebraska authorized a joint committee of the two houses to make a study of the administrative organization of the state. The report of this committee, which was made the following year, showed the need for reorganization and recommended that the legislature provided for a survey as a means of working out a consolidation plan. The legislature took no immediate action, but both Governors Moreland and Neville in their messages to that body recommended the adoption of a plan of administrative consolidation and the establishment of an effective budget system. The platform upon which the present governor was elected pledged the party to the realization of a consolidation plan and budget system. Accordingly, the 1919 legislature under the leadership of Governor McKelvie passed a law, known as the " civil administrative code," which provides for the consolidation of most of the statutory administrative agencies of the state.

Organization Under the Civil Administrative Code

The Civil Administrative Code creates and establishes the following administrative departments:

Department of finance; department of agriculture; department of labor; department of trade and commerce; department of public welfare; department of public works.

This reorganization comprehends practically all the changes in the administrative organization of the state which can be made without constitutional amendment. Excepting the governor, there are seven constitutional officers; namely, lieutenant governor, secretary of state, treasurer, auditor of public accounts, attorney general, commissioner of lands and buildings, and superintendent of public instruction.   There are also four constitutional boards — the state railway commission, composed of three members elected for terms of six years; the board of regents, composed of six members elected for terms of six years; the board of commissioners of state institutions, composed of three members appointed by the governor with the consent of the Senate for terms of six years, and the board of educational lands and funds, composed of *ex officio* membership. Two statutory boards — namely, the state board of equalization and the state board of agriculture — continue in existence and are attached to the department of finance and the department of agriculture respectively.

Department Heads and Subordinates

Each of the six departments has a single head known as a secretary, who is appointed by the governor with the approval of the Senate for a term of two years from the first Tuesday after the first Monday in January following the election of the governor. The code prescribes an annual salary of $5,000 for each of these secretaries, which is twice that received by the governor.

Under the code the governor is required to confer with the department heads relative to appointments and to appoint such deputies, assistants, employees, and clerical help as shall be necessary or essential to the proper management of the departments. Each secretary and appointee in each department is required to devote his entire time to the duties of his office and to render not less than eight hours' service during each regular working day.

The secretary of each department is empowered to prescribe regulations not inconsistent with law for the government of his department, conduct of his employees, and the performance of the business of his department. Each department is required to maintain a central office at the capitol of the state and may establish branch offices upon the approval of the governor.

The secretaries of the departments are required to devise a practical and working basis for coöperation and coördination of work, eliminating duplication and overlapping functions. They are required to coöperate with each other in the employment of help and in the use of quarters and equipment.

Each department created by the code is given the power through its secretary to make a thorough investigation of all books and records of any person, firm, or corporation under the control of, doing business with, or being regulated by the state.

Functions of Departments

The department of finance prescribes and installs uniform accounting in the other departments. It supervises and examines the accounts and financial reports of the other departments and keeps summary and controlling accounts of the expenditures of these departments. It approves or disapproves all vouchers, bills, and claims of the other departments.   The adjustment of duplication of work among the departments, as well as the publication of information with reference to the administration, is a function of the department of finance.   This department also acts as a staff agency to the governor in the preparation of the budget; it prescribes uniform rules governing the specifications for the purchase of supplies; it is given supervisory powers over taxation, the work of the state board of equalization being merged into the department.   The work of this department consists mainly of new functions.   Only the functions of one previously existing office — that is, the state printer — have been taken over by this department.

The department of agriculture exercises the powers and duties originally performed by the food, drug, dairy, and hotel commission, the live-stock sanitary board, the board of survey and public welfare, and deputy game warden.   The state board of agriculture, which is a statutory board, was not abolished by the code, but was made advisory to this department.   In addition to the functions performed by these boards and officers a new function of markets and marketing has been added to the department of agriculture.

The department of trade and commerce exercises the powers formerly vested in the state banking board; the state insurance board, and deputy fire commissioner. The state railway commission, a constitutional and elective board, coöperates with this department in the exercise of its functions.   This department also administers the "blue sky" law with reference to corporations.

The department of labor assumes the powers and duties formerly vested in the compensation commission and deputy labor commissioner.   It administers the workmen's compensation law, prepares industrial statistics, and maintains a free employment bureau. It is also charged with the administration of the child labor law, the health and sanitary inspection, and the safety regulation of factories and other places of employment in the state. A state board of mediation and investigation is created in connection with the department of labor, which consists of the governor and the secretaries of the six code departments. This board is charged with the mediation and adjustment of disputes arising between employers and employees within the state.

The department of public works discharges the functions vested by law in the state board of highways, irrigation, and drainage. It also takes over the licensing of motor vehicles from the office of the secretary of state. The construction of all highways, irrigation works, and drainage within the state is under the supervision of this department.

The department of public welfare performs the functions of the state board of health, the child welfare commission, and the board of pardons and parole. It is charged with the execution and enforcement of all laws relating to food inspection, sanitation, and the prevention of contagious and communicable diseases. The department conducts examinations for the licensing of physicians, surgeons, chiropractitioners, dentists, nurses, pharmacists, optometrists, embalmers, and veterinary surgeons. It has the enforcement of laws relating to weights and measures. It supervises the registration of vital statistics. The regulation of maternity homes and the placing of dependent and delinquent children are under the supervision of this department. The state system of public charities and corrections is also under the direction and control of the department of public welfare.

What the Code Accomplishes

The code eliminates eight boards and commissions and consolidates ten departments that have similar functions into six main departments, the heads of which are appointed by the governor and confirmed by the Senate. The plan thus distinctly locates accountability, coördinates administrative effort, and gives the governor authority over nearly all the administrative functions which are not vested in constitutional agencies. It gives the governor no power that is not provided by the constitution or the law. He makes fewer major appointments under the code than he made under the old laws.

Unlike the codes of Illinois and Idaho, the Nebraska code brings together and codifies the administrative law of the state. In this way the overlapping functions between the newly created departments have been eliminated by revision and numerous new duties essential to the successful operation of the several departments have been added.

Nebraska has followed the same general plan in the adoption of her code as those of Illinois and Idaho. As in the other two states a thoroughgoing centralization of the administration is impossible without constitutional amendment.

CHAPTER XI

Preliminary Surveys

THE Massachusetts legislature of 1912 created a commission on economy and efficiency consisting of three members. At first the state auditor was *ex officio* a member and the other two members were appointed by the governor. Later (1914) all members were appointed by the governor with overlapping terms of three years each. Among other things this commission made a study of the administrative organization and submitted to the governor in November, 1914, a comprehensive report on "the functions, organization, and administration of the departments in the executive branch of the state government." This report contained no constructive proposals for reorganization and consolidation. Later, however, the commission made recommendations for the reorganization of the administration of the militia, the state normal schools, and the transfer of certain functions among the existing departments. In 1916 the commission was abolished by the legislature and its functions given to the newly created supervisor of administration.

The 1917 legislature created a joint special committee on finances and budget procedure and authorized it to "investigate and consider the matter of the consolidation and abolition of commissions." This committee made a report to the 1919 legislature in which it stated that the administrative work of the state was performed by two hundred and sixteen more or less independent agencies —

179

one hundred and ten of which had a single official in charge; three of which had a single official with an advisory council; and one hundred and three of which were headed by boards or commissions. The committee proposed a tentative plan of consolidation which did not affect the constitutional administrative officers, but grouped the remaining administrative agencies under eleven departments, the heads of which were to be appointed by the governor with the approval of the council.

Constitutional Amendment Providing for Consolidation

The Constitutional Convention of Massachusetts, which held its final sessions during the summer of 1918, took up the subject of administrative consolidation. Although no further detailed study had yet been made of the administrative agencies of the state, the Convention agreed upon a proposed amendment to the constitution designed to bring about more efficient administration of the business of the state. This amendment was submitted to a vote of the people on November 5, 1918, and was ratified. The amendment reads as follows: " On or before January 1, 1921, the executive and administrative work of the commonwealth shall be organized in not more than twenty departments, in one of which every executive and administrative office, board, and commission, except those officers serving directly under the governor or the council, shall be placed. Such departments shall be under such supervision and regulation as the general court may from time to time prescribe by law." (Amendment No. 19.)

While the economy and efficiency commission of 1912 had made an investigation similar to those made in Illinois and New York some years prior to the adoption of this amendment, there was, nevertheless, at the time the amendment was discussed, no definite plan of reorganization before the convention. The subject of reorganization was therefore considered as a broad question upon its merits and was not hindered by the rivalry and jealousy of the existing officers in the departments or by political bickering over the details of the plan. No one in the convention knew definitely what administrative agencies were to be created or abolished. For this reason the opposition was unable to offer concrete objections to the general proposal.

Reorganization Proposed by Supervisor of Administration

Preceding the beginning of the 1919 session of the legislature, the supervisor of administration made a re-survey of the administrative agencies of the state as result of which he proposed a plan of consolidation which was submitted to the 1919 legislature together with a number of bills designed to carry the plan into effect. This plan proposed no changes in the offices of the elective constitutional officers except the addition of a few new functions. Five of the departments proposed were to be headed by constitutional officers, namely: (1) Governor and council; (2) secretary of the commonwealth; (3) treasurer and receiver general; (4) auditor of the commonwealth; (5) attorney general. The office of supervisor of administration was placed under the governor and the council. The remaining administrative agencies of the state were grouped under fourteen departments, as follows: (1) Department of tax commissioner and commissioner of corporations; (2) department of public utilities; (3) department of public health; (4) department of accounting, banking and insurance; (5) department of industrial accidents; (6) department of labor and industry; (7) department of education and registration; (8) department of public works; (9) department of agriculture; (10) department of institutions; (11) department of public welfare; (12) department of public safety; (13) department of civil service; (14) department of metropolitan districts. Thus all the administrative agencies of the state were grouped by the supervisor under nineteen proposed departments.

In the bills which the supervisor of administration submitted to the legislature and which were designed to set up his proposed reorganization, political expediency rather than a consistent plan seems to have been followed in working out the overhead organization of the several proposed departments. Some of the departments were to be administered by single heads and others by commissions. The proposed departments of registration and education, public works, agriculture, accounting, banking and insurance, institutions, welfare and public safety were to be headed by directors appointed by the governor with the approval of the council for terms varying from three to five years, the term of the governor being two years. Some of these departments were to have advisory boards appointed by the governor with the consent of the council, consisting of from five to eight members with overlapping terms varying from three to five years. The departments of public utilities, metropolitan district, and civil service were to be headed by commissions composed of three members, each appointed by the governor with the consent of the council for overlapping terms varying from three to five years. The department of labor and industry was to have a director as administrative head appointed by the governor with the consent of the council for a term of four years, and three commissioners to act as a board of arbitration and concilation appointed by the governor with the consent of the council for overlapping terms of three years.

In addition to the proposals for reorganization submitted by the supervisor of administration, several other proposals were submitted by members of the legislature in the 1919 session.

After rather lengthy consideration of the proposed plans as embodied in the separate bills before the legislature, it was decided to frame a single bill which would contain the entire consolidated organization. Accordingly, this bill was prepared by the legislative committee on administration and commissions to which had been referred Governor Coolidge's recommendations and all bills pertaining to administrative reorganization. This bill was introduced in the legislature on June 6, passed with a few minor changes, and received the approval of the governor on July 23d. Its provisions became effective on December 1, 1919.

Organization under the Consolidation Plan

The Administrative Consolidation Act of Massachusetts groups the executive and administrative functions of the state, "except such as pertain to the governor and the council, and such as are exercised and performed by officers serving directly under the governor or the governor and council," into the departments of the secretary of the commonwealth, the treasurer and receiver general, the auditor of the commonwealth, and the attorney general, headed by constitutional elective officers, and the following departments created by the act: agriculture, conservation, banking and insurance, corporations and taxation, education, civil service and registration, industrial accidents, labor and industries, mental diseases, correction, public welfare, public health, public safety, public works, public utilities, and a metropolitan district commission. The plan, therefore, establishes twenty departments, excluding the governor and council — the maximum number permitted under the constitutional amendment.

Complicated and Involved Scheme

The general scheme of organization, as will be seen later, is very complicated and involved. Practically all the officials connected with the existing administrative agencies have been retained, their offices being continued in existence and placed under the several departments without alteration either in personnel or duties.   Seven boards, which apparently did not fit into the scheme elsewhere, are placed under the governor and council.   The military and naval functions, the office of supervisor of administration, and the newly created superintendent of buildings are also placed under the governor and council. The superintendent of buildings cares for the statehouse and manages the purchasing of supplies for the departments.   All appointments made by the governor must have the approval of the council, an independent elective body of nine members.   The administrative officers are appointed in nearly all cases for terms of three or five years, and the members of the administrative and other boards are usually appointed for overlapping terms varying from three to six years.   In all cases, except those of the elective constitutional officers, the terms of the principal administrative officers are longer than that of the governor, his term being fixed by the constitution at two years.

Status of Constitutional Officers

Few changes have been made by the Consolidation Act in the work of departments which are headed by the four constitutional officers.   To the department of the secretary of the commonwealth have been added the functions performed by the commissioner of public records and the bureau of statistics, both of which are abolished. The existing board of retirement and the commissioners on firemen's relief are placed under the department of the treasurer and receiver general, where they continue to exist and to perform their present functions.   The departments of the auditor of the commonwealth and of the attorney general continue as previously organized.

Administrative Machinery of the Statutory Departments

The department of agriculture is under the supervision and control of a commissioner assisted by an advisory board of six members, all of whom are appointed by the governor with the approval of the council. The commissioner will serve for a term of three years and the members of the advisory board for overlapping terms of three years, two being appointed each year. The annual salary of the commissioner is not to exceed $5,000 and the members of the advisory board are to receive $10 per diem and traveling expenses. The commissioner must organize the department into at least five divisions: dairying and animal husbandry, plant pest control, ornithology, markets and reclamation, soil survey and fairs, and may add other divisions. He may appoint and remove the director of each division.

The department of conservation is under the control of a commissioner appointed by the governor with the approval of the council for a term of three years at an annual salary not to exceed $5,000. He is designated by the governor as director of one of the three divisions into which the department is divided, namely: forestry, fisheries and game, and animal industry. However, provision is made for the retention of the old commissioner of animal industry in the capacity of director of the division of animal industry, his appointment to office being made hereafter as formerly provided by law. The director of the remaining division is appointed by the governor with the approval of the council for a term of three years, and should he serve as head of the division of fisheries and game, he will receive a salary not to exceed $4,000 per year. The directors act as an advisory council to the commissioner.

The department of banking and insurance is organized into three divisions, a division of banks and loan agencies, a division of insurance, and a division of savings-bank life insurance. Each division is under the control of a commissioner, the commissioner of banks and the commissioner of insurance are appointed by the governor with the council's approval for terms of three years at annual salaries not to exceed $5,000 each. The commissioner of savings-bank life insurance is one of the board of trustees of the corporation known as the general insurance guaranty fund, his term of office to be that of his appointment as trustee. Since it is obvious that this 'department has triple heads, the act provides that the commissioners "shall act as a board in all matters concerning the department as a whole." The three divisions are really independent agencies nominally brought together. The existing boards of bank incorporation and of appeal on fire-insurance rates are continued under the division of banks and loan agencies and the division of insurance, respectively.

The department of corporations and taxation consists of the office of tax commissioner and commissioner of corporations as formerly organized. The old tax commissioner and commissioner of corporations is the commissioner of the department at a salary not to exceed $7,500 per year. The department is organized into an income-tax division, a division of corporations, a division of inheritance taxes, a division of local taxation, and a division of accounts. The commissioner appoints, subject to the approval of the governor and council, a director at the head of each division and also fixes the salaries of such directors.

The department of education is under the control of a commissioner and an advisory board of six members appointed by the governor with the approval of the council. The commissioner's term of office is fixed at five years with an annual salary not to exceed $7,500. The members of the advisory board will serve for overlapping terms of three years, two being appointed each year. At least two members of this board must be women, one of whom shall be a teacher. The department will be organized into such divisions as the commissioner with the approval of the governor and council may determine, but must include a division of public libraries, a division of education of aliens, and a division of the blind. The division of public libraries consists of the board of free public libraries as formerly organized, the chairman acting as director of the division. The division of education of aliens consists of a director, who may be a woman, and an advisory board of six members appointed by the governor with the approval of the council, the director for a term of five years, and the board members for overlapping terms of three years. The division of the blind consists of the commission for the blind as formerly organized, the head of the commission acting as director of the division. Such other divisions as may be organized will have a director in charge appointed by the commissioner with the approval of the advisory board. Hence the department of education consists of three divisions, administratively independent of each other, and a possible group of divisions with heads appointed by the commissioner. The old boards of trustees of five schools and the teachers' retirement board are continued in existence and are placed in the department.

The department of civil service and registration is organized in two divisions, a division of civil service and a division of registration. The division of civil service is under the control of a commissioner and two associate commissioners appointed by the governor with the council's approval for overlapping terms of three years, the commissioner to receive not more than $5,000 annually and the associate commissioners not exceeding $2,000 each. The three constitute a board for the preparation of rules and regulations and the holding of hearings on civil service matters. The division of registration is under the supervision of a director appointed by the governor and council for a term not to exceed two years at an annual salary of $1,500. As a possible means of coördinating the work of the department, the act provides that the commissioner of civil service and the director of registration "shall act as a board in all matters affecting the department as a whole." Ten state registration boards are continued in existence and are placed under the division of registration.

The department of industrial accidents consists of the old industrial accident board as formerly organized with its duties and functions unchanged.

The department of labor and industries is under a commissioner, an assistant commissioner, who may be a woman, and three associate commissioners, among whom must be a representative each of labor and employers. All are appointed by the governor with the council's approval for terms of three years, the associate commissioners' terms being overlapping. The commissioner receives $5,000 annually and the assistant and associate commissioners, $4,000 each. The associate commissioners constitute a board of conciliation and arbitration.

The department of mental diseases consists of the present Massachusetts commission on mental diseases. The commissioner of mental diseases is the administrative head of the department.

The department of correction is under a commissioner appointed by the governor with the council's approval for a three years' term at an annual salary not to exceed $6,000. The commissioner, with the approval of the governor and council, may appoint, remove, and fix the salary of two deputy commissioners.

The department of public welfare is under the supervision of a commissioner and an advisory board of six members, two of whom must be women, all appointed by the governor with the council's approval. The commissioner's term is five years, and the members of the advisory board are appointed for overlapping terms of three years, two each year. The commissioner is *ex officio* a member of the advisory board and receives an annual salary not to exceed $6,000. The department is organized into three divisions, namely: aid and relief, child guardianship, and juvenile training. Each division has a director, the directors of aid and relief and of child guardianship being appointed, removed, and salaries fixed by the commissioner with the consent of the governor and council. The director of juvenile training is a member of the board of trustees of the Massachusetts training schools, designated by the governor, and serves without compensation. This officer is, therefore, practically independent of the commissioner. The commissioner prepares and presents for the consideration of the advisory board rules and regulations governing the conduct of his department which become effective upon approval by a majority of the members of this board. Several previously existing boards are continued and placed in this department.

The department of health is the old department of health as now organized and the head of the old department becomes its commissioner.

The department of public safety is under the supervision of a commissioner appointed by the governor with the approval of the council for a term of five years at an annual salary not exceeding $5,000. The department is organized into three divisions — a division of state police, headed by the commissioner, a division of inspection, under a director known as chief of inspections, a division of fire prevention, under a director known as state fire marshal. The two directors are appointed by the governor and council for terms of three years at annual salaries not to exceed $4,000.

The department of public works is under the control of a commissioner and four associate commissioners, all appointed by the governor with the approval of the council. The commissioner serves for a term of three years, and the associate commissioners for overlapping terms of two years. The department is divided into a division of highways and a division of waterways and public lands. The governor designates two of the associate commissioners to have charge of each of these divisions, thus making a dual-headed administration of the divisions. The commissioner appoints, with the approval of the governor and council, a registrar of motor vehicles.

The department of public utilities is under the management of a commission of five members appointed by the governor with the consent of the council for overlapping terms of five years. The governor designates one of the commissioners chairman, who receives an annual salary of $9,000. Each of the other commissioners receives an annual salary of $8,000.

The metropolitan district commission is composed of a commissioner and four associate commissioners, all appointed by the governor with the approval of the council. The commissioner serves for a term of five years at an annual salary of $6,000, and the associate commissioners for overlapping terms of four years at $1,000 each per year.

Plan Violates Principles Establishing Executive Responsibility

In summing up, it can be said that the Massachusetts plan of consolidation and reorganization is inconsistent with the principle of making one person fully responsible for the administrative work of each department. As has already been pointed out, it proposes single heads, either elective or appointive by the governor and council, for the administration of some departments, and for the administration of other departments it sets up boards appointed by the governor and council. Two departments — department of banking and insurance, and department of civil service and registration — are headless; however, each is nominally unified by a provision requiring the independent division heads to " act as a board in all matters concerning the department as a whole."

The Massachusetts plan also departs from the principle that department heads and other chief administrative officers should not be given a longer term of office than that of the governor. It provides that practically all administrative officers shall serve for terms of three or five years, and the members of all administrative boards shall be appointed for overlapping terms of from three to six years. Since the constitution fixes the governor's term of office at two years, he will never be able to control his administration by appointment, even if he is not blocked by action of the council, except he hold office for at least two successive terms, and perhaps then he will not have gained control until it is too late for him to accomplish anything.

Finally, the governor can exercise practically no control over the expenditure of appropriations under the plan of administrative organization set up by the Massachusetts Consolidation Act. The governors of Illinois, Idaho, and Nebraska have the power through the general control vested in their departments of finance and by reason of the greater authority which they exercise over the administration because of the organization under consolidation plans to enforce the proper execution of the appropriations.

There is in Massachusetts, as in the other states having administrative codes in operation, great need for constitutional revision. A comprehensive and consistent plan of administrative consolidation — one that establishes executive responsibility — cannot be adopted until the people decide in their own minds whether they want a responsible executive at the head of the state. They seem to have decided this in the affirmative but have not been willing to trust their ability to enforce responsibility, and therefore have retained all of the trappings of an irresponsible party system, irresponsible bosses, and irresponsible government. If they really want responsible government, this end cannot be attained until (1) a number of administrative officers have been removed from the list of the elected and made appointive by the governor, (2) the existing council of nine elective members which share to a large degree the governor's responsibility in the administration of the state has been abolished, and (3) a procedure has been provided for which will bring the head of the administration before the representative appropriating body each year to give an account of himself and stand or fall on his ability to command the support of a majority — with a right of appeal to the voters of the state.

CHAPTER XII

OREGON, Delaware, California, and New York have recently had under consideration, or in the process of evolution, plans for the centralization of executive responsibility. Several other states have given serious thought to the subject.

PROPOSED OREGON PLAN

People's Power League

In 1909 and again in 1911 the People's Power League of Oregon proposed a plan for the reorganization of the state government, which concentrated executive power in the hands of the governor — checked only by an elective auditor — and established close relations between the governor and the legislature. In 1912 and 1913 the League submitted parts of its plan to the voters, which were defeated. Later it proposed to abolish one house of the legislature, to give the governor a seat in that body, to destroy " logrolling " by giving him the power to initiate the budget with only power to decrease in the legislature, and to centralize administrative authority in the governor. These proposals, however, did not meet with success.

Commissions to Investigate Administration

At length the legislature became interested in the reorganization of the state government. During the 1915 session a joint committee was appointed by the legislature for the purpose of eliminating and consolidating offices, boards, and commissions, but this committee did not accomplish anything. The 1917 session, however, provided for a " commission of seven business men " to study the state administration with a view to the consolidation and elimination of useless administrative agencies. This commission was duly appointed by the governor and became known as the consolidation commission. It was instructed to report to the 1919 legislature. After its organization it secured the assistance of three of the state colleges in making a survey of the state administrative agencies. Later it engaged Professor John M. Mathews of the University of Illinois and Mr. Fred Topkins of Portland to put the report in final shape.

Report of Consolidation Commission

The report of the consolidation commission, as submitted to the 1919 legislature, gives in the space of forty-four pages a concise statement of the present administrative conditions and lays down specific recommendations for a plan of consolidation. It points out that under existing statutes there are three principal ways of choosing state officials: (1) By election of the people; (2) by appointment of the governor; (3) by appointment of the governor, secretary of state, and state treasurer; in addition, many appointments are made by sundry boards and commissions. It states that "no efficient, businesslike administration of state affairs in Oregon can be expected unless some one officer who is fully responsible to the people can control all the important departments of the administration, with the possible exception of the auditing and treasury departments. The governor does not do so at present, however, for three main reasons: (1) Because there are too many elective officers; (2) because the administration is split up into too many departments for the governor to exercise adequate control over them; (3)

because the appointing power is too often shared with other officials, boards, and commissions." It further asserts that " It is commonly supposed that the state of Oregon has only one governor, just as there is but one President of the United States. This supposition, however, is a mistake . . . instead of one governor, Oregon has a multitude of governors." In commenting upon this condition, the report says: " All of the elective officers derive their authority from the same source that the governor himself does, and he, therefore, has no real power of control over them. The election of so many heads of administrative departments exerts a subtle influence in dividing the administration, developing friction, and causing a lack of harmony and coöperation between the various departments. It also causes the injection of political considerations and ambition into the management of elective offices which are not conducive to efficiency and economy. There is no logical reason inherent in the character of the position or the nature of the duties why some offices should be elective and others appointive. . . . The sharing of the governor's appointing power with other state officials, if anything, exerts a still more subtle influence in producing friction and causing lack of harmony and coöperation. Most frequently it results in a division and shifting of responsibility both among those having the joint appointing power as well as with the one appointed."

The following general principles are laid down by the report as a guide in the preparation and consideration of the plan of reorganization: (1) That the governor should appoint all heads of administrative departments under the reorganized and consolidated administration; (2) that in making appointments the governor should be privileged to act in all cases without confirmation by the Senate and should have unhampered power of removal; (3) that all minor officers of the department should be chosen under the civil service regulations.

The consolidation commission proposes to consolidate all existing administrative agencies of Oregon into ten departments, which consolidation will involve both constitutional and statutory changes. The proposed departments are as follows: (1) finance department; (2) law department; (3) tax department. (4) department of education; (5) department of labor; (6) department of health; (7) department of agriculture; (8) department of trade and commerce; (9) department of public welfare (institutions); (10) department of public works. The two hundred and fifty officials under the present scheme of administration would, it is claimed, be reduced by this consolidation to forty officials.

Departmental Organization

The proposed finance department is to include the present functions of the secretary of state, state treasurer, state printer, and six *ex officio* boards. The secretary of state now acts as state auditor. The report recommends that the function of auditing be separated from the office of secretary of state and that the office of state auditor of public accounts be created to be either appointed by the legislature or elected by the people. The report is not very clear as to the overhead organization of the department. A chart of the proposed organization indicates that this department is to be under the control of a finance commission, composed of the governor, secretary of state, and state treasurer. The finance department is to be charged with the preparation of the budget for the governor, the assessment and collection of taxes, the custody of funds, the registration of motor vehicles, and the purchasing of supplies.

The department of law is to remain as at present constituted except that the attorney general is to be made appointive by the governor instead of elective by the people. This change is recommended because he is an administrative rather than a judicial officer, his important function being in the capacity of legal adviser to the governor and various state administrative departments.

The present state tax commission, composed of three *ex officio* members (governor, secretary of state, and state treasurer) and the state tax commissioner appointed by the governor, is to be reorganized by eliminating the *ex officio* members and will then constitute the proposed tax department. The head of this department is to have the assistance of two deputies appointed by himself.

The proposed department of education is to be headed by the superintendent of public instruction appointed by the governor. He is to have the advice and assistance of a board of education consisting of seven members, of which he is to be an *ex officio* member and chairman. The members of this board are to be appointed by the governor for overlapping terms of six years each. The six existing educational boards are to be abolished.

The proposed department of labor is to assume the functions of all the existing labor agencies which will be abolished. The head of this department is to be the director of labor appointed by the governor. He will appoint, with the approval of the governor, two deputy directors. The three will constitute a board to handle all deliberative or quasi-judicial functions of the department.

The proposed department of public health is to be under the control of a director of public health appointed by the governor. There is to be created an advisory health council of seven members appointed by the governor of whom the director of public health is to be *ex officio* a member and chairman. The examination and registration of physicians, surgeons, chiropractors, optometrists, pharmacists, nurses, dentists, and barbers is to be under the administration of this department.

The agricultural and related functions, such as the management of fairs and the licensing of veterinary surgeons, are to be brought together under the proposed department of agriculture. This department is to have a director appointed by the governor. Attached to the department is to be an unpaid advisory council of agriculture composed of five practical farmers in the state at large, appointed by the governor, representing different agricultural interests, and not excluding the director of the agricultural experiment station.

The proposed department of trade and commerce is to include the insurance, banking, and public service functions as well as the regulation of pilots and weights and measures. This department is to be administered by a director appointed by the governor. He would have the assistance of four deputies who would act as heads of bureaus within the department. A public utilities commission is to be composed of the director of the department and two deputies appointed by him, or two technical experts now serving under the public service commission designated by the director. This commission will perform the quasi-judicial work in connection with the administration of public utilities.

The department of public welfare is to have at its head a director of public welfare appointed by the governor. Attached to the department is to be an advisory unpaid board of five members appointed by the governor, at least one of whom is to be a woman.

The proposed department of public works is to be placed under the administration of a director of public works appointed by the governor. This director is to appoint six deputy commissioners to head the proposed bureaus. Associated with the department is to be an advisory unpaid board of three highway commissioners to be appointed by the governor to advise the state highway department engineer in the performance of his duties. The conservation agencies of the state will be included in this department.

The commission estimates that a saving to the state will be made by the adoption of its plan of consolidation amounting to from $500,000 to $800,000 annually.

No definite action was taken by the 1919 legislature upon the plan proposed by the consolidation commission.

PROPOSED DELAWARE PLAN

During the summer of 1918 the Delaware State Council of Defense engaged the New York Bureau of Municipal Research to make a complete survey of the state administration, as well as the governments of the three counties of the state and the city of Wilmington. This survey was completed by the end of the year and a report was submitted to the council for its approval and presentation to the legislature.

Findings of Survey Report

It was found in making this survey that the administrative branch of the state government includes one hundred and seventeen separate agencies, which are in most cases independent of each other and without any direct and effective overhead supervision. Of these agencies, the heads of six are elected by the voters, eighty-three are appointed by the governor (in most cases with the Senate's approval), two are appointed by judges of the superior court of the state, twelve are appointed by boards and administrative officers other than the governor, and fourteen are *ex officio* bodies. Fifty four of the total number of agencies are headed by boards or commissions. Much duplication of work as well as scattering of functions exists.

It is pointed out in the report that Delaware has fifty-four boards and commissions that exercise administrative powers of which forty-two are appointed by the governor with the advice of the Senate, two by the judges of the superior court, and eight are composed of *ex officio* members. The board system of administration, the report maintains, is not only unbusinesslike but irresponsible. The reasons for this statement, as set forth in the report, are as follows:

(1) Boards seldom show any real initiative and, therefore, businesslike leadership in improving services is not to be expected from them. They are a check on good work, not a spur to invention and activity.

(2) In addition to being a drag upon administration, the boards and commissions are so constructed that definite responsibility for action or inaction cannot be located. In fact, board government in general may be regarded as a clever means of escaping accountability and consequently criticism or blame. Hence the board system appeals particularly to a certain class of administrative officials who wish to shift responsibility from themselves.

(3) The board system tends to delay and to inefficiency. Boards, meeting as they do only periodically, cannot exercise effective supervision and control. They must fail as administrative agents because they are not " on the job " all the time.

(4) In addition to its inherent defects, the board system of Delaware is so organized as to deprive the governor of the control which he must have if he is to be responsible for the state's business. The board members usually have overlapping terms, hence each governor may appoint only a minority. Each board is, therefore, a government within itself.

The report further points out that Delaware's present administrative system is not adapted to unified financial planning and financial control. It says: " The existence of a hundred or more separate and distinct agencies, uncontrolled and competing with one another for public support and public funds, militates against the development of a businesslike planning for appropriations to support the functions of the state government — against a budget system . . . Even if the governor should be empowered to prepare the budget of the state for legislative consideration, he could not do the work effectively if he had to deal with one hundred different agencies. That number of men could not sit around a council table and discuss in a matter-of-fact way the merits of their respective demands upon the treasury of the state. A cabinet of one hundred members is unthinkable and a cabinet is necessary to financial planning."

General Recommendations

Among the general recommendations are the following:

(1) The governor should be the only elective administrative officer in the state government. Election of other administrative officers produces decentralized hide and seek in which responsibility for the work of the state cannot be fixed. It places each officer on an independent footing subject to little or no severe administrative control. In the popular election of administrative officers other than the governor, the people do not, as a rule, choose, but merely vote for the names that follow the governor's on the ballot. Officers so chosen usually lack the necessary qualifications for good administration. Such officers usually belong to the same political party as the governor, hence from the political point of view it makes little difference whether they are elected or appointed. . . .

(2) The governor should have the sole power to appoint and remove all executive officers. To require the consent of the senate is to make this power conditional and to permit responsibility to be shifted. It allows the governor to avoid public criticism by laying the blame of inefficient and unworthy officers upon mem-

bers of the Senate who are responsible to their respective constituencies and not to the people of the whole state.

(3) The responsibility for preparing the budget of the state should be placed squarely upon the governor.

(4) The office of lieutenant governor should be abolished. The duties of this office are so slight that the state might as well save the $6.00 a day which it pays him as the President of the Senate and the $100 per annum which it grants him as a member of the board of pardons. Except in the case of succession to the governorship on the death, resignation, or inability of the governor, the lieutenant governor plays an insignificant rôle in Delaware. The Senate should choose its own presiding officer . . . The secretary of state might well be designated governor in case that office should become vacant. This is now the practice in several states. Moreover, the elimination of the lieutenant governor is no radical innovation, for a number of states have already dispensed with that officer.

(5) It is proposed that the present organization of the central authority in the state militia should remain unchanged. The state constitution quite properly makes the governor commander in chief of the militia and requires him to select the staff, of which the adjutant general is the principal officer.

In recommending the reorganization and consolidation of the administration of Delaware, the report says: " In order to avoid duplication of effort, to eliminate waste, to draw clear and positive lines of authority connecting all work of the state in one unified plan, to establish the responsibility of the governor and the chief officers to the people, it is recommended that the work of all the existing officers, boards, commissions, and other agencies should be distributed among the following nine departments, each to be headed by an officer appointed by the governor and responsible to him:

"Department of state; department of finance; department of labor and industry; department of health; department of public welfare; department of agriculture; department of highways and drainage; department of education; department of law."

With reference to the creation of new administrative agencies in the future, the report recommends "that a constitutional provision be adopted requiring the legislature to assign all newly created administrative functions to one or more of the departments enumerated. Failure to establish this constitutional principle would leave the legislature free to continue in the future as in the past; to establish new agencies and undertake new functions without any reference to agencies and work already in existence."

The existing administrative agencies of the state are grouped under the departments into which it is proposed to consolidate them; and considerable space is given in the report to a discussion of their organization and functions. The general organization of each of the proposed departments is outlined and a chart of such proposed organization is included. Charts are also included in the report showing the present organization as well as the proposed organization of the entire state administration.

Departmental Organization

As already pointed out, the report recommends for each of the nine proposed departments single heads, called commissioners, to be appointed by the governor without let or hindrance by the Senate; it recommends that the subordinate officers of each department be appointed by the department head. In the case, however, of the department of finance, the governor is to act as head *ex officio* of the department and the four bureau heads are to be appointed by him. In the case of the department of labor and industry the commissioner and his two bureau heads are to sit as an industrial board for the exercise of quasi-judicial powers. The departments of public health, public welfare, and agriculture are each to have advisory councils composed of six members, appointed by the governor, and the commissioner of the department *ex officio*. These councils are to have no administrative duties but are to advise with the department head with reference to the work of the departments.

While the 1919 legislature did not take any definite action upon the plan as a whole, it authorized the appointment of a commission of five members to study the proposed reorganization and to report to the next legislature. This commission, known as the state survey commission, has been appointed by the governor and is working upon the plan of consolidation.

PROPOSED CALIFORNIA PLANS

Plan of the Taxpayers' Association

During 1918 the Taxpayers' Association of California prepared a plan of reorganization for the state administration. This plan, as published in the *California Taxpayers' Journal* for January, 1919, does not involve the elimination of any function now performed by the state government; does not eliminate any constitutional officer or board (although constitutional amendment is recommended for later consideration) ; and can be adopted in its entirety by statutory enactment. In grouping the existing administrative agencies under the proposed plan the functional unit has been used as a basis for coördination. The administrative functions are grouped under two main heads; namely, protective and constructive. " Protective " is subdivided into administrative, preventative, curative, conservative, and defensive; and " constructive " into developmental, reclamatory, and educational. These subheads are divided and redivided. It is claimed that the methods used elsewhere in the regrouping of administrative agencies for the purpose of consolidation have largely overlooked functional lines. In this report is printed an elaborate functional analysis of the work of the present administrative agencies alongside which is the proposed reorganizational grouping.

The consolidation plan of the Taxpayers' Association proposes the setting up of twelve administrative departments in addition to the offices of governor, lieutenant governor, and secretary of state. These departments are finance, law, sanitation and hygiene, commerce and labor, charities and welfare, corrections, care of defectives, conservation, defense, public works, natural resources, and education. The departments of law, charities and welfare, care of defectives, defense, and public works are to be administered by single heads appointed by the governor and directly responsible to him. The other departments are to be administered by boards, the members of which are appointed by the governor. However, in the departments of finance, natural resources, and education certain elective officials are to be members of the administrative boards. In most cases where the departments are headed by boards the members will serve as division chiefs.

Plan of the Committee on Efficiency and Economy

In November, 1918, Governor Stephens appointed a committee on efficiency and economy, consisting of eleven persons, some of whom were state officers. This committee made a report on administrative consolidation which the governor submitted to the legislature on March 20th. Its report sets down certain principles which it deems essential to efficient governmental management: Centralization of responsibility; coöperation of the larger organization units; and coöperation of agencies which perform similar or allied functions. These principles have been carried into the proposed plan by creating a governor's cabinet, composed of departmental executives appointed by him; by insuring coöperation of various departments by bringing their administrative officers together in an executive council; and by placing in departments, under one executive head, those agencies which perform similar or allied functions. The report holds that because of the great diversity in the nature of the state's activities it is impracticable to correlate all administrative agencies into larger administrative units. Therefore, nine elective officers and agencies and thirty other administrative agencies, the latter dealing with registration of trades and professions, regulation of financial corporations, local problems, military affairs, pardons and reprieves, civil service, and minor affairs are not included in the plan of consolidation. The remaining seventy administrative agencies are grouped under ten departments as follows: Finance, trade and corporations, public works, agriculture, natural resources, labor, education, public health, institutions, and social service. The departments of public works, agriculture, natural resources, labor, and institutions are to be under the administrative control of directors appointed by the governor and holding office at his pleasure. The department of finance is to have a director of accounts and expenditures and a director of receipts and supplies, both appointed by and serving at the pleasure of the governor, and a board of finance composed of the two directors and the state comptroller. The president of the railroad commission is to be the director of the department of trade and corporations. The department of education is to be under the control of a board, consisting of five lay members, and the superintendent of public instruction as chief executive officer. The department of public health is to be under the control of a board of five licensed and practicing physicians, appointed by the governor for overlapping terms of four years. The department of social service is to be administered by an unpaid board of seven members appointed by the governor for overlapping terms of four years. The governor's cabinet is to be composed of the directors of seven departments and the chairmen of the administrative boards of three departments.

Upon submitting this report to the legislature, Governor Stephens declined to give it his full indorsement, consequently no action was taken upon it by the legislature.

On March 27th, a bill was introduced in the legislature embodying the consolidation plan proposed by the Taxpayers' Association. Since the end of the legislative session was near, the bill failed to receive any very serious consideration. It is understood that the association will continue to emphasize the need for administrative consolidation and will make an early attempt to bring its plan before the voters by means of the initiative process.

NEW YORK PLAN OF 1919

Report of Reconstruction Commission

Soon after his inauguration in January, 1919, Governor Smith appointed a reconstruction commission, consisting of thirty-five members, which was organized into a number of committees, each charged with the investigation of an urgent need or immediate problem in connection with the administration of the state's affairs. The committee on retrenchment of this commission, with the assistance of a staff, conducted a study of the organization of the entire state administration and published in October, 1919, a four-hundred-page " Report on Retrenchment and Reorganization in the State Government."

This report maintains that administrative consolidation is one of the most effective means of retrenchment. It, therefore, outlines a comprehensive plan of administrative

reorganization for the state of New York. Briefly, the
principles upon which the report bases the plan of consolidation are as follows: Grouping of all administrative
agencies into a small number of departments, each headed
by a single officer except where quasi-legislative, quasi-
judicial, inspectional, or advisory functions require a
board; giving the governor the power to choose with
the Senate's approval the department heads who are to
constitute his cabinet; extending the governor's term to
four years and making the terms of department heads
coterminous with his; making appropriate subdivisions
of departmental work; and establishing an executive
budget system.

Departmental Organization

The report proposes to consolidate the one hundred
and eighty or more administrative agencies of the state
into sixteen groups, composed of eighteen departments
and two public service commissions. The departments
are executive, audit and control, taxation and finance,
attorney general, state, public works, conservation, agriculture and markets, labor, education, health, mental
hygiene, charities, correction, banking, insurance, military
and naval affairs, and civil service. The plan involves
constitutional changes; it recommends that only the governor, lieutenant governor, and comptroller shall remain
elective. The comptroller would be head of the department of audit and control and his department will exercise
only strictly auditing functions. Under the executive
department would be a bureau of administration charged
mainly with the preparation of the budget and the conducting of special investigations for the governor. The
departments of taxation and finance, attorney general,
state, public works, conservation, banking, insurance, and
health would be under the control of single heads appointed by the governor with the approval of the Senate.

Attached to the department of public health would be an
advisory council of six members, appointed by the governor for overlapping terms of six years, and the department head *ex officio*. The department of military and
naval affairs would be headed by the governor, who
would appoint as his deputy an adjutant general. A commission of five and ultimately of three members, appointed by the governor with the Senate's approval for
five years, would be head of the department of labor.
The department of agriculture and markets would be
under the control of a council composed of one representative from each of the nine judicial districts of the
state, one representative at large, and the commissioner
of markets of New York City *ex officio*; the ten members
would be elected by the legislature for terms of ten
years. This council would select a commissioner to be
administrative head of the department. The department of education would be under the control of the
board of regents of the University of the State of New
York, composed of twelve members, one from each
judicial district and three at large, appointed by the
legislature for overlapping terms of twelve years. The
regents would appoint a commissioner as executive head
of the department. The department of hygiene would
be under the direction of a commission of three members
appointed by the governor, two for terms of six years
and the other to serve during good behavior. The department of charities would be under the control of a
board of twelve members, one from each judicial district
and three additional from New York City, appointed
by the governor for overlapping terms of six years, two
to be appointed each year. The department of correction
would be headed by a single commissioner appointed by
the governor with the Senate's approval. Attached to
this department would be an advisory council of five members appointed by the governor for overlapping terms of

five years, and a board of parole and probation of three members would in turn be appointed by the advisory council and serve at its pleasure. The three departments of mental hygiene, charities, and correction would be co-ordinated in their work by a council of public welfare composed of the chairmen of the controlling boards, of two of the departments and the head of the other department, also the commissioners of health and education. The department of civil service would be directed by the chairman of a board of three appointive members. There would be two public service commissions, one for New York City and one for the remainder of the state, each composed of a single commissioner appointed by the governor with the consent of the Senate.

The proposals for administrative reorganization are clearly a compromise between those humanitarian forces that would retain government by commission and those who would centralize responsibility in the governor and provide the means of popular control.

Recommendations are made in the report for the establishment of an executive budget system, for centralized purchasing of materials and supplies, for better control of state printing, and for the standardization and grading of the personal service of the state. It is expected that this report will be used by Governor Smith as a basis for executive recommendations to the 1920 legislature.

TENDENCIES IN OTHER STATES

In addition to the states noted above, which are giving serious consideration to the adoption of administrative consolidation plans, the legislatures of about a dozen more states have had the subject of administrative reorganization brought before them. During the present year much emphasis has been laid upon the need for administrative reorganization, it being recognized that this is necessary to effective planning of work and finances and that budget making and administration must go hand in hand.

Ohio

The 1919 legislature of Ohio authorized the appointment of a joint committee to conduct investigations and to prepare a plan of administrative reorganization for consideration by the next legislature. An appropriation of $30,000 was made to carry on the study.

Indiana

Governor Goodrich of Indiana in his message to the legislature of 1919 recommended the abolishing of the elective offices of state superintendent of public instruction, clerk of the Supreme Court, state statistician and state geologist, and the combining of their present functions under suitable departmental agencies. He also recommended that the attorney general be no longer an elective officer, but that he be made appointive by the governor. In defense of this proposal he said:

" There is little force in the argument that the appointment of an attorney general by the governor is dangerous because of the centralization of power involved. The attorney general is now possessed of no material power which might be misused or abused by any executive, except, possibly, that of bringing unjust prosecutions under the criminal statutes, which misuse or abuse is quite as likely to happen whether the attorney general is elected or appointed. The appointment of the attorney general by the governor adds little to the power exercised by my last two predecessors in the appointment of the legal clerk, attorneys for the various commissions and boards of the state, but it will result in saving large sums of money and make this office a more efficient instrument of public service."

Vermont

Governor Clement of Vermont in his inaugural message to the 1919 legislature recommended a reorganization and centralization of practically all the present administrative agencies. The reasons for his recommendation are very striking.

He said: " In 1901, as shown by the auditor's comparative statement, state activities were less than thirty in number, and the grand total of state expense was less than $800,000. To-day state activities have reached a total of over fifty and the expense has risen to $2,250,000 per year. So within the knowledge of every member of this assembly, we have nearly doubled our state activities and trebled our state expense. The state has not increased in population. There is no more taxable property now than in 1900, although the valuation for taxation purposes has been increased. In fact, the reduction in tilled areas of farm land would indicate that the farm property as a whole has deteriorated in value. How, then, have these additional sums been raised? The answer is by the taxation of banks, railroads, corporations, and other indirect forms of taxation, the sources of which have now been thoroughly exploited.

" We have reached our taxing limit in this direction and your predecessors, the legislature of 1917, found it necessary to impose a state tax of twenty cents on the dollar of the grand list in order to meet the expenses of the war and the increased cost of doing public business. The war is over, but the expenses of it are not paid, and you are not only faced by the same conditions, but the report of the budget committee — which you have before you — indicates that the continuation of this direct tax of twenty cents is not only necessary, but if this legislature passes any special appropriations of any kind, an increase in that state tax will be necessary.

" Every administration for the past twenty years has been confronted by this problem of increased state expense, and various attempts have been made to consolidate state institutions, departments, and activities. Your predecessors and mine have made some important progress in that direction, but the net result has always been that we have had every year more state activities and greater expense, with no proportionate gain in the public convenience, or the public benefit therefrom, or the public ability to pay therefor."

North Carolina, New Mexico and Others

Governor Bickett of North Carolina recommended to the 1917 legislature the reorganization of the state administration, which recommendations he reiterated in his message to the 1919 legislature. In his later message he said:

" There is something attractive to the popular mind in the theory that all the people select (administrative) officials, but the truth is that the people do no such thing. A few men, an average of not more than three, select themselves as candidates and then the people are accorded the privilege of saying in the primaries which of these three is least objectionable. There never was a more tragic delusion than the one that the people select these officials.

" But if the people should be actually consulted it is plain that all the people cannot secure sufficient information about the qualifications of a man for these administrative offices to enable them to arrive at a conclusion satisfactory to themselves.

" There is no more reason for electing the governor's council than there is for electing the President's cabinet. I take it that no one would favor electing the president of the university by a vote of all the people, and yet people can pass upon his qualifications quite as well as they can upon those of the state superintendent of public instruction. . . .

" I have supreme faith in the judgment of all the people when they know the facts. They can know the facts about a few men on the ticket. They should vote for these few, and then hold them responsible for results.

" Only the governor and the lieutenant governor should be elected, but a complete change would require a constitutional amendment, and hence as a start in the right direction I urge this General Assembly to enact a law that all state administrative officers whose election by the people is not required by the constitution shall hereafter be appointed by the governor."

Governor Lindsey of New Mexico is a member and chairman of a committee of five appointed by the Taxpayers' Association to formulate a plan for the reorganization of the state government and report the same to the association for its adoption and advocacy to the 1921 legislature.

The governors of Michigan, Minnesota, Nevada, and North Dakota made recommendations upon the reorganization and centralization of administrative agencies to their 1919 legislature.

PART III. DETAILED ACCOUNTS OF THE
CHARACTERISTICS AND OPERATION OF
RECENT STATE ENACTMENTS PRO-
VIDING FOR A BUDGET PROCEDURE

CHAPTER XIII

MASSACHUSETTS CONSTITUTIONAL AND STATUTORY
BUDGET PROVISIONS — A PRODUCT OF MIXED POLITI-
CAL EMOTIONS

Legislative Organization and Procedure

As in other states, the representative branch of the government, here called the general court, is composed of two coördinate deliberative bodies, the concurrence of which is required to reach a decision on any matter brought before them. The Senate has 40 members; the House has 240. The organization differs from that of the representative branch of the government of many other states in this: From the very earliest days, the practice in Massachusetts has been to have the membership of both houses parceled out or appointed to *joint* standing committees for the initial consideration of matters coming before either house; whereas the more usual practice is to organize standing committees in each house for the initial consideration of matters presented there — and it is only after action taken in one house that it goes to the other house to be taken up *de novo* in a corresponding standing committee of its own. In 1919 there were thirty-two of these joint committees. There are but three committees of significance which are not joint committees; each house has its committee on ways and means, rules, and judiciary. In practice these corresponding committees of the two houses are often fused for more prompt and effective action.

The fact that in Massachusetts the membership of both houses is combined in joint committees, instead of each house having its own separate standing committee, has not given to Massachusetts a characteristically different result. The machinery may have been a little more productive; there may have been a little less friction between the houses, and a little less delay in making deliveries; but the product delivered has been the same. The added facilities afforded have been for something that the people did not want — more legislation. Instead of demanding more legislation the popular demand has been for less legislation, better considered and understood. In fact, the citizenry of the states have been so much dissatisfied with these enlarged facilities for production that they have tried sabotage in every form to slow down and reduce the output without actually putting their law mills out of commission. They have limited the periods during which the legislatures could sit; they have given to them biennial instead of annual sessions; they have required the grist to be ground over by two mills; and then, in case the governor did not approve, required it to be ground again by both mills. A form of organization within these law-making mills which had the effect only of permitting them to speed up could not prove effective to cure the cause of popular dissatisfaction. The net effect of creating thirty-two joint committees is to provide thirty-two hoppers and thirty-two sets of burrs where the grist could be ground once instead of twice — the function of the regular session in each house being to give the members a chance to audit the toll and approve the grist on the statements made by the foremen and crews appointed to take charge of the operation of the thirty-two jointly operated mills.

By reason of the fact that a large part of the legislation of to-day is to provide for public service of one kind or another each of these thirty-two streams of legislation involves expenditures. With the initiative in the hands of so many legislative leaders, none of whom is responsible for administration, it is necessary to provide some means of coördination. In so far as there may be said to be a common plan or central management, this comes through the majority " party " caucus, and through the rules committees and the committees on ways and means. The " party " caucus rises superior to the committees, in that it is through this agency that the committees are organized; but the " party," as in all other states, is irresponsible. The rules committees are the adjusters used for keeping the machinery in condition to execute the orders of the " party " leadership — the presiding officer of each house being chairman of the rules committee. The ways and means committees operate as a sieve. Neither of the houses makes use of a committee-of-the-whole procedure, as it is quite foreign to the system of inquest, discussion, and determination of matters of policy.

This in general is the organization and procedure developed in past years for the conduct of the duly constituted forum of the people — the representative reviewing and appropriating body of Massachusetts. It is mentioned in passing not because it is essentially different from that of the other states and the National Government, but to get it clearly in mind before taking up the recent enactments for a budget procedure. The steps taken for revision of procedure for the exercise of control over the House in no material way affected the organization or the methods of the legislature; it did not undertake to develop responsible leadership; it was not devised to establish an open-forum practice.

Constitutional and Statutory Budget Provisions

The essential features of the budget system as enacted into law by constitutional amendment and statute in 1918 are in substance as follows :[1]

---

[1] The sections in italics are constitutional provisions; those not in italics are provisions of statute law. Constitutional Amendments, Art. LXIII: General Acts, 1918, Ch. 244.

Preparation of Estimates:

(1) Estimates for the ordinary maintenance of departments, institutions, and undertakings receiving annual appropriations from the commonwealth shall be prepared by the officer or board in charge and submitted to the supervisor of administration by October 15th. These estimates " shall not include any estimate for any new or special purposes or objects not authorized by statute."

(2) Estimates for all other financial needs of the departments and institutions shall be submitted by the department head to the supervisor by October 15th, separate from the above.

(3) Estimates of requirements for interest and debt service for deficiencies and for all claims and other such expenditures authorized by the statutes shall be prepared by the auditor submitted to the supervisor and to the clerk of the House by December 26th.

(4) Estimates of receipts from ordinary and other revenues, of unencumbered balances, and of all other resources available for appropriation shall be prepared by the auditor and submitted to the supervisor and the clerk of the House by December 26th.

(5) A tabulated itemized statement of estimates submitted under (1) above, together with the comparative appropriations of the previous year and the expenditures of the three previous years, shall be submitted by the auditor to the supervisor and the clerk of the House by December 26th.

Revision of Estimates and Preparation of Budget:

(1) The supervisor of administration shall revise all estimates and prepare for the governor a budget " setting forth such recommendations as the governor shall determine." No date is fixed for the completion of the supervisor's work. The supervisor is required to " make

such investigations as may be necessary," and under his general powers is authorized to make any investigations authorized by the governor and council, and to compel the production of books and papers and the giving of testimony.

(2) *"For the purpose of preparing his budget, the governor shall have power to require any board, commission, officer, or department to furnish him with any information which he may deem necessary."* He may call on the auditor for information and assistance in preparing the budget.

Contents and Form of Budget:

(1) The budget shall contain *" a statement of all proposed expenditures of the commonwealth for the fiscal year, including those already authorized by law, and of all taxes, revenues, loans, and other means by which such expenditures shall be defrayed."* It shall include also " definite recommendations of the governor as to the financing of the expenditures recommended and the relative amounts to be raised from ordinary revenue, direct taxes, or loans."

(2) The budget shall be classified to show separately estimates and recommendations for: (a) expenses of administration, operation, and maintenance; (b) deficiencies or overdrafts in former appropriations; (c) new construction, additions, improvements, and capital outlays; (d) interest on the public debt and debt requirements; (e) all new and other requests for expenditures.

(3) *Except for the requirements of (2) above, the governor is left to determine the form and arrangement of the budget.*

Submission of Budget to Legislature:

(1) " Within three weeks after the convening of the general court," the governor shall submit his budget to

the legislature. The time within this period is fixed, by
law, as on or before the second Wednesday in January,
or within one week of the convening of the general court.
This is the only point at which the two budget provisions,
one of law and one of the constitution, conflict, if indeed
these are to be considered contradictory.[1]

(2) With the budget the governor shall submit such
messages and supplemental data as he deems necessary.

Supplementary Budgets:

*The governor may at any time submit to the general
court supplementary budgets. He shall recommend the
term for which any loan shall be contracted.*[2]

Restrictions on Legislative Procedure:

(1) " *All appropriations based upon the budget to be
paid from taxes or revenues shall be incorporated in a
single bill which shall be called the general appropriation
bill.*"

(2) " *The general court may provide for its salaries,
mileage, and expenses, and for the necessary expenditures
in anticipation of appropriations, but before final action
on the general appropriation bill it shall not enact any
appropriation bill except on recommendation of the governor.*"

(3) " *The general court may increase, add, decrease,
or omit items in the budget.*"

(4) *The commonwealth may borrow money to repel
invasion, suppress insurrection, defend the commonwealth,
assist the United States in case of war, and in anticipation
of receipts from taxes or other sources. For other purposes the commonwealth may borrow money only by a*

[1] General Acts of 1919, Ch. 52, brought the two into agreement.
[2] Constitutional Amendments, Art. LXII.

vote taken by yeas and nays, of two thirds of each house present and voting.[1]

(5) *" After final action on the general appropriation bill, or on recommendation of the governor, special appropriation bills may be enacted. Such bills shall provide the specific means for defraying the appropriations therein contained."*

Veto of Items:

(1) *" The governor may disapprove or reduce items or parts of items in any bill appropriating money. So much of such bill as he approves shall upon his signing the same become law."*

(2) *" As to each item disapproved or reduced, he shall transmit to the house in which the bill originated his reason for such disapproval or reduction, and the procedure shall then be the same as in the case of a bill disapproved as a whole."*

Fiscal Year:

(1) The fiscal year begins on December 1st.[2]

Votes on Account:

(1) " Boards, commissions, officers, and officials having charge of expenditures in behalf of the commonwealth may continue expenditures in each year at the rate of the appropriation authorized for the preceding year until the general court makes an appropriation therefor or otherwise provides." [3]

Treasury Receipts and Payments:

(1) *" All money received on account of the common-*

---

[1] Constitutional Amendments, Art. LXII.
[2] Acts of 1905, Ch. 211.
[3] Chapter 20, General Laws of 1919, passed on March 5, 1919.

wealth from any source whatsoever shall be paid into the treasury thereof."

(2) *" No moneys shall be issued out of the treasury of this commonwealth and disposed of (except such sums as may be appropriated for the redemption of bills of credit or treasury notes, or for the payment of interest arising thereon) but by warrant under the hand of the governor for the time being, with the advice and consent of the council, for the necessary defense and support of the commonwealth; and for the protection and preservation of the inhabitants thereof, agreeably to the acts and resolves of the general court."* [1]

(3) " No public functionary shall make any purchases or incur any liabilities in the name of the commonwealth for a larger amount than that which has been appropriated by law for the service or object." [2]

Transfers:

(1) Transfers between appropriation items are illegal.

(2) The governor's emergency fund of $100,000 may be used, among other things, as a fund from which transfers may be made to cover deficiencies in other appropriations, on approval of the governor and council, after certification by the auditor of the necessity.[3]

(3) There is placed at the auditor's disposal annually an appropriation of $1,000 " For small items of expenditure for which no appropriations have been made, and for cases in which appropriations have been exhausted or have reverted to the treasury in previous years." [4]

Position of the Governor in the Administration

The discussion leading up to the administrative reor-

[1] Constitution, Ch. II, Sec. 1, Art. XI
[2] Acts of 1858, Ch. 71.
[3] Acts of 1908, Ch. 549.
[4] Acts of 1916, Ch. 222.

ganization described in a foregoing chapter, and the budget discussion and enactment, hold out the view that executive responsibility should be made more definite and certain through the governor. But this view was not carried out either in law or in fact. The governor is not the responsible head of the administration; he is not placed in a position to exercise leadership. In practice, under the new budget law, he did not undertake to perform the function of leader. Both an elected executive council and the legislative organization and procedure stand in the way if this were attempted; and the supervisor of administration who is charged with the duty of preparing the estimates is responsible to a ten-headed executive, the " governor and council."

Filing of Estimates with Supervisor of Administration

Estimate blanks issued to the departments and institutions in 1918 for the 1919 budget were prepared by the supervisor of administration. In conformity with sections 1 and 2 of the budget law, one set of estimate sheets is prepared for the maintenance and other ordinary expenses already authorized by law and another set for extraordinary expenses, for capital outlays, and for objects not already authorized by law. Because of the essential difference between information required from departments and from institutions, separate maintenance estimate blanks are used for the two. In the case of normal schools, still another set of blanks is furnished to allow for the boarding hall.

Estimates Reviewed and Budget Prepared by Office of Supervisor of Administration

The deputy supervisor of administration took personal charge of the revision of estimates and the preparation of the 1919 budget. He followed in the main the procedure he had worked out in 1918, and called the department heads in to go over with him the estimates they had submitted. A stenographic record was kept of some of these conferences, while of others a memorandum only was kept covering the main questions involved. In each case the deputy dictated a brief statement of his tentative decisions with regard to the estimates involved. All of the memoranda, with such other material as was pertinent, were bound with the related departmental or institutional estimates in a large loose-leaf binder. All of the estimates filled three such volumes. These were the deputy's private files and contained many pencil notations and references on the estimate sheets.

The deputy supervisor received altogether departmental and institutional estimates amounting to $40,577,-481.27. Of this amount he eliminated $4,847,546.62 or 11.9 per cent. and recommended for appropriation a total of $35,739,934.45. A large part of the departmental estimates for special purposes was filed too late to allow for the necessary study before the supervisor made recommendations for the governor's budget. Over $2,000,000 of the amount listed here as budget cuts is made up of this item.

The tentative budget for 1919 was submitted to the governor on January 3, 1919. Governor Coolidge had the document in his possession from that time till its submission to the general court on January 8th. A Saturday and a Sunday intervened to reduce the time still further. No conferences were held, so far as could be ascertained, either with officials or with the public.

The 1919 budget as submitted to the legislature by the governor was the identical document handed to him by the supervisor a few days before. It was prefaced by a four-and-a-half page letter of transmittal signed by the governor. A careful examination of this letter does not disclose a single phrase which might even be construed as committing the governor to any definite recommendation contained in the budget. He did not even mention the total amount recommended by the deputy supervisor, though he mentioned the total of amounts requested by the departments. The governor contented himself with saying: " The estimates for expenditures have been studied by the supervisor of administration, and *his recommendations* are embodied in the summary of financial statements submitted with this budget."[1]   In the part of the letter dealing with the subject of capital outlays, he again refers to the " recommendations of the supervisor of the administration," assuming no responsibility therefor, though the budget law requires the supervisor to prepare a budget for the governor " setting forth such recommendations as the governor shall determine."

The governor's refusal to take any of the responsibility for the 1919 budget is all the more significant in the light of the recommendations of his inaugural address, delivered the week previous to the submission of the budget.   In that address there are no less than thirteen major recommendations which either belonged in the 1919 budget or deserved mention there.   Take for example the recommendations for the welcome of returning troops, for the subventions to public schools, for the instruction of aliens in English, for a survey of the street-railway situation, for the improvement of the port of Boston, for the Plymouth exposition, and for the creation of a loan fund to encourage home owning. These were not dealt with at all in the letter of transmittal nor were they among the estimated financial requirements of the fiscal year.   This gives further evidence of the fact that the budget submitted was not the plan of the governor.

The policy of the governor appears to have been cal-

[1] The italics are the author's.

culated to avoid the possibility of arousing prejudice in the minds of the members of the legislature against him and against the new budget system.   Such a breach was foreshadowed in the remarks of more than one legislator and was successfully avoided by the governor's tact and the leadership of Representative Benjamin Loring Young, chairman of the House committee on ways and means.

Form and Content of the 1919 Budget

Eliminating the governor's letter of transmittal, the 1919 budget is composed of:

(1) A seven-page statement by the supervisor explaining in detail the recommendations for capital outlays contained in the subsequent pages.

(2) The estimated revenues for 1919, as furnished by the auditor.

(3) A summary of general fund treasury transactions for 1918.

(4) A statement of the condition of state debt, showing the direct and contingent debts separately.

(5) A six-page statement of the recommended appropriations for 1919 by spending units, classified as for salaries, for expenses, and for capital outlays, and showing the source from which the appropriations are to be financed.

(6) A general summary of estimated receipts by sources, showing the amounts to be credited to general fund, special funds, and the total.

(7) A balance sheet as of the end of the fiscal year for which the 1919 budget provides.

(8) A detailed estimate of proposed expenditures for 1919 for the state government, including the legislative and judicial departments.   (This statement covers eighty-five pages, and contains 507 enumerated items many of which are further subclassified.   While this is as detailed material as is printed, it must be remembered that the .

supervisor's private file of departmental and institutional estimates goes into much greater detail.)

(9) An index of the entire document.

House Ways and Means Committee Remake Budget

The 1919 budget was referred immediately to the House committee on ways and means when received from the governor on January 8th. Representative Benjamin Loring Young was chairman of this committee, and the budget when it came out was virtually his measure.

Said Mr. Young to the House in his budget speech: " Immediately on receipt of the budget, the committee sent a notice to each state department, setting aside two weeks for public hearings and inviting all persons interested to appear. The committee also requested that statements in writing be filed. Open hearings continued for two weeks and a further week was devoted to executive sessions."

During the time that the estimates were before the committee the deputy supervisor of administration, who had prepared the budget sent in by the governor, and the first deputy auditor were in constant attendance. The deputy supervisor had with him his personal estimate files, both for his own information and for the use of the committee.

After the hearings and the executive sessions, the committee arrived at its revisions, and the deputy supervisor, acting under the guidance of Mr. Young, drew up the general appropriation bill. The bill contained provisions for appropriations amounting to $34,944,664.22, or $795,360.23 less than recommended in the budget; $400,000 of this amount represented cuts by the committee in the maintenance recommendations of the governor. This large decrease was made possible partly because of the fact that the estimates upon which the budget was based were drawn in the main before the signing of the armistice, and represented guesses based on a rising commodity market.

On February 10th, Mr. Young reported out of the ways and means committee the general appropriation bill. It contained appropriations for maintenance and capital outlays, both for the state and for the metropolitan districts. The 515 numbered items were grouped by spending units, except in the case of interest, debt service, and deficiencies.

In presenting the budget bill, Mr. Young delivered one of the most significant addresses that had ever been heard in the Massachusetts legislature on the finances of the state and the fiscal program for the following year. Mr. Young gave this outline of his speech as an introduction:

" My remarks will naturally divide themselves under four heads —

" I. An explanation of the constitutional amendment for a state budget recently adopted by the people, and a brief statement of the various modifications in the financial procedure of the House and of the general court which would seem to be made necessary or advisable by its adoption.

" II. An explanation of the appropriation bill now reported to the House by the committee on ways and means, and a brief discussion of several of its more important features. This discussion may serve to point out to the members of the House some of the more difficult problems which confronted the committee, those in which the members will probably be most interested, and with regard to which they have a right to demand complete, detailed, and satisfactory information. It is my hope that before this bill is passed to be engrossed every question of doubt in the mind of any member may be satisfactorily answered by the committee, and that no member can justly say that he has not been given an opportunity to know and understand every detail thereof.

" III. An explanation of the general financial policy outlined by his excellency the governor in his budget recommendations (House Document, No. 185), and the manner in which the bill now under consideration carries out that policy in part, together with a brief survey of the additional appropriation bills as may reasonably be expected to come before the general court after final action on the present bill either through submission of supplementary budgets by the governor or otherwise.

" IV. A statement of work accomplished by the committee on ways and means, and of the methods adopted by it during its consideration of the budget."

In the course of discussion on the first point, Mr. Young outlined no unusual changes in the legislative procedure, except to call attention to the fact that bills based on the budget or on supplementary budgets have the right of way over all other appropriations in the legislature. He reproved the departments which had failed to submit their estimates in time for the budget and had then attempted to secure their appropriations through private petitions. Of these departments, he said: " They have refused to enter the open door of the budget, and now seek to obtain entrance to the treasury through the back door of special legislation. If the budget system is to stand, these special bills should receive no consideration at this time."

Mr. Young placed great emphasis on the responsibility of the governor for the budget. He said in part:

" The statute and the constitutional amendment taken together make the governor, so far as finances are concerned, the actual executive head of the state in practice as well as theory. In place of an irresponsible government by boards and commissions, each anxious to augment its own importance and its own financial needs, we have lodged full responsibility with the governor, whose viewpoint is not limited to a particular department or to a particular locality, but extends to the entire state government of which he is the responsible head."

That Mr. Young has a full appreciation of the function and significance of the budget is evident from the following paragraph of his budget speech:

" The budget is not a mere document; it is not a mere appropriation bill. The budget is the plan for financing the state government for the current year, which has been prepared under the direction of the governor and has been submitted by him to the general court for its consideration. The budget contains an appropriation program, a social program, a revenue program. It is a complete plan for the government of the commonwealth."

In disposing of his remaining three points, Mr. Young is equally clear and forceful. His discussion of the main issues involved in the general appropriation bill is particularly valuable. When Mr. Young told the House that he hoped that debate on the budget bill would result in " thorough, frank, and pertinent discussion of the budget proposals," he seemed to be thoroughly in earnest.

In addition to the general appropriation bill, there was presented with the budget speech a balance sheet as of the end of the fiscal year, a table showing the individual cuts and increases made by the committee on ways and means, a table showing the recommended appropriations compared with those of 1918, and a table of the per capita weekly costs for maintenance of the state institutions.

Chairman of House Committee Gives News Value to Budget Issues

When Governor Coolidge presented the 1919 budget to the legislature early in January, there was no dramatic incident. There was no " news " to attract attention. The document went to the clerk of the House, the clerk read the title with the drone of routine business, the document was referred to the ways and means committee and thus for the time being was lost from sight. A few of the papers mentioned the fact, but even these missed the meat of the matter. The *Boston Herald,* for example, ran the headline on the seventh page, " Budget of $11,000,000," when as a matter of fact the budget carried $35,739,934.44.

The situation was quite different when the appropriation bill was reported and sponsored by Mr. Young. His personal presentation of the bill, together with his concise and straightforward discussion of the issues involved, before an open session of the House, introduced enough of the dramatic element to carry the budget into almost every paper of the state. The *Christian Science Monitor,* the policy of which is to exclude matters of sectional interest, devoted almost a column to Mr. Young's budget speech, quoting liberally from him, and stressing the four major issues he had raised. The *Boston Globe* of February 10th and the *Springfield Republican* of the 11th cover the incident in their news columns. The *Boston Transcript* not only covered the event as news, but devoted an editorial to a commendation of Representative Young and his budget speech. The editorial was headed, "Loring Young's Contribution," and among other observations said: " He has associated with his comprehensive view of the state's proposed expenditures a comprehensive view of the state's whole legislative program, thus equating, as it were, problems in the distribution of cash with problems in the distribution of the general court's energies as a state-governing and state-building body."

Following the presentation of the budget bill and the budget speech, the better part of a week was devoted to the debate on the bill. During this time Mr. Young was continually on his feet explaining items, answering questions, and defending the budget. As a result of this discussion, and as the result of later information, the ways

and means committee itself put forward a number of
amendments.   Three of these were textual, one decreased,
while five increased the bill.   Nine private members'
amendments were offered to strike out or reduce, and
two to increase the appropriation for band concerts in
Boston.   All the amendments put forward by the committee were adopted by the House; Mr. Young accepted
the'private amendments to reduce, and they were adopted
by the House; Mr. Young, however, refused to accept the
two amendments to increase the budget and they were
defeated.

The general appropriation bill was received in the
Senate on March 5th.   It was immediately referred to
the Senate committee on ways and means.   Here it was
held till March 28th, when it was reported with twenty
amendments.   Of these five were textual, one segregat-
ing an item by splitting it in two, two decreasing items
in the bill, and the remaining twelve making increases.
On April 2d, all of these amendments were adopted, and
at the same stage three private members' amendments to
increase items were adopted.   Two of these restored items
were cut out in the house, and the third increased the
appropriation for band concerts in Boston by $5,000.
The net result of the Senate's seventeen amendments was
a decrease of $230.

Action of Senate Calls Forth Conference Committee

The House, under the leadership of Mr. Young, refused
to accept five of the amendments made in the Senate.   A
conference committee, however, worked out a compromise
eliminating two of the Senate amendments to increase,
and the two houses agreed on the measure, enacted it,
and sent it to the governor for his approval, which it received on April 23d and became Chapter 153 of the Special Acts of 1919.   As the bill finally passed it contained
but one amendment to increase which had not been put

forward by the House or the Senate ways and means committee. It carried but $115,711.25 more than the budget as drawn by the House ways and means committee, almost all of which represented items amended on recommendation of the committee subsequent to its reporting of the bill.

Form of General Appropriation Bill

The general appropriation bill based on the budget is a document of thirty-five pages. It contains 515 numbered items, 15 lettered sub-items, and a score or so unlettered sub-items. The general principle of lump-sum appropriation is followed, though in certain cases, where a greater control is wanted, some segregation is made. The average item is over $60,000, while five of the items are for over $1,000,000 and sixty-seven items are of $100,000 or more. The item numbers follow the item numbers of the budget throughout, and the same classification by spending units is followed. All amounts appropriated are from the general fund except where specified.

Two Supplementary Budgets Submitted by Governor

The budget amendment to the constitution provides: "The governor may at any time recommend to the general court supplementary budgets which shall be subject to the same procedure as the original budget." In accordance with this provision, Governor Coolidge submitted two supplementary budgets to the legislature in 1919.

The first supplementary budget carried $2,932,865.10, almost all of which was for capital outlay. It disposed of the items which had been received too late for consideration in the budget, and added a number of others in accordance with the governor's recommendation that an extended public works program be initiated as a means of lessening unemployment. The governor's letter transmitting the first supplementary budget is more in accordance with the law.   The success of the original budget seems to have made the governor more ready to admit his legal responsibilities, and we find him saying:

"In the general appropriation act based on *my original budget recommendations,* approximately $1,600,000 was appropriated for capital outlay.   To this sum I now recommend an addition of $2,479,285.50."

The second supplementary budget carried $1,019,013.18. It provided for the needs created by the new laws of the 1919 session — the salary increases, the various investigations, the enlarged services, and the capital outlays authorized since the preparation of the previous supplementary budget.   It is dated July 14th, ten days before the prorogation of the general court.   A large part of this supplementary budget may be said to be made up of non-administration measures, or measures accepted by the governor because there was no other way out.   The largest single item is for $120,500 to meet the increase in legislative pay in accordance with Chapter 239 of the General Acts of 1919, which was passed over the governor's veto.   The next largest item is for $100,000 recommended by the supervisor "in connection with several bills pending for special highway improvements." These are nothing more nor less than the traditional "private road bills" and were opposed by the governor though he did not veto the acts authorizing them nor exclude them from his last supplementary budget.   No harbor bills got through in 1919.

The supplementary budgets were prepared by the deputy supervisor of administration as had been the case with the original budget.   They seem not to contain anything which Mr. Young had not already approved.   As in the case of the budget, the governor made no alterations in the substance of the supplementary budgets.   The entire initiative was left with the deputy supervisor and Mr.

Young, the governor assuming the position of recipient and not of leader.

Additional and Special Claims Appropriations

In addition to the budget and the two supplementary budgets, the Massachusetts legislature was called upon to make appropriations:

1. Through special messages from the governor, and
2. Through petitions filed by private citizens, by public officials, and by members of the legislature.

Governor Coolidge addressed a number of special messages to the legislature asking that immediate appropriations be made for the following emergencies:

Purpose	Appropriated	By Chapter
Welcome of soldiers	$ 10,000	1
Soldiers and sailors commission	10,000	112
Parade of 26th Division	300,000	119
Influenza epidemic	5,000	1
Suppression of corn borer	30,000	135
Total	$355,000	

There was no marked decrease in 1919 in the number of private petitions filed with the general court asking for appropriations of one kind or another. As has been common heretofore, a dozen or more departments attempted to secure through private petition appropriations which they had deliberately or accidentally failed to file with their departmental estimates. This was severely dealt with by Mr. Young and the committee on ways and means, and will probably not be repeated. Not allowing for duplications, the number of private petitions filed involving a charge on the treasury in 1919 was 212; they carried requests for appropriations aggregating $36,491,-865.21, not to mention those which carried indefinite amounts.

While some of these were finally carried through to

enactment, it was only by being taken up in the governor's supplementary budgets, or by being inserted by the legislature in the bills used on his budgets. Insertions of this kind took place only with the last budget, where an 18.6 per cent. increase was made. Nevertheless, almost the entire amount of this increase is due not to insertions but to the $150,000 increase in the item recommended by the budget for the administration of the bounty for soldiers.

Total Appropriations Carried in Seven Acts

During the 1919 session of the Massachusetts General Court total appropriations amounting to $39,337,913.63 were passed by the legislature and signed by the governor. These appropriations are contained in seven separate acts, three of which were based on the governor's three budgets; and four on his special messages. The following table indicates the basis of the various appropriations and the amounts carried by each.

APPROPRIATIONS OF 1919 SESSION

Basis	Amount	Per Cent. of Total Appropriation
Budget	$35,060,375.47	89.2
First Supplemental	2,713,802.15	6.9
Second Supplemental ..	1,208,736.01	3.0
Special Messages	355,000.00	.9
Total	$39,337,913.63	100.0

Summary of Facts

The significant facts with regard to the 1919 Massachusetts budget procedure are:

1. All appropriations were based on budgets as contemplated in the law or on executive messages. Not a dollar was otherwise appropriated in 1919. There were no "private appropriation bills." This must not be taken, however, as meaning that there were no private bills

which found their way into the treasury. It simply means that the only channel of entry they were able to find was through the budget bills.

2. The general appropriation bill carried almost ninety per cent. of the total appropriations of the session.

3. Ninety-seven per cent. of the total appropriations were disposed of a month before the end of the session. The appropriations of the last week were but three per cent. of the total appropriations, and these represented almost entirely matters which had been authorized by act or resolve earlier in the session. Ninety per cent. of the appropriations were passed soon after the middle of the session.

4. The general appropriation bill includes the appropriations for the legislative and judicial departments.

5. The total appropriations passed differ from the totals recommended by the House committee on ways and means by less than $20,000. They are, however, some $300,000 lower than the governor's recommendations.

6. The governor did not exercise his right to veto items in appropriation bills or to reduce items. He accepted every change made by the legislature.

7. The maintenance appropriations were not passed until almost five months after the beginning of the fiscal year to which they relate. In the interim the government was run on credit, at the rate authorized the previous year. This provision enables the budget makers and the legislature to have before them, when considering the budget, a full statement of the actual expenses for the immediately preceding fiscal period.

CHAPTER XIV

THE state in which the operation of the " executive budget " idea has been most fully exemplified in American law and practice to date is Illinois. It has operated more fully here than in the other twenty-two states which have declared in favor of the principle and passed laws for its adoption: (1) because it fitted best — was better adapted and adjusted to the state governmental machine; (2) because the public opinion of the state was better informed as to what the executive budget was expected to do.

Recent Administrative Reorganization Makes Possible Operation of Executive Budget

The better adaptation and adjustment of the state machine on which the executive budget was fitted as a means of control came about through the adoption of the new administrative code, described above (Chapter X). Many other states that have adopted the executive budget as an instrument or mechanism of control have old types of administrative machinery on which the new controlling device does not fit and into which it cannot be geared to make it function effectively.

The better information and more favorable public opinion of the state was the direct result of a campaign of education conducted by Governor Lowden and his party organization in seeking the votes which brought him into office. His party was pledged to a thoroughgoing reorganization of the administration around executive leadership, and to the adoption of an executive budget as a means of controlling leadership. The installation therefore as made in 1917 was more nearly complete, and was better understood, than other plans were in states where a new budget procedure was talked about and adopted as if it were a specific for all political ills — the thought being that any budget, which had been recommended and that had the trade name " executive " on it, would fit any administrative system.

Legislative Organization and Procedure Unchanged

While Illinois had a brand-new administrative machine, it had an old form of legislative organization and procedure. As in other states, the legislature had a set of rules governing its action which had been developed when the state was using the old administrative machine. It was very much like a company adopting steam tugs for canal transport, and retaining the rules governing the use of the canal and the control of its pilots which had been worked out when mules were used as the motor power.

The legislative organization and practice in Illinois was similar to that of Massachusetts, described above, in this: Its grist was actually ground by a multitude of standing committees, each of which had a separate hopper, and special burrs and bolts, for handling different kinds of material and products. It differed, in that each house had similar or corresponding committees, and contemplated that the same grist should be put through the committee mill twice: first in one house, then in the other; then if there was failure to agree on the grist a joint committee came together to put the stamp of approval on a mix that would be acceptable to the " party " steering committee which determined in the main what would be sent to the governor to have the trade-mark of the state affixed to it.

This was the more usual practice developed in state

legislatures under the operation of the bicameral, standing-committee type of organization.   Illinois, however,
differed in that a large proportion of the membership was
on the appropriation or finance committees, the Senate
appropriation committee being composed of forty-four
out of forty-nine members (one member having died).
Why the other five were left off does not appear to the
uninitiated.   Of these, thirty were Republicans and fourteen were Democrats — about two of the majority to one
of the minority party.   The House committee was composed of forty-three members out of a total of 153.   This
made a very large committee, although a much smaller
percentage of the whole than in the Senate.   Of these,
27 were Republican and 16 were Democrats.   When a
matter was taken before the Senate committee in charge
of appropriations therefor, it was like taking it up in
" committee of the whole," without provision being made,
however, for the drama of contest between party leaders
as is the case where inquest in the " committee of the
whole " is made an essential part of a budget procedure.

Legislative Reference Bureau

The Illinois General Assembly of 1913 passed a measure, taking effect on July 1st of that year, which created
a joint legislative reference bureau, composed of the
governor and the chairmen of the committees on " appropriations " and " judiciary " of the Senate and House.   It
was made the duty of this bureau to prepare, print, and
distribute for the use of the members of the legislature a
compilation of the estimates as submitted to it by the
various spending agencies, together with a comparative
statement of the sums appropriated by the succeeding
legislature for the same purposes.   The work of this
bureau proved unsatisfactory on account of the lack of
executive control, the multiplicity of detail, and the fail-

ure to provide the proper authority for amendment or revision.

Department of Finance

The legal provisions of the present Illinois budget are a part of the civil administrative code adopted in 1917. This code, as has been pointed out, consolidated practically all statutory administrative agencies into nine departments with a director at the head of each department. One of these is the department of finance, the duties of which are described in Chapter X. This department is not only regarded as the most important of the new departments, but it is in American practice a new conception since it took over very little work performed by previously existing administrative agencies. In brief, the functions of this department are: (1) To prescribe and install a uniform system of bookkeeping, accounting, and reporting; (2) to examine into the accuracy and legality of accounts and expenditures of other departments; (3) to examine and approve or disapprove all bills, vouchers, and claims against the other departments; (4) to prepare a budget for submission to the governor; and (5) to formulate plans for better coordination of the departmental work. In addition to these departmental functions, the director of finance acts as the financial adviser for the governor and all the departments directly under the governor's control. Practically all powers of the department are vested in the director, who by rules and regulations provides how such powers shall be administered.

Through the department of finance a centralized control of the expenditures made by the agencies responsible to the governor is effected. While this department has no direct control over the expenditures made by any department other than those created by the code, yet it is authorized and required to study the entire field of governmental needs in order to prepare the budget.

Statutory Budget Provisions

The provisions of the civil administrative code with reference to budgetary procedure are as follows:

The director of finance is required by September 15th of the even-numbered years to distribute to all spending agencies, including the elective officers, University of Illinois, and judicial department estimate blanks in such form as he may prescribe. He must procure information of the revenues and expenditures for the two preceding fiscal years, the appropriations made by the previous legislature, the expenditures therefrom, the encumbrances thereon, amounts unencumbered and unexpended, estimates of the revenues and expenditures for the current fiscal year, and estimates of revenues and amounts needed by several spending agencies for the succeeding biennium. All spending agencies, not later than November 1st, must file with the director of finance their estimate of receipts and expenditures for the succeeding biennium. Such estimates must be accompanied by written explanations.

The director of finance may approve, disapprove, or alter the estimates. He may at his discretion make inquiries and investigations. He is required by January 1st to submit to the governor in writing his estimates of revenues and appropriations for the next biennium.

The governor has, by the code, imposed on him the duty of submitting to the legislature a budget for the biennial period. The budget so submitted must contain the amounts recommended by the governor to be appropriated to the several spending agencies; the estimated revenues from taxation and from sources other than taxation, and the estimated amount required to be raised by taxation. Together with the budget, the governor is required to transmit the estimates of receipts and expenditures received by the director of finance from the elective officers in the executive and judicial departments and from the University of Illinois. These submissions are to be made to the General Assembly not later than four weeks after its organization.

An important feature, not to be overlooked, is this: Each department is required, before an appropriation for such department becomes available for expenditure, to prepare and submit to the department of finance an estimate of the amount required for each activity to be carried on, and accounts shall be kept and reports rendered showing the expenditures for each such purpose. This permits the director of finance, and, through him, the governor, to exercise continuing supervision over expenditures; and in practice the departments, so far as practicable, are required to submit monthly requisitions to be approved.

Budget Staff in Department of Finance

In the department of finance, under the supervision of the director of finance, is a superintendent of budget. Both of these officers are appointed by the governor with the approval of the Senate for terms of four years, beginning on the second Monday in January following the election of the governor. The superintendent of budget receives $3,600 per annum. The present incumbent of the office was for several years a statistician in the old department of charities which existed before the creation of code departments. He is assisted in his work by one accountant and one stenographer, and may call on other employees of the department of finance for help when necessary.

The work of preparing the first state budget, which was presented to the 1919 legislature, was begun in the summer of 1917. An analysis of the cost of operating the several departments and their respective divisions was made. Standard accounts, as provided by the action of the preceding legislature, were installed and controlling ledgers were set up and kept by the department of finance upon this basis. The appropriations made by the two preceding legislatures were classified and tabulated. This work not only simplified but aided greatly the preparation of the budget.

Estimates and Other Information Gathered by Department of Finance.

Estimate forms were prepared by the department of finance, which classified the past and proposed expenditure according to the ten standard accounts already adopted. These forms were submitted to the departments and other spending agencies about August 1, 1918, although the law does not require the department of finance to send them out until September 15th. Being the initial operation, it was deemed advisable to send them out at an earlier date so as to give ample time to assemble the required data and to prepare the estimates. Three copies of the estimates were required, two of which were filed with the department of finance and the third copy retained by the agency making the estimates. No difficulty was experienced in getting the estimates filed in the time required by the law — November 1st.

During a period of about six months prior to the time of sending out the estimate forms, the superintendent of budget visited all institutions and studied their needs and the per capita cost of their maintenance. In addition, a person employed and supervised by the architect of the department of public works and buildings visited all institutions and looked over the condition of the buildings, making written recommendations to the department of finance as to the amounts needed for repairs. The supervising engineer also took an inventory of the machinery and estimated the amounts needed for repairs and replacements. The director of finance has announced his intention, in the near future, to work out a building program, and also a plan of standardization of personal service.

Review and Revision of Estimates by Director of Finance

The estimates, as filed with the department of finance, together with all other budget data, are submitted by the superintendent of budget to the director of finance, whose duty it is to review and revise the estimates before submitting them to the governor for his recommendations thereon to the legislature. As a matter of actual practice, the director of finance and the superintendent of budget checked up all the estimates and then called into conference the department heads and bureau chiefs of the code departments and the independent state officers at which time the estimates were reviewed carefully and revised by the director of finance in his discretion. This period of review and revision occupied the time between November 1st and January 1st. The revised estimates were then submitted to the governor, who went over them carefully for his own information, called further conferences, and made whatever changes he deemed necessary. The estimates as approved by the governor are printed as the budget — all the estimates and data received up to that time being considered as preliminary and not official.

Budget Speeches Delivered to Legislature

The Illinois legislature of 1919 met about January 10th, and under the provisions of the code, the governor's budget recommendations must be presented to the legislature not later than four weeks after its organization. Accordingly, the budget was printed and submitted to the legislature about February 10th. Besides the letter of transmittal which the budget carried, explaining briefly the needs of the state, the governor and the director of finance both appeared before a joint session of the two houses of the legislature at the time the budget was presented and made short speeches relative to the budget program.   Immediately upon its presentation to the legislature, the governor's budget was referred to the appropriation committees of the two houses.   Each member of the legislature was furnished with a copy of the governor's budget.

The Budget and Budget Supplements

The budget, as submitted, was summary in form.   The amounts appropriated for the biennium, 1917–1919, the actual expenditures for the fiscal year 1917 and the estimated requirements for the next biennium, 1919–1921, were given; also the actual and estimated revenues for the same periods were stated.   These, however, were not recapitulated as a balanced statement by years or for the two bienniums; neither were the summaries of expenditures and estimates supported by an exhibit of detailed information showing how the totals were arrived at by the governor when his budget was prepared.   While the annual report of the auditor, an independent elective constitutional officer, was printed and before the legislature, it was of little value, since the auditor's office has not been developed as a critical agent of the legislature.   Very soon a number of the legislators asked for more detailed information; and in response to this request a detailed supplement to the budget, called the "Book of Estimates," was printed.   This supplemental document contained the detailed information (1) of the estimates as submitted by the various non-code spending agencies to the department of finance, and (2) the details as finally agreed to by the governor in conference with the *code* departments.   The estimates of the code departments as prepared by the department heads under the governor were not sent to the legislature, as the governor took the stand that these were merely preliminary, and to serve the purposes of data to assist the governor in coming to a conclusion as to what amounts would finally be considered adequate after conference—the theory being that it is against public policy to require the governor to go over with the legislature any controversies which might have arisen between him and his subordinates.

At the time the budget was prepared, which was directly after the signing of the armistice, it was thought that prices for supplies would drop soon, but on the contrary they actually advanced in some instances. Therefore, before the budget was finally acted on in June by the legislature, the code department heads were obliged to ask the governor, through the department of finance, to request larger appropriations than had been planned. In such cases as appeared to the governor meritorious this was done in the form of a typewritten supplement to the budget submitted to the chairmen of the appropriation committees. This accounts for many of the changes made in the governor's first budget recommendations and for most of the increases while before the committees. The non-code departments also submitted requests for revision to the department of finance, which were sent to the legislature with the recommendations of the governor.

Legislative Procedure and Action on the Budget

During the consideration of the proposed appropriations the House committee was divided into small subcommittees, known as visiting committees, which made trips to the charitable and penal institutions of the state. The Senate committee did no visiting. The committees, mainly the House committee, held a number of hearings. A few of the hearings were conducted by the Senate and House committees sitting jointly. The hearings before the committees ended about May 15th. These hearings were conducted under the usual rules which obtain in the

American states for the conduct of hearings in the consideration of measures by standing committees; that is, they were considered as closed meetings. They differed, however, from those held by previous legislatures in that a representative of the governor, the superintendent of budget of the department of finance, was present.

After the hearings were completed the work of bill drafting was begun. The secretary of the legislative reference bureau, the regular bill-drafting agency, assisted by the superintendent of budget, drafted the appropriation bills for the appropriation committees. In fact, the superintendent of budget worked with the appropriation committees while they were considering the proposed appropriations. It is stated that this coöperation helped greatly to coördinate the work of the department of finance with that of the legislative committees in making the appropriations.

Many Emergency Appropriation Measures Passed

Before the regular appropriation bills were submitted, nineteen emergency appropriation measures had been passed by the legislature. Eleven of these were for expenditures other than by code departments, and eight were for expenditures of code departments under the governor. Of the former, six were for legislature expenditures, one for the Constitutional Convention, and four were for constitutional offices which went directly to the legislature. Of the latter (the emergency appropriations to code departments) all of them were for deficiencies except two, one for Federal-aid roads, and another for a free employment bureau growing out of the conditions of war. Two of these were recommended by the governor in his budget, and the other six were submitted with his knowledge and consent.

General Appropriation Bills

Illinois does not have a single appropriation bill covering the proposals of the governor's budget, but a number of appropriation bills, the drafting of which is left to the legislature with the assistance of the legislative reference bureau and the superintendent of budget. In fact, even if it were desirable under an executive budget plan, it is impossible under the present constitutional provisions for Illinois to have a single appropriation bill. The most important of these bills are: (1) the omnibus bill, containing the appropriations made for the departments and other administrative agencies (not included in other bills) and the courts; (2) the officer's bill, which, under the provision of the constitution, contains appropriations for the pay of members and officers of the General Assembly and for salaries of the officers of government, and being further provided that it shall contain " no provisions on any other subject "; (3) the charitable and penal appropriation bill; (4) the normal school bill; and (5) the University of Illinois bill. Usually there are separate bills providing for the legislature, for roads, and for the national guard. These may be regarded as the regular appropriation bills. In addition there are numerous other bills covering reappropriations, claims, special and miscellaneous appropriations besides emergencies. There were seventy-nine appropriation measures passed in the 1919 legislature. Seven of these were vetoed by the governor, leaving a total of seventy-two to become laws.

The history of the omnibus appropriation bill in the legislature may be noted briefly. This bill (H. B. No. 754) was introduced in the House on June 6th, at which time it had its first reading, and was ordered printed for a second reading. It was printed and on the desks of the members on June 9th. On June 11th, thirty-six amendments were offered by the chairman of the House appropriations committee, mostly affecting salaries, all save one of which were adopted; whereupon the bill passed the House. It then went to the Senate and was read a second time on June 13th, when seventy-nine amendments were reported from the Senate committee on appropriations affecting salaries, all except one of which were adopted. Two amendments were offered by members of the Senate which were rejected. Immediately the bill passed the Senate as amended. On June 16th the bill was reported to the House as amended, and the House refused to concur in the Senate amendments. A conference committee, consisting of five members from each house, was then appointed. This committee reported to the legislature on June 20th, recommending that the House concur with the Senate in forty-five of the Senate amendments and that the Senate recede from the remaining thirty-three of its amendments. The conference committee also offered ninety-one new amendments largely affecting salaries. Some of these amendments amounted to rewriting whole schedules of the appropriation act. Both houses adopted the conference committee's report on June 20th and recessed until June 30th, in which time the governor was required, under the constitution, to act on the bill. On June 30th, Governor Lowden approved the bill, except six items totaling $116,800; $6,600 of which was for salaries due to failure in the passage of supporting legislation, $50,000 was for the purchase of submerged lands, and the remainder for armories and armory sites. During the passage of this bill through the legislature there was a little debate on the floor of the House occasioned by one or two amendments, but no debate occurred in the Senate.

Effect of Legislative Action on Governor's Proposals

In the action of the legislature upon the governor's budget recommendations it is stated that one decrease was made against numerous increases, most of which were for personal service. It is to be noted, however, that there was much pressure brought for increasing salaries between the time the budget was prepared and the time the appropriation bills were passed both in the governor's departments and in those not under his direction and control—practically all the changes proposed in committee being of this sort. Nevertheless, it is to be assumed that all of those affecting the code departments were with the governor's knowledge and consent, as these departments were given to understand that there should be no proposals for increases except through executive channels.

Control by Department of Finance Over Expenditures

Before the appropriations become available for expenditure, each department is required to prepare and submit to the department of finance an estimate of the amount required for each activity to be carried on, and accounts are set up and reports rendered showing the expenditures for each such purpose. The finance code, passed by the 1919 legislature, enlarges these powers of the department of finance.

Conclusions

In conclusion it may be said that Governor Lowden was the dominating force in the preparation of the budget and in following it through the legislature. Under the administrative code he has absolute control over the code departments. For example, the amount requested and appropriated ($50,000) for submerged lands was placed in the omnibus appropriation bill by the legislative committees, without consulting the governor, to be expended under the control of the director of one of the code departments.   This amount was vetoed by the governor when he approved the bill.   The governor's power, however, is advisory in the preparation and submission of estimates and requests by independent elective officers.   They may and do go over the governor's head to the legislature for appropriations.

The coöperation between the departments, which is brought about by the code administration and consolidation, is a great help in budget making and effects a great saving in the operation of the state's functions.   For example, the superintendent of purchases in the department of public works coöperated with the department of finance in making the budget recommendations for supplies for the various departments and institutions of the state.

The handling of the budget by the legislature is the part of the procedure that is most open to criticism.   The governor's budget goes to separate appropriation committees in the two houses, which work independently of each other in the preparation of the appropriation bills, and they are not inquired into initially in such manner as to make the consideration of the budget an open-forum procedure.   The result is that no opportunity is given to sound out the membership by taking an informal vote department by department.   The open-forum discussion on appropriation measures is delayed until the closing days of the legislative session when usually there is too little time left for discussion.   In case of disagreement between the two houses over proposed amendments and adjustment, the only way open is by reference to a conference committee.   In other states as New Jersey, New York, and Wisconsin, the claim is made that it is more satisfactory to have the appropriation committees of the two houses coöperate and work together as a joint committee in the consideration of the budget.   It is urged that this saves duplication of work and obviates the necessity of the undesirable conference committee. But whatever the procedure is in standing committees, this does not serve the purpose of giving publicity to discussion.

CHAPTER XV

As has been pointed out in Chapter VIII, the controlling thought in Wisconsin in bringing about the changes in its public law has not been a desire to strengthen and make vital the processes of popular control over the government, or even to seek to establish executive responsibility. Rather, it has been to promote the operation of the various decentralized boards and commissions in charge of state administration, and to protect them from domination or interference either by the governor or the legislature.

"Government by Commission" Seriously Limits Power of Governor

The board form of government, as it is being developed in Wisconsin, has been in the direction of removing from the governor his power and control over the state administration. The members of these boards have in practically all cases overlapping terms which are very much longer than the two-year term of the governor. The result is that the governor can never control the boards, because he cannot appoint a majority of the members during his short term of office. More than this, all appointments made by the governor must be approved by the Senate. Since the legislature, under the Wisconsin plan, is the controlling factor in matters of administration, in so far as control may be exercised at all, and the board of public affairs is the controlling body in budget making, the governor can do nothing more than nominate to office those persons who stand well in the favor of the Senate and exert an influence in the preparation of an administrative and financial program for the state. Had the bill recently passed by the legislature which gave that body the power to vote a " lack of confidence " in any public official whereupon his office would become vacant and a new appointment would have to be made — had this bill not been vetoed by the governor, the executive power would have been still farther curtailed. In that event the real head of the administration would have been the leader of the majority in the legislature.

In financial matters the governor has very little power. He may concur with or dissent from the proposals of other members of the board of public affairs (all excepting three of which are elective like himself) in preparing budget recommendations which are made to the legislature. Even then the legislature may disregard his recommendations altogether and not even discuss them. He may then send special messages to the legislature, as Governor Philipp did last year (1919), calling attention to the mounting appropriations and urging the legislature to curb its action. Finally he has the power of veto, which, however, under the system of continuing appropriations may amount to little.

The State Board of Public Affairs

Reform of procedure in preparation of estimate dates back to 1909, when the legislature authorized the tax commission to make an investigation of state finances. This was done in a rather lengthy report which was submitted to the legislature of 1911. Among other things, this report recommended that the state-spending agencies prepare estimates in advance of the legislative session to be submitted to a committee of both houses of the legislature and possibly the presiding officers of the Senate and

House. This body was to prepare the budget and submit it to the legislature.

By act of 1911 the state board of public affairs was created consisting of the governor as chairman, the secretary of state, the president *pro tem.* of the Senate, the speaker of the House, the chairman of the Senate and House committees on finance, and three members appointed by the governor and confirmed by the Senate, subject to removal by the governor. Provisions were made for the employment of a secretary and such experts and other employees as might be necessary. This was an experimental organization, as it was to expire by limitation on June 30, 1913. But the temporary device has been continued with little change except in personnel. The 1913 legislature provided that the board should continue in office for a term of two years and a second term of one year. In 1915 the board was further continued in office, this time for one term of two years and a second term of one and a half years.

Statutory Provisions for Budget Procedure

A definite budgetary procedure was adopted in 1913 (Chap. 728, Laws of 1913) ; this, as revised in 1915 and 1917, provides:

1. That the state board of public affairs shall furnish estimate blanks to each public body not later than July 1st, which in turn, not later than September 1st, shall present to the board its estimates for the ensuing biennium.

2. That the board shall cause the estimates to be compiled forthwith and reviewed through such field examinations, interviews, or correspondence as may be necessary to obtain full information.

3. That the board, as a whole, between November 10th and December 1st shall consider and review the results of the preliminary examinations, together with the estimates and explanations.

4. That the governor elect shall have the right to attend the review meetings, personally or through a representative, and to receive all reports and information sent to members of the board.

5. That the budget shall show comparisons of estimates for the ensuing biennium with each year of the current biennium and each of the three years next preceding; the amount of each item recommended; whether the amounts recommended are equal to above or below the amounts requested and the amounts for the first year of the preceding biennium; reasons for recommended allowances or disallowances; a record of the vote on each recommendation that is not unanimous; and any recommendation which a minority of the board or the governor elect may wish to have included.

6. That the board shall accompany the conclusions or recommendations of all its reports with a summary of the facts upon which its conclusions or findings are based, the names of the members approving the report, and the summary of the investigation pursued to obtain the facts.

7. That the board shall recommend a budget to the legislature not later than December 15th, and not later than January 1st shall distribute copies of the estimates with its recommendations thereon to the members of the legislature.

8. That the board shall have such supervision over every public body as is necessary to secure uniformity and accuracy of accounts, and it may devise uniform systems of accounts and uniform accounting procedure for all such public bodies.

9. That the board shall also investigate duplication of work, inefficiency of organization and administration, and shall formulate plans for better coördination and the improvement of administration in general.

Budget Staff

The present secretary of the state board of public affairs has been with the board since 1912. His salary is $4,500 per annum. He is by profession an accountant, having received his training at the University of Wisconsin. A special examiner is employed by the board at a salary of $4,500 per year. He has been four years with the work. Four permanent accountants are employed by the board at salaries ranging from $1,000 to $2,700. During the preparation of the last budget three extra accountants were employed. From two to four stenographers are engaged in the office of the board.

Preparation, Filing, and Review of Estimates

Mimeographed estimate sheets are prepared by the staff of the board, which are sent out to various spending agencies about the middle of August of the even-numbered years. Before these forms are sent out the actual and itemized expenditures of the agency, as shown by the controlling accounts of the board, are inserted for each of the three years preceding the year then current. Each spending agency upon receipt of these forms is required to insert the estimated allotment of appropriations for the current year and its requests for each year of the succeeding biennium. The estimates are usually returned to the board by September 15th.

The estimates are reviewed by the staff directly upon being filed. Then field examinations are made; usually each institution and department is visited by a member of the staff, the secretary of the board directing the examinations. Conferences are held with the institutional heads and other officers. The information thus obtained is recorded for later use by the board and for presentation to the legislature. These investigations are usually finished in about one month.

Public Hearings on Estimates

The board of public affairs usually begins to hold public hearings upon the estimates about the fifteenth of November and continues for some three or four weeks. About fifty hearings were held in 1918. The time the hearings are to be held is announced in the newspapers and occasionally a reporter is present. The heads of the departments and institutions appear at these hearings and present the facts upon which their estimates are based. The members of the board have presented to them at the same time the information collected by their own staff. This procedure supplies facts both from the point of view of the agency seeking an appropriation and from the point of view of the trained and independent investigator. Having both sides of the question before it, the board goes into executive session after the hearing is concluded and determines upon the amount of its recommendations to the legislature.

The Compilation of Estimates

The hearings are usually finished by about December 15th. The estimates are then brought together and compiled by the staff of the state board of public affairs. Mimeographed copies are produced and bound in a volume about fifteen by eighteen inches in size. This volume is usually ready for distribution to the members of the legislature by January 1st.

The compilation, as presented to the 1919 legislature, contained the following information: (1) a report of actual receipts and expenditures for the three fiscal years prior to July 1, 1918; (2) departmental estimates of receipts and expenditures for the current year, 1918–1919; (3) estimated treasury balances as of July 1, 1919; (4) departmental estimated receipts and expenditures for the biennial period beginning July 1, 1919; (5) appropriations available beginning July 1, 1916, and (6) appropriations requested by state departments, boards, institutions, and commissions for the biennium, July 1, 1919, through June 30, 1921. It was expressly stated that the appropriations requested in this document were not those recommended or approved by the state board of public affairs, but that its recommendations were contained in a separate report attached to the compilation.

The purpose of this compilation of estimates (called a budget), it is stated, is to give the legislature full and complete information relative to financial facts; also to help that body in determining policies, in working out a definite fiscal program, and in drafting the necessary appropriation measures. Furthermore, it is intended to show the legislature clearly the limitations within which appropriations must be kept to avoid a general purpose tax levy.

Budget Recommendations of Board of Public Affairs

Prior to 1917 the state board of public affairs made no budget recommendations, as it believed its duty to be the gathering of estimates and of facts relating thereto in advance of each legislative session and the submission of this data, organized in a systematic manner, to the legislature. In 1917 the board reviewed each request and made recommendations thereon, with the exception of the requests relating to educational institutions which were examined and passed upon by the state board of education. In 1919 the board considered not only the departmental but institutional requests as well.

The recommendations of the board, as has already been stated, were included in a mimeographed pamphlet of about twenty pages, which was inserted in an envelope attached to the back cover of the compilation of estimates. An introductory statement to this document asserts that " the board in no wise takes unto itself any of the legislative functions, but has gathered this information in the hopes of being of greatest possible assistance to the legislature." A statement then follows in which the requests for appropriations and the anticipated revenues are balanced, showing a deficit of almost two million dollars for each year of the biennium. The recommendations of the board, it is stated, reduce the requests until they come within the estimated income of the state for the biennium. The legislature is cautioned against appropriating in excess of the total amount recommended by the board of public affairs, since such action will necessitate the levying of a direct tax for general purposes. Most of the recommendations of the board are for the continuation of the present appropriations, a large number of which are by law continuous in their operation until the statute is repealed. In conclusion, the board offered the use of all its files and budget information to the joint committee on finance of the legislature.

Organization and Work of Joint Committee on Finance

The finance committees of the two houses of the legislature act jointly, a procedure similar to that of New Jersey. This joint committee on finance is composed of nine members from the House of one hundred members and five members from the Senate of thirty-three members. Of the fourteen members composing this committee all were Republicans except two — a Democrat and a Socialist.

The board of public affairs has coöperated with the joint committee on finance since 1913. Its staff, assisted by the legislative reference bureau, has drafted appropriation measures for the committee since 1915. It has been the practice for the secretary of the board to work with the joint committee upon all matters relating to state finances.

The joint committee on finance is usually organized

about ten days after the beginning of the legislative session. Immediately thereafter the budget is presented to the committee by the secretary of the state board of public affairs. Very soon the committee begins to hold public hearings, the purpose of which is to bring out any information that may be used to check up the recommendations of the board of public affairs. As a matter of fact, the public hearings are of little interest except to those who are interested in increasing appropriations and improving the service of the particular department under consideration. More than one hundred such hearings were conducted by the committee during the past session of the legislature. Members of the committee also visited the charitable and penal institutions of the state, using the week-ends for five or six weeks for this purpose.

The Appropriation Bills

Usually there are from fifteen to twenty regular appropriation bills passed each session of the legislature. These include the appropriation bill for the University of Wisconsin, the bill making appropriations for the normal schools, the bill for the charitable and penal institutions of the state, and from twelve to fifteen departmental and miscellaneous bills. An attempt to require a single bill has been made, it being thought that this is the only way to get the whole plan before the membership and keep it before the people while appropriations are under discussion — and with such a plan as Wisconsin has there is much force in the contention.

The regular appropriation bills are usually introduced by the joint committee on finance and may go to either house for introduction. These bills are prepared by a committee as rapidly as it can take action on the estimates and the information placed before it by the state board of public affairs. For example, the appropriation bill for the University of Wisconsin was prepared and

introduced into the Senate on March 14th, the normal
school appropriation bill was introduced in the House on
March 18th, and the bill for charitable and penal institutions was introduced in the House on April 10th.   The
legislature did not adjourn until almost the close of July.

The Wisconsin System of " Continuing Appropriations "

It should be kept in mind that since Wisconsin has a
system of continuing appropriations, all appropriation
measures, except those making appropriations to newly
created agencies, must be in the form of amendments to
various sections of statute law previously passed.   Only
where changes are made in the appropriations as previously authorized is any action taken by the legislature.
While the estimates are presented in detail, the appropriation bills propose action only on certain items and totals.

Expenditures are classified under three heads; namely,
operation, maintenance, and capital.   Operation appropriations are those authorized for meeting the ordinary
running expenses and upkeep of the state departments,
boards, commissions, and institutions.   Maintenance appropriations are those authorized for repair and upkeep
of permanent property, including lands, buildings, machinery, and equipment.   Separate appropriations are
made for operation, maintenance, and capital expenditures.   Under the system of continuing appropriations,
those for operation recur annually for the departments
and institutions of the state which are considered permanent and integral parts of the state government.   Appropriations for maintenance and capital purposes are
made for the ensuing two years only.   Practically all of
the appropriations are non-lapsible.   Only positive action of the legislature can affect or modify an appropriation when once it is made.   That is, a majority of both
houses of the legislature and the approval of the governor, or two thirds of the members of the legislature in

case of executive veto, are necessary to modify or abolish these appropriations. Thus it is asserted " the burden of proof for changes in established law·or organization has shifted from the administration to the legislature, and changes can be effected only by positive action of the law-making agencies." Thus, it is contended, the administrator is made to feel reasonably safe and he may continue to perform his administrative duties instead of " cajoling and jollying legislators in the lobby of the hotels of the capital city or in the lobby of the legislature." Moreover, it is contended that " legislative pressure is not likely to be so effective because the source of its momentum is gone and particularly minority control is ineffective."

The Result of " Government by Commission"

The Wisconsin budget procedure is based upon the principle " that the function of the administration, including the executive, in budget making is preliminary, preparatory, advisory, and the function of the legislature is determining and conclusive." [1] The governor, as has already been explained, is practically without power over the state administration because of the board system of organization. Whatever financial recommendations he makes to the legislature are made through the board of public affairs. In the final analysis all recommendations of this board are merely advisory to the action of the legislature. The joint finance committee of the legislature formulates the expenditure program after it has examined the data submitted by the board of public affairs and the various state spending agencies. In the meantime, the several state agencies may go directly to the leg-

---

[1] For defense of the Wisconsin practice, see "Budget Making in a Democracy," by E. A. Fitzpatrick. This is the best treatise extant on the commission budget idea.

islature and use whatever influence they may have to secure additional appropriations.

When once the functions of an agency have been classed as a permanent service and the agency has been put on the basis of a continuing appropriation, it need have little fear of its appropriation being reduced by the legislature. The governor cannot reduce the appropriation even if he finds the service incompetently managed, or its needs are much below its former requirements. He may recommend a decrease, but that is all. In case the legislature takes no positive action — that is, makes neither an increase nor a decrease in the continuing appropriation of an agency — the governor's veto is absolutely useless. The whole financial administration of the state is, therefore, practically out of the hands of the elected representatives of the people.

" Government by commission " is thereby rendered safe both by establishment in the public law, and by vesting the budget-making power in a super-commission; but the people are at the same time removed one step farther from control over the administration. In operation the service results have been favorable, as is the case also in Massachusetts — as favorable as in any of the states. But the extent to which the people will rest content with this form of government must depend on the extent to which they are willing to accept anything short of responsible leadership. The system is one which adopts the autocratic principle for purposes of commission management, and the decentralized, independent, specialized soviet principle for purposes of control. The mind of the people must operate, if at all, through private agencies of publicity and discussion, too often the tools of special interests. The method of inquest and determination is that of class rule, not the method of democracy.

CHAPTER XVI

THE "LEGISLATIVE BUDGET" IDEA AS EXEMPLIFIED IN NEW YORK

WHILE in New York the humanitarian civic forces (those which sought to express their souls through " government by commission ") and the boss (hoping to keep up the fences of his political preserves) combined to defeat the proposals of the Constitutional Convention in 1915 — as soon as the matter of vote getting was settled in their favor, they separated like oil and vinegar from an emulsion. They were only temporarily held together by adhesion, not by chemical affinity. The civic secretary and his committee or board returned to their specialized field of service; the boss and his plutocratic oligarchy returned to their political preserves to plan campaigns for " big game " or to turn to " head-hunting."

Vacillating Party Positions on New York's Budget Issue

As matters turned the campaign of education which had been carried on in favor of centralization of authority as a means of locating responsibility, but without any thought being given to processes by which the popular will could be ascertained and be made to function, all the high educational value of the Constitutional Convention was turned to account by the managers of the majority political " party." The history of the legislative budget in New York is of interest not alone as a political experiment, but as evidence of the fact that the budget issue, the question as to whether one form or another of budget procedure is advocated or adopted, is not a matter on which our irresponsible political parties have taken sides or have any friendly interest except in so far as advocacy may be to the advantage of the " party " in power on the one hand, or to the advantage of a " party " in opposition on the other.

To illustrate this point: when in 1912 President Taft proposed an " executive budget " for the national government it was not put forward as a " party " measure; it was in support of recommendations of the President's commission on economy and efficiency, three of whom were Democrats, two of whom were Independents, only one of whom was a Republican. But President Taft was a candidate for renomination on the Republican ticket; and there was a strong hostile Democratic majority in Congress which for party reasons would be against anything coming from the President which would redound to his credit. There was also another reason why members of Congress might be opposed, viz.: the out-working of an " executive budget," if effective, would threaten the supremacy of the standing committee system. Through the leadership of the Democratic party in Congress, a " legislative budget " was urged in opposition to President Taft's " executive budget " proposal. But note what happened in New York. When, in 1916, Governor Whitman sought to capitalize public opinion favoring an " executive budget," and for partisan reasons the leaders of his party jockeyed this proposal around so that in the race the " executive budget " went lame and quit at the half-mile post, giving a favorable decision to the " legislative budget " by default in the councils of the governor's party — when this, the identical proposal urged by the Democrats in Congress against Mr. Taft, came before the legislature as a Republican measure, the leaders of the Democratic party just as lustily shouted for a decision favorable to the " executive budget " as they had shouted it down at Washington. Thus, in 1916, we have this spectacle: the Republican national party managers entered the race for votes on a platform, one plank of which was the " executive budget "; and in New York the Republican managers went before the legislature standing on a platform in which this plank had been slyly taken out in the secrecy of the committee room, and a legislative budget law was slipped into its place.   The same year the Democratic party, " pointing with pride," went before the national electorate and won standing on a platform with a "legislative budget" plank in it; and in New York State when the Republican party organization proclaimed its intention to make this a part of the permanent law, the Democrats damned the idea as a device suitable only to the uses and purposes of " invisible government."

Need for Administrative Reorganization

The administrative machinery of the New York State government contains a miscellaneous collection of more than one hundred and seventy-five offices, boards, commissions, and other agencies — nearly all of them are independent of each other and most of them subject to no direct or effective supervision by the governor.   In a few cases the governor has the power of appointment and removal; but the whole subject and method of appointment and removal was peculiarly designed to confuse and defeat executive responsibility and power.   The governor is free to appoint only about ten minor and temporary agencies out of more than one hundred and fifty making up the state administration.   There are in the state thirteen methods of appointment and six methods of removal. Most of the administrative officers are appointed by the governor with the " advice and consent " of the Senate.   There are more than a dozen boards and commissions which are composed partly of members appointed by the governor and of members serving in an *ex officio* capacity.   About an equal number of boards and commissions is made up entirely of *ex officio* members. The legislature appoints and has full control over several important administrative agencies. Some offices are filled by bringing in the courts; others require the coöperation of unofficial agencies. While there are several single-headed departments among the administrative agencies of New York State, there are also a large number of boards and commissions. Members of most of these boards and commissions are appointed for long overlapping terms. Quite a few of them duplicate functions performed by others. Similar groups of functions are usually split up between a large number of agencies. There are no direct lines of responsibility, either to the governor or to the legislature.

Governor not a Chief Executive

The governor of New York, because of his short term of office and the various indirect methods of appointing and removing administrative officials, has little power over the state administration. In fact, the state comptroller, especially from the standpoint of political patronage, exerts greater power and control than the governor. Several of the other independent and elective administrative officers exercise power almost equal to that of the governor.

Not only is the governor of New York not a chief executive, but, in the formulation of the financial program of the state, he has practically nothing to say. Governor Whitman submitted a budget in 1916 which met with the same fate in the legislature at the hands of the managers for his own party that President Taft's budget, submitted to Congress in the early days of 1913, did at the hands of the opposition. In New York the governor may recommend appropriations to the legislature, but the legislature was not compelled to act upon his recommendations either before or since the enactment of

the new " legislative budget " procedure.   The legislature,
therefore, generally disregards the governor's proposal
as gratuitous advice.   The general procedure is similar
to that which has been in vogue for years in Congress.
The estimates are collected and transmitted by the comptroller.   The governor is permitted to submit recommendations.   The finance measures are prepared by the
standing committee of the legislature.   They receive their
main consideration and discussion in the committee room;
are brought out on the floor at the eleventh hour to be
voted by the legislature; and go to the governor for his
approval.   In New York there is a joint committee, and
the legislature usually remains in session so as to override the governor's vetoes, in case he should veto items
of the general appropriations.   In the control of the
expenditure of the appropriations, the comptroller is
given almost complete power to construe the laws, and
he operates independently of the governor.

Efforts of Governors Hughes and Sulzer

Governor Hughes' effort in 1910 did not have the budget vision; his was simply a proposal to secure a more
orderly handling of public business.   A law was passed
which required all requests for appropriations to be filed
with the comptroller and tabulated by him in advance of
the legislative session for the use of the governor and the
legislature.   The effort of Governor Sulzer was clearly
one to strengthen public confidence in him when he appointed, in 1913, a committee of inquiry to investigate
into the management of state departments and institutions.
This committee gave special attention to the method
of making appropriations and submitted recommendations designed to improve the existing procedure.   The
background for the recommendations of the committee
was partly the New York City practice and partly the
proposals of the Taft Commission.   These recommen-

dations provided, among other things, for the creation of a state board of estimate, consisting of state officials whose duty it was to prepare the appropriation bill; also the establishment of a department of efficiency and economy, charged with the power to examine into all expenditures of the state and to make recommendations along the lines of efficiency and economy. The legislature of 1913 enacted laws creating the agencies thus recommended. By 1915 the work of both the board of estimate and the department of efficiency and economy had come to be considered a failure because neither of them could find a place in the then existing political system; and the laws creating these agencies were repealed.

Budget Provisions of Proposed Constitution of 1915

As has been said, the proposed constitution of 1915 contained provisions for the establishment of a budget system of the " executive " type. And this was to be put on an administrative machine of an " executive " type — it being assumed that the legislative practice would be adjusted to the exercise of control through the budget over the executive — thereby controlling all questions of public policy of an administrative or financial character. All public service, *i.e.*, administrative departments of the state were to be reorganized under the governor, and as a measure of preserving executive discipline were to be required to submit to the governor itemized estimates of their financial needs. Responsibility of the executive to the people was to be enforced through the legislature. After public hearings upon the estimates the governor could revise them according to his judgment thereby making the administrative program the governor's. The estimates of the legislature and the judiciary were to be included in the budget without revision, although he could make recommendations relating to these. This, it is to be observed, was the plan which was later made law

in Illinois.   By February 1st the governor was to submit
to the legislature an itemized budget containing all proposed expenditures and estimated revenues, together with
appropriation bills, proposed taxation measures, and other
data relating to the fiscal year and the two years preceding.
The budget and the administrative appropriation bills
were to be presented, explained, and defended by the governor or his representative to the whole membership of
the legislature and for this purpose a committee-of-the
whole procedure was provided for.   The procedure was
to be provided by the statutes, but the constitution laid
down the principle that the governor and the heads of
departments were given the right and it was made their
duty to appear before the legislature.   In order not to
confuse responsibility for administration proposals members of the legislature might propose to amend by striking
out or reducing items but might not introduce new provisions or propose measures except for legislative functions or for the judiciary.   Not until the appropriation
bills proposed by the governor had been acted upon by
both houses could the legislature consider any further
or added provisions of organic law involving appropriation and then only in the form of separate bills, each
for a single object and subject to the governor's veto.
Such were the proposed constitutional provisions defeated
at the polls in November, 1915.

Governor Whitman's Budget Conference and Recommendations

At the preceding election Mr. Whitman was chosen
governor.   He immediately won state-wide applause by
the statement that there was one proposal that he would
put through as governor; budget procedure could be established without constitutional amendment, and he proposed to devote himself to this cause.   And after he was
fairly seated he set about proposing a budget.   For this

purpose he requested estimates from all the spending agencies and in November following his inauguration he appointed a conference committee of the chief executive officers of the state for the revision of these estimates. The result of the work was that on the first day of January he sent to the legislature a volume of tabulated estimates, together with a draft of an appropriation bill containing the governor's recommendations in itemized form, based upon his conference review and revision of the estimates. The budget bill as proposed by the governor, if it had contained nothing but the proposed items of appropriation, would have been a measure of a few pages made up of authorizations of total sums to be made available to each department or service, subdivided by items; one for salaries and wages, one for supplies, etc., making from two to six items under each administrative unit. But the bill was not so written; to each item was subjoined a large number of minor details making up the total that were to operate as schedules binding upon the department head but which could be changed or shifted from time to time as circumstances might require with the approval of the governor. This proposal was made to enable the legislature to have before them every detail making up the amounts asked for, and at the same time leaving to the executive the exercise of discretion where this could be used to advantage in the conduct of public business — the governor to be made responsible for approving changes requested, and accountable to the next legislature. For example: a total amount would be appropriated for salaries and wages for a department, to which a complete schedule of positions and salaries authorized was attached; in case it were found desirable to use more employees of a class at a lower salary rate, or in case certain employees were to be promoted or other changes seemed desirable, with the approval of the Civil Service Commission and under its rules, this could be done on application to the head of the department subject to review and approval by the governor.

When, however, this bill came out of the standing committee to which it was referred, by the change of a few words of the text not noticed even by many of the members of the legislature itself, every item of the supporting schedules was made items of appropriation, thereby making the act itself a document of several hundred pages with thousands of detailed items of appropriation. But the importance of the change is found in the fact that the whole civil service, every position and salary in it, was made the subject of legislative committee determination. The whole subject of administrative personnel was shifted to a basis of committee-room bargaining. In this revised form the bill was submitted to the legislature with the statement that it was the governor's measure " somewhat improved " as a result of committee inquiry. And in this form it was passed and was approved by the governor — the governor coming forward in a statement defending it and claiming it as among his political successes. The governor had completely surrendered every principle involved, and rested his laurels on a bill passed which was so similar in textual form that by the casual reader it was not recognized as an entirely new and an essentially different creature of law.

The Present Budget Law and Its Provisions

At the same time the standing-committee leaders made sure of their victory by passing a law for the institution of a " legislative budget." The bill by means of which this was accomplished was sponsored by Senator Sage. This was simultaneously introduced into the assembly by Mr. Maier — hence called the Sage-Maier Budget Bill. It passed the legislature and received the signature of Governor Whitman. By this law, three agencies: namely, the governor, Senate finance committee, and the Assembly ways and means committee were designated to be concerned with the preparation of the budget. The 1910 law requiring the comptroller to receive and compile estimates was not repealed. Hence, altogether as the statutes of the state now stand there are four agencies. However, the two legislative committees, under a provision of the budget law, very soon combined as a joint legislative budget committee and began with a joint staff ignoring the governor's and comptroller's functions to work together in the preparation of the budget. As will be seen from the provisions of the budget law, a summary of which follows, the budget recommendations of the governor and comptroller are considered as merely advisory to the joint legislative budget committee.

The chairman of the finance and ways and means committees may each appoint a clerk, also an accountant and a stenographer to assist each clerk. The clerks receive an annual salary of $4000, together with traveling and other necessary expenses. They are engaged at the work throughout the year. Other provisions of the budget law are:

(1) That the state spending agencies shall through their proper officers or deputies furnish such data, information, or statements as may be necessary for carrying into effect the provisions of this article.

(2) By November 15th of each year all state spending agencies shall file with the comptroller a detailed statement of all requests for appropriations to be made at the next legislative session. (State Finance Law, Sec. 48-49, or Chap. 149, Laws of 1910.)

(3) The comptroller shall prepare a report of expenditures for the first six months of the fiscal year. (State Finance Law, Sec. 4, Sub. Sec. 6, or Chap. 118, Laws of 1916.)

(4) The chairman of the joint legislative budget com-

mittee may name subcommittees to perform such duties as they may prescribe in gathering information relating to the financial needs of the several state spending agencies.

(5) The clerks of the joint legislative budget committee shall (a) compile information and financial data relating to the state spending agencies; (b) prepare tables of appropriations previously made by the legislature for the use of the joint budget committee; (c) procure statistics relating to the revenues of the states; (d) make a record of all information and correspondence concerning the budget; (e) investigate and report on requests for appropriations; (f) aid the committee and the legislature in making investigations pertaining to expenditures of state funds; (g) assist in the preparation of the annual budget; (h) have access to the offices of all spending agencies for the purposes of obtaining information as to their operation and their financial needs.

(6) The comptroller shall tabulate the estimates, together with itemized statement of the actual expenditures made during the preceding year, the appropriations made for the preceding year, the appropriations desired for the coming year, and the estimated income of the state. (State Finance Law, Secs. 48-49, or Chap. 149, Laws of 1910.)

(7) The Senate finance committee and the Assembly ways and means committee, acting jointly or separately, shall annually prepare a budget.   (In practice they act jointly.)

(8) The budget shall specify the unit of organization under whose control or supervision the moneys appropriated shall be expended for which appropriations are made.   It shall contain a detailed estimate of the probable revenues of the state and an estimate of the amounts which it shall be necessary to raise by direct tax; also a

statement containing such information as the committees may deem advisable to submit.

(9) The comptroller shall transmit the consolidated tabulation of estimates to the governor by December 15th and to the legislature on the opening day of the session (in January of each year). (State Finance Law, Secs. 48-49, or Chap. 149, Laws of 1910.)

(10) The governor shall annually within one week after the convening of the legislature submit to the Senate and Assembly a statement of the total amount of appropriations desired by each state spending agency, and may at the same time make such suggestions for reductions or additions thereto as he deems proper. As a part of such statement he may also submit an estimate of the probable revenues of the state.

(11) The comptroller shall present to the legislature by February 1st of each year a report of expenditures for the first six months of the current fiscal year. (State Finance Law, Sec. 4, Sub. Sec. 6, or Chap. 118, Laws of 1916.)

(12) The legislative budget committee shall, not later than March 15th, present to their respective houses with the budget a single bill providing the appropriations contained in the budget.

(13) The appropriation bill when reported shall be referred to the committee of the whole of the Senate and advanced to the order of second reading in the Assembly, and shall thus remain five full legislative days, on each of which it shall be the special order of the day. While the bill is being thus considered the head of any spending agency may, and upon request by the majority vote of either house, shall appear and shall be heard and answer questions pertaining to the bill. All meetings of either house for the consideration of the appropriation bill shall be open to the public.

(14) While the appropriation bill is before the committee of the whole of the Senate or on the order of second reading of the House it may be amended by introducing additional items or by increasing, reducing, or eliminating the items; but on third reading no amendment except to reduce or eliminate an item shall be in order except by unanimous consent. When advanced to the order of third reading in either house the appropriation bill shall be a special order of the day for at least three full legislative days.

The Joint Legislative Budget Committee

The joint legislative budget committee is the chief budget-making agency of New York. This committee is formed by union of the Senate finance and the Assembly ways and means committees. In 1919 the Senate finance committee was composed of sixteen members and the Assembly ways and means committee of fifteen members, making a total of thirty-one members. In the Senate committee there were twelve Republicans and three Democrats, giving a total of twenty-four members of the joint committee to the majority party and seven members to the minority party.

Most of the minority members of the joint legislative budget commission were absent from the discussion of the estimates and took no part in the drafting of the appropriation bill. In fact, the majority members gave little attention to the making up of the appropriations, the work being done mainly by the chairmen of the committees and their budget clerks.

Form and Preparation of Estimates

In collecting the data for the 1917 budget, each of the three budget agencies — the comptroller, the governor, and the joint legislative budget committee — used a separate set of estimate forms. The preparation of so many forms, twenty-one in all, created a great deal of confusion among the various state agencies, and the information thus submitted was without uniformity. A set of estimate forms was jointly prepared and agreed upon by the three budget agencies for the preparation of the 1918 budget. These forms have since been used with some slight modifications.

The estimate forms are usually sent out in September. The spending agencies are required to prepare six copies of the estimates and transmit them to the budget agencies — two copies to the governor's budget bureau, three copies to the joint legislative committee, and one copy to the comptroller — not later than October 15th. The majority of the estimates were usually completed and filed promptly with the budget officials. Each year a few of the spending agencies do not submit their requests for appropriations until it is too late to tabulate them in the proper classification of the volume of requests for appropriations as compiled by the joint legislative budget committee and submitted to the legislature. These belated estimates are printed as an appendix to the volume. A number of deficiency estimates are usually filed with the legislative budget committee during the month of January and February and are incorporated in the emergency bills.

Budget Staffs

Both the governor and the joint legislative budget committee have staffs to assist them in their duties. The governor's budget staff was organized by Governor Whitman in 1916 and is composed of a budget secretary, stenographers, and other clerical help. In addition the governor's private secretary usually directs the work. This bureau tabulates the governor's compilation of estimates and makes up his tentative appropriation act. Governor Smith, who came into office January 1, 1919, did not get his bureau organized in time to perform the work that is usually accomplished.

The staff of the legislative budget committee, as provided for under the budget law, consists of two clerks, two accountants, two stenographers, and some additional help. This is a permanent staff and works throughout the year.

Three Compilations of Estimates

The compilation produced by the legislative budget committee is a volume of more than a thousand pages. The compilation of the comptroller is more summary in form and usually about a hundred pages. Until the past year, the governor has had the estimates compiled into a volume which he presented to the legislature on the opening day of the session. This year, however, Governor Smith did not assume the duties of his office in time to direct the preparation of such a volume, but he presented a summary compilation prepared by the comptroller. All three of these compilations are presented at the beginning of the session, a sufficient number of copies being printed to supply one to each member. During the three years that the budget has been in operation, the cost of printing these three compilations of estimates has ranged between five and ten thousand dollars annually. The compilations are of little value for comparison purposes because they do not follow uniform classifications in setting up their information.

Review of Estimates—Hearings

The comptroller does not hold hearings in the review of the estimates. In fact, he only makes very general recommendations and his work is done merely to comply with the 1910 law. Practically the only service of any value which he renders in making up the budget is his estimate of the anticipated revenues of the state. This statement he furnishes to both the governor and the legislative budget committee, besides publishing it in his digest of the estimates.

Each year, hearings on the estimates are conducted by the governor's budget bureau. These hearings usually continue for a month, beginning the latter part of November. The representatives of the various standing agencies of the state are called to appear before the governor's budget staff. In this manner the information contained in the estimates is supplemented and the relative importance of the various requests is determined. Sometimes members of the governor's budget staff go into the field and make examinations. During the past year, however, owing to a change in the administration, very little was done by the governor's budget staff and Governor Smith did not submit any budget recommendations to the legislature. Previously Governor Whitman had made recommendations in the form of a tentative appropriation act, which he presented to the legislature along with his compilation of the estimates and a small document called the governor's budget estimate.

The most effective work of reviewing the estimates was done by the budget staff of the joint appropriation budget committee. During the summer and fall of each year the clerks and the chairman of the Senate finance committee and the chairman of the House ways and means committee visit all the institutions and departments of the state. In this way they gather first hand information as to the needs of the various spending agencies. This information is used to supplement the data contained on the estimates. Beginning in January and continuing until the first week in March, the joint legislative budget committee holds hearings upon the estimates. Besides the representatives of the spending agencies in question, usually only the chairmen of the joint committee and the two clerks are present. These hearings are not public.

It is stated by those in charge that the technical work of budget making — that is, the preparation of a financial plan, which is later submitted to the people for criticism and approval through their representatives in the legislature — can gain nothing by public hearings by the staff or committee — instead, the progress of the work may be greatly impeded.   But under a "legislative budget" plan or a "commission budget" plan there is no other way of giving the semblance of publicity.

The General Appropriation Bill

When the joint legislative budget committee has finished its hearings on the estimates, the clerks of the committee proceed to prepare the general appropriation bill. Following the precedent set by the legislature, and continuing the enlargement on this practice in converting Governor Whitman's "schedules" into items, this bill is highly and rigidly itemized.   The first fifty pages attached to this bill constitute the nearest approach to a budget of any of the documents produced by the three budget agencies.   It is a brief summary of the proposed expenditures in comparison with previous expenditures, together with an attempt to balance the anticipated revenues and proposed expenditures for the period to be financed. The general appropriation bill is required by the budget law to be introduced in the legislature on or before March 15th.   Usually ten days or two weeks elapse after the introduction of the bill before its passage.   While a committee-of-the-whole procedure for the consideration of the bill in the Senate has been provided for, such procedure is rarely ever used, and by its very conditions must prove a dead letter.   Usually the bill passes to third reading before there is any debate upon its contents by either house.   The debate usually lasts little more than an hour in each house and ordinarily is of the most perfunctory character.   The criticisms of the minority are uninformed and ineffective. The newspapers give little space to reporting the discussion on the appropriation bill. When the bill comes to the governor for his approval, the joint legislative committee may have drafted its sections in such a manner that it is impossible for him to exercise his veto should he think it advisable to reduce the appropriations. Furthermore, the legislature always remains in session in order to consider the governor's vetoes in case he does not approve of the bill in its entirety.

Scores of Special Appropriation Bills

No restrictions are placed upon the introduction and passage of special appropriation bills by the New York budget law. Such bills are passed throughout the session; the majority of them, however, are usually passed after the final consideration of the general appropriation bill, or budget so-called. The general appropriation bill usually goes to the governor about the last week in March and the legislature remains in session until about the middle of April. It is during the last week of the session, and even the last day, that the majority of the special appropriation bills are rushed through, and consequently go to the governor as "thirty-day" bills. It is to be noted that the passage of special appropriation bills has increased rather than decreased since the budget law began to operate in 1917. In 1916, thirty-nine such bills were passed and became laws; in 1917, the first year under the budget law, there were eighty-one; in 1918 there were eighty-nine; and in 1919 there were eighty-seven. Each one of these bills was reported, considered, enacted, and signed by the governor separately.

The general, or annual, appropriation bill of 1919 carried only $59,390,811.95 of the $95,538,303 appropriated by the legislature and approved by Governor Smith. The difference between these two amounts, or a total of

$36,147,492.05, was scattered through eighty-seven other appropriation bills. By deducting the amount of the debt service, or $13,341,678.42, from this amount there remains $22,805,713.63 carried by special appropriation bills, most of which were passed during the rush and confusion of the last week of the legislative session.

No Definite Revenue Plan

Since the total amount actually appropriated by the legislature is not known until at least thirty days after the legislature has adjourned, when the governor has acted upon all the " thirty-day " bills, it is impossible for the committees on taxation and retrenchment of the legislature to measure accurately the proposed expenditures and to provide revenues for meeting them. Under the present budgetary procedure, these committees work blindly in their efforts to provide revenue for a budget, the total expenditures of which they can only roughly approximate. For example, an income tax was laid upon the people of the state by the 1919 legislature without knowing, in the first place, what the state would expend for the next fiscal year, and consequently how much additional revenue was needed; and, in the second place, how much revenue such a tax would produce.

Responsibility for Budget Scattered

Under New York's budget procedure the joint legislative budget committee, or, to make it more definite, the chairmen of the finance and ways and means committees and their budget clerks, control the formulation of the budget. Of course they receive budget recommendations from the governor, but they are at liberty to disregard them if they choose, and they usually do so. The only recourse left to the governor is to exercise his constitutional right of veto; but since the legislature manages to pass the more important appropriations a

sufficient length of time before its adjournment to repass
them in case of the governor's disapproval there remain
only the "thirty-day" appropriation bills upon which the
executive veto may be effective.

Both houses pass the budget practically as submitted to
them by the chairmen of the joint legislative budget committee. But the budget is not final, as no one knows
what it will be till the governor gets through with it.

When it comes to the execution of the budget, or the
carrying out of the provisions attached to the appropriations, complete control is centered in the comptroller's
office, which acts on departmental matters independently
of the governor. The budget law prescribes no procedure for the execution of the budget. Provisions that,
in practice, govern this stage of budgetary procedure are
to be found in the state finance law which is evolved out
of the legal regulations applicable to the expenditure of
appropriations during more than a century prior to the
time of the adoption of the budget law. Under the
finance law the comptroller is authorized, among other
things, to "superintend the fiscal concerns of the state,"
to settle accounts, to liquidate claims, to approve all
contracts above $1000, and to receive an invoice of all
supplies and materials furnished to state agencies. His
power is further increased by a section of the general
appropriation acts of the past three years authorizing him
to promulgate definitions of the expense classification by
totals, "defining the purpose for which moneys appropriated under each title may be expended," and giving him
the further power "to amend such definitions from time
to time as in his judgment becomes necessary for the
proper conduct of the fiscal affairs of the state." The
comptroller is elective and the organization of his office
is independent of both the governor and the legislature.

The payment of state obligations is made by the treasurer, who has the custody of the state funds. All his

disbursements, however, are both authorized and audited by the comptroller. Although an elective officer, the treasurer may be suspended by the governor.

In brief, under the financial system of New York State, the budget is both prepared and enacted by the legislature, a body without responsibility for the expenditure of the appropriations and is then reënacted by way of revision downward by the governor. The execution of the budget is placed in the hands of the comptroller, an independent elective officer, who has the power to authorize expenditures and to reclassify appropriations. The governor performs no definite function in the budgetary procedure other than that of revision downward, approval or veto of appropriations.

The New York System Resembles the Present National Plan

The legislative procedure and appropriative practice of New York State bear a striking resemblance to that of the National Government. In its essential features it is a formulation into statute law of standing-committee domination over both the administrative branch and members of the representative deliberative branch of the government. The New York plan is an exemplification in practice of the proposals of Congressmen Fitzgerald of New York and Sherley of Kentucky, who as leaders of their party in Congress, proposed, the one a single standing appropriation committee, the other a super-committee to prepare a budget for the National Government. These were the proposals offered in opposition to President Taft's recommendation. Out of the forty-four other states which have passed budget laws since 1911, only one, Arkansas, has adopted the plan of New York.

CHAPTER XVII

THE OHIO, MARYLAND, AND NEW JERSEY BUDGET PLANS

In Illinois, Wisconsin, and New York are seen the three best American examples of three essentially different kinds of representative government. Illinois, as reorganized in 1917, is a type which seeks to develop an efficient public service and at the same time makes provision for a strong, responsible executive leadership. While it has provided for giving strength to administrative leadership accountable through a representative body devoted to inquest, open discussion, and initial decision, it has not taken the steps necessary to make this accountability reach to the people. Wisconsin has adopted a method which is suited to the development of efficient service, but it has frankly abandoned the principle of representative and electoral control, the legislature having placed the control of the purse in the hands of an oligarchy whose decisions the representative body and the people are asked to accept largely on faith. This has been in defense of the *status quo* as it has come to find expression in the erection of a multitude of boards and commissions — a device adopted to defeat boss rule. New York has incorporated and fortified the irresponsible standing-committee domination under which has grown up the worst features of boss rule, pork-barrel politics, patronage, and spoils.

The new budget plans of Ohio, Maryland, and New Jersey are examples of attempts to put a new and foreign device on a machine to which it is not and cannot be adapted without material and radical change both of structure and fundamental design. An executive budget assumes executive leadership and a means of making this leadership accountable and responsible both for past acts of the whole administrative service and for future proposals. In none of these states was the executive in a position to take leadership; in none of them was there a procedure for holding him to account; in none of them were steps taken to readjust the organism of government with these ends in view. Maryland proceeded by constitutional amendment, Ohio and New Jersey proceeded by change in statute law. The changes were made to satisfy a demand of the people for visible and responsible government. They were majority party measures taken by the leaders to secure or maintain popular support, due care being taken, however, not in any manner to disturb the *status quo*.

OHIO

Disintegrated Administrative System

The Ohio state administration, like that of many other states, is made up of numerous independent officers and agencies. Several of these officers and agencies are constitutional; the majority of them, however, have been created from time to time by the legislature without any conception whatever of a well coördinated administrative plan. The result is a multitude of offices, boards, and commissions over which no responsible or effective authority can be exercised. However, as has already been pointed out, the 1919 legislature authorized the appointment of a joint committee to investigate all administrative agencies of the state with a view to reorganization and consolidation.

The constitution provides that the following officers shall be elected by the people: governor, lieutenant governor, secretary of state, auditor of state, treasurer of state, and attorney general. All these officers serve for a term of two years except the auditor, whose term is four years. In addition to these officers, the constitution provides that there shall be a superintendent of public instruction and a superintendent of public works, each appointed by the governor, the former serving for a term of four years and the latter for one year. Provisions are made in the constitution for the appointment by the governor with the approval of the Senate of a board of trustees for the state institution; also for the establishment of an *ex officio* board composed of the auditor, secretary of state, and attorney general, called the commissioners of the sinking fund.

Ohio has about one hundred statutory administrative officers, boards, commissions, and other agencies. The majority of these are independent of each other. The more important ones, however, are the boards and commissions. They usually consist of from three to ten members, appointed by the governor with the approval of the Senate for overlapping terms varying from three to seven years. Sometimes the membership is entirely *ex officio*, as, for example, the commissioners of public printing and the emergency board. Practically all of the administrative officers, who are appointed by the governor, must have the approval of the Senate, and in nearly every case they serve longer terms than that of the governor.

Limited Power of the Governor

While the governor is given the power to name the department heads and the members of numerous boards and commissions, he must in practically every case secure the approval of the Senate before such appointments become valid. His power of control over such officers is further reduced by the fact that their terms are fixed and are in nearly every case much longer than the two-year term of the governor. Furthermore, such officers may be removed only for cause, and consequently the governor's hands are tied in that he cannot impress executive leadership on the departments.

The governor is required by statute to present a budget to the legislature, but he has no power to put his recommendation into the form of an appropriation bill for the consideration of the legislature. He is given the power of vetoing items in appropriation bills even after the legislature has adjourned, but he is not given the power of setting any limit above which his budget recommendations cannot be raised by the legislature.

Organization and Procedure of the Legislature

The constitution requires the state legislature to meet on the first Monday of January in the odd-numbered years. It also provides that the legislature shall be organized on the bicameral plan, having a House of Representatives composed at present of 128 members and a Senate of thirty-six members. Each house has forty-one standing committees and two joint committees. In the Senate the committees are elected by the members and in the House they are appointed by the Speaker. The lieutenant governor is the presiding officer of the Senate, and the Speaker chosen by the House is the presiding officer of that body. The power of confirming appointments is vested in the Senate.

In the matter of handling appropriation measures, it is customary for the general appropriation bill to be introduced in the House; however, other appropriation bills are introduced in the Senate as frequently as in the House. The general appropriation bill is usually drafted in committee and is brought forth and introduced at the discretion of the committee. In general the procedure of the Ohio legislature in passing money bills does not differ from its procedure in passing other bills. The budget law makes no provisions for legislative procedure, hence practically the same procedure is followed at the present time as was practiced before the passage of the budget law in 1913. The appropriation committees of the two houses continue to work separately. As a result the houses frequently disagree on the contents of appropriation bills and have to resort to conference committees as a means of adjustment.

Provisions of the Budget Law

In 1913 Ohio adopted a budget system which displaced the compilation of departmental estimates by the auditor of the state and made the governor the chief budget officer with authority to appoint competent assistants to serve under his direction and control. The procedure laid down by this law (S.B. No. 127, Laws of 1913) is as follows:

1. The governor is required to furnish blanks on which the various chief officers of the government shall present requests for appropriation.

2. Every spending agency is required to prepare estimates and submit them on or before November 15th in the even years.

3. The auditor is required to submit a report to the governor on or before November 15th in the even years, showing: (*a*) Balance to the credit of the several spending agencies at the end of the last fiscal year; (*b*) monthly revenues and expenditures from each appropriation account in the twelve months of the last fiscal year; (*c*) annual revenues and expenditures for each of the last fiscal years; (*d*) monthly average of expenditures from each of the several appropriation accounts for the last fiscal year.

4. The governor is authorized, through his assistants, (budget commissioner and staff) to examine without no-

tice the affairs of any branch of the state government and to call witnesses and require the production of books and papers and to present findings and recommendations relative to the promotion of economy and efficiency.

5. The governor is required to submit to the General Assembly at the beginning of each regular session his budget of current expenses of the state for the ensuing biennium, together with the estimates of the several branches of the state government.

The Budget Commissioner and Staff

The first budget document prepared under the Ohio budget law was produced in 1913 and was the basis for an appropriation bill covering the fiscal year from February 16th, 1914, to February 14, 1915. At the next session (1915) of the legislature the fiscal year was changed to begin on July 1st and the budget was prepared covering the biennium following that date. Since then two budgets have been prepared.

The provisions of the budget law would suggest a board of examiners with certain auditing functions, rather than a single officer or budget commissioner, with special power to compile the estimates and to produce the budget. However, immediately following the passage of the law, the governor determined upon the appointment of a budget commissioner with a staff under his control. Since 1913 there have been four budget commissioners. The present commissioner was appointed by Governor Cox in 1919. His staff consists of an assistant budget commissioner, one secretary, and a stenographer during the period of the budget preparation. The budget commissioner receives a salary of $4000 per year. The assistant budget commissioner receives a salary of $1800 a year. The commissioner as well as the assistant commissioner, are appointees of the governor and are exempt from civil service regulation.

Filing and Review of Estimates

The estimate forms are prepared by the budget commissioner and are usually sent out about August 1st of the even-numbered years. The forms are printed on heavy calendar paper and are somewhat unwieldy in size. Under the budget law the estimates are required to be filed by November 15th; however, the spending agencies usually begin returning them in October and continue until the latter part of November. The state auditor is required to furnish the budget commissioner with a statement of the anticipated revenues of the state, which he usually produces about November 15th.

Beginning in August and continuing until the latter part of November, the budget commissioner and his assistant visit the various institutions and departments of the state for the purpose of investigating their equipment, facilities, and general needs. During November and December the budget commissioner holds informal conferences with the heads and superior officers of the several departments and institutions requesting appropriations from the state. These conferences are in the nature of hearings but are not public. In fact the commissioner states that he is inclined to discourage publicity at this time. It is only when one of the institutions decides to make its demands public that any information concerning the estimates gets into the newspapers. As a rule the governor is never present at these conferences or hearings before the budget commissioner. However, in case a dispute arises between the commissioner and a spending agency, the governor may take the matter up and settle it so far as the budget to be submitted is concerned.

Upon the basis of the data gathered by visits and conferences and the information furnished by the estimates, the budget commissioner makes up tentative recommendations for appropriations which he presents to the governor for his approval.   In making up these recommendations, the commissioner does not attempt to balance the proposed expenditures with the anticipated revenues.   For example, in the budget submitted to the 1919 legislature, the recommendations for appropriations far exceed the estimated revenues of the state.

Budget Commissioner Prepares Budget Document

While the law requires the budget to be presented to the legislature at the opening of the regular sessions, it was not submitted until March 1st, in 1919.   The legislature had been in session for about two months before the commissioner succeeded in getting the document printed and puting it into the hands of the members of each house of the legislature.   This tardiness in its presentation to the legislature greatly reduced the usefulness of the document, since the information contained in the budget was not available to the members of the legislature and to the public until the financial program of the appropriation committees had begun to assume definite shape. There were also similar delays in the presentation of the budget document to the legislature during the 1915 and 1917 sessions of the legislature.   When submitted, the budget is in practice referred to the appropriation or finance committees of the two houses.   Very little attention is given to the budget document by the members of the legislature, inasmuch as they have learned to look to the appropriation committees and not to the governor for the definite appropriation proposals.

In practice the governor relies almost wholly upon the commissioner's judgment as to budget recommendations. The recommendations contained in the budget, as presented to the legislature, are therefore largely the recommendations of the budget commissioner.   The budget document contains a summary statement of actual and estimated revenues for the biennium to be financed and for the four years prior thereto. It also contains a summary of the expenditures for the same period. No new sources of revenue are suggested in case a deficit is shown between the proposed expenditures and the anticipated revenues for the biennium, as was the case in the budget prepared for 1919-1921. The budget, as presented to the legislature of 1919, showed a deficit for the biennium of more than three and a half million dollars. It contains a graphic presentation of the revenues and of the expenditures for the fiscal year just ended. Most of the document is taken up with an abbreviated transcription of the estimate sheet, showing the amounts requested, the recommendations and the decreases. The estimates of each organization unit are printed separately for each year of the biennium, when they might easily be combined and reduce the size of the budget document by practically half.

The Appropriation Committees and Their Work

The Senate finance committee is composed of twelve members, eight of whom for the 1919 session were Republicans and four were Democrats. The House appropriation and finance committee, consisting of fifteen members, was made up of ten Republicans and five Democrats. It is stated that the Democratic members of the two committees were rarely ever present at the hearings conducted by the committees and took little part in the appropriation procedure. The result was that the minority was unable to offer any effective criticism or constructive suggestions at the passage of the general appropriation bill.

It is the custom for the appropriation committee of the House to lead in the procedure for handling the general appropriation bill. However, the Senate appropriation committee never coöperates or works jointly with the

House committee.   All hearings, sessions, and junkets
of the committees are conducted separately.   This results
in a duplication of work between the two committees,
as well as a repetition of most of the work done by the
budget commissioner and his staff.

During February and March the appropriation committees of each house conducted hearings on the estimates
independently of each other.   It is stated that about
seventy-five hearings were held by each committee.
These hearings were always held behind closed doors,
only the members of the committee, the budget commissioner or his assistant, and the representatives of the
spending agency in question being present.   Immediately
upon the conclusion of each hearing the committee decided
upon the amount of the several items of appropriation
to be allowed the spending agency, and the budget commissioner, or his assistant, recorded the recommendations
of the committee on the estimate sheets or in a copy of
of the budget.   During the 1919 session of the legislature
the budget commissioner worked principally with the
Senate finance committee, while his assistant worked with
the House appropriation committee.

During about two months of the 1919 legislative
session, the appropriation committee of each house spent
its week-ends from Friday until Monday visiting the
institutions of the state.   The committees never made
joint visits to the institutions.   It is the usual procedure
for each committee to make a round of the state institutions every legislative session.   So far as could be learned,
the information which is gathered as a result of these
visits is superficial and adds little to the data already in
the office of the budget commissioner.

The staff of the budget commissioner, it is stated, does
practically all of the work in connection with the drafting
of the general appropriation bill.   The staff also does
the proof reading and comparison in connection with the

printing of the bill. This coöperation increases to some degree the influence of the budget commissioner's judgment over the recommendations for appropriations as made by the appropriation committees.

Legislative Handling of General Appropriation Bill

The general appropriation bill for the biennium, 1919-21, following the usual procedure, was first introduced into the House. This was on May 5, 1919. The bill had its first and second readings, was ordered engrossed and placed on the calendar on the same date. On May 9th the bill was printed and laid on the desk of each member of the House, and three or four hours later went to a third reading and was passed with practically no discussion. On the same day, May 9th, it was sent to the Senate, where it immediately went to a second reading and was referred to the finance committee of the Senate. This committee had already framed up a set of proposed amendments, and on May 10th the bill was reported out with these amendments. It immediately went to a third reading as amended and was sent to the Senate. When the bill was returned to the house for concurrence in the Senate amendments, the House refused to concur and upon request of the Senate a conference committee was appointed consisting of three members from the appropriation committee of each house. The conference committee spent its time from May 10th to May 28th modifying the proposed amendments and agreeing upon new amendments. On the latter date the bill was reported with amendments to the Senate and was accepted. On the same day the report of the conference committee was adopted by the House.

Immediately upon its passage by the legislature the general appropriation bill went to Governor Cox, who refused to sign it because of the numerous changes which had been made in it by the conference committee. Since the legislature continued in session the bill became a law in ten days without the governor's signature. The governor's veto messages on appropriation bills are usually prepared by the budget commissioner.

Prior to 1919, the general appropriation bill has usually been acted upon the last week or even the last day of the legislative session. The present year, however, the legislature refused to adjourn. In order to thwart the desires of the governor, it decided to recess from time to time with the intention of meeting again in December.

As a result of the numerous changes made by the House committee, the Senate committee, and the conference committee, the governor's recommendations for appropriations for the biennium were decreased between two and three million dollars. Most of the changes were made in the personal service schedules. About half a million dollars was added to the governor's recommendations for permanent improvements.

Such provisions as were made for additional revenue were framed without reference to the total amount that had been appropriated by the legislature. In fact, the total amount of appropriations could not be ascertained until the governor had finally acted upon all the appropriation measures passed by the legislature.

Numerous Special Appropriation Bills Passed

More than fifty bills carrying special appropriations, other than those included in the general appropriation bill, were introduced in the legislature during the 1919 session and more than a dozen of these bills passed and became laws. The total appropriated by these special bills is not known at the time of this writing. Some of the bills were enacted early in the session, even before the governor's budget had been received by the legislature. One such measure was a deficiency appropriation bill amounting to several million dollars.

Using the report of the sundry claims board as a basis, a sundry appropriation bill was prepared and introduced in the legislature following the enactment of the general appropriation bill. The two houses of the legislature, however, failed to agree upon the appropriations included in this bill and as a result it was not acted upon before the legislature recessed to meet again in December, when it was taken up and passed after considerable wrangling between the two houses. For the past two or three regular sessions of the legislature, the sundry claims bill has been the cause of a deadlock in the legislature.

Provisions for Transfers and Emergencies

In order to provide for some flexibility in the expenditure of appropriations, section four of the general appropriation act constitutes a controlling board, consisting of the governor or the budget commissioner (in practice always the budget commissioner), the chairmen of the two appropriation committees, the attorney general, and state auditor. This board is empowered to authorize transfers within the appropriation accounts of any organization unit upon application.

An emergency board, created by statute, consisting of the governor, auditor, attorney general, and chairmen of the finance committees of the legislature, is empowered to authorize the expenditure of money for emergency purposes, which has not already been appropriated by the legislature.

Under a law passed in 1917 (Vol. 107, p. 639) the budget commissioner is authorized to receive statements from the spending agencies of proposed expenditures preceding the month in which such expenditures are to be made. These statements, when approved by the commissioner, permit expenditures to be made from the authorized appropriations. This is one of the most effective provisions of the law, since by this means, in a well-organized administration, the commissioner would be able to veto a part of an appropriation item and it would permit the governor, through the commissioner, to be effective in the supervision of departmental expenditures. But because of lack of authority of the governor over the department heads and lack of coöperation on the part of the state auditor this plan does not seem to work very effectively.

Governor Cox Condemns Present Budget Procedure

In his message to the 1919 legislature, Governor Cox stated that the budget procedure of Ohio was ineffective as a means of checking the injudicious appropriation of money by the legislature. He asserted that the executive proposals for the appropriations had always been increased rather than decreased by action of the legislature. He recommended that provisions for a budget system should be written into the constitution, which would set limitations upon the power of the legislature to increase the governor's proposals or to enact special and supplementary appropriations, similar to those of the Maryland budget amendment. A joint resolution (H.J.R.No.62) was introduced into the 1919 legislature, proposing an amendment to the constitution and providing for the adoption of a budget system. Its provisions were in accord with the recommendations of Governor Cox, but it failed of any consideration on the part of the legislature.

The Ohio System Fails to Fix Responsibility or to Provide Publicity

The governor's budget recommendations, or rather those of the budget commissioner, are usually mutilated beyond recognition in their passage through the legislative committees. As a result, no one knows whose judgment the appropriation act represents; the governor cannot be charged with responsibility — responsibility is dissipated.   During the recent legislative session the governor and the legislature were at loggerheads most of the time, the result being that the legislature practically had its way in financial matters.

Under the present procedure the financial program, indefinite as it is, gets practically no consideration by the legislature as a whole.   The consideration is by committees behind closed doors.   Furthermore, these committees do not work jointly.   This results in frequent disagreements, whereupon resort is made to conference committees for adjustment.

The advantages of executive control over the budget are destroyed when the legislature is permitted promiscuously to pass supplementary appropriation bills, as under the Ohio procedure.   A number of such bills are passed every session of the legislature.

In brief, the budgetary procedure of Ohio fails in the first place to establish definite executive responsibility, and in the second place to provide publicity in the legislative action on money measures.

MARYLAND

Scattered and Uncontrolled Administrative Agencies

The administrative branch of the state government of Maryland includes about eighty separate offices, departments, commissions, and other agencies, most of which are independent of one another and subject to no direct and effective control by the governor.   While the governor has in several instances the power of appointment and removal, most of his important appointments are made with the approval of the Senate which thus shares with him the conduct of the administration.   Several of the constitutional officers, as well as many of the officers created by statute, are not even brought under this nominal executive control.

There are nine administrative officers or agencies provided for in the constitution; namely, governor, secretary of state, attorney general, comptroller, treasurer, state librarian, commissioner of the land office, adjutant general, and board of public works. The governor and attorney general are each elected for a term of four years. The comptroller is elected for a two-year term, and the treasurer is appointed by the two houses of the legislature for a like term. The secretary of state, the state librarian, and the commissioner of the land office are appointed by the governor with the approval of the Senate for terms equal to that of the governor. The governor appoints, with the approval of the Senate, the adjutant general. The board of public works is composed of the governor, the comptroller, and the treasurer acting in an *ex officio* capacity.

The board type seems to predominate among the statutory administrative agencies of Maryland. Usually the members of the boards are appointed for overlapping terms longer than that of the governor. In some cases these boards are made up entirely of appointive members, and in other cases of both appointive and *ex officio* members. A few examples may be pointed out. The public service commission, the state tax commission, and the state industrial accident commission are each composed of three members which are appointed by the governor for overlapping terms of six years. The state board of prison control, having charge of the penal institutions of the state, consists of three members appointed by the governor with the approval of the Senate for overlapping terms of six years. The three members of the conservation commission are appointed by the governor for overlapping terms of four years. The motion-pictures censors, consisting of three persons, are appointed by the governor, with the approval of the Senate for overlapping terms of three years. The governor appoints six members, composing the board of state aid and charities, each having an overlapping term of four years. The state board of health consists of the attorney general, health commissioner of Baltimore, and four persons appointed by the governor, with the approval of the Senate. The state lunacy commission is made up of the attorney general and four members appointed by the governor for overlapping terms of four years. The state board of forestry consists of the governor, comptroller, president of Johns Hopkins University, president of Maryland Agricultural College, state geologist, and two members appointed by the governor for a term of two years.

The statutory administrative officers are appointed in some instances by the governor, in others by the governor with the approval of the Senate, and in others by the board of public works. The superintendent of public buildings and grounds is appointed by the governor. The board of public works appoints the state auditor, the bank commissioner, and the insurance commissioner — the first two for terms of two years each and the last for a term of four years.

Maryland has approximately 120 independent agencies, such as institutions, associations, and societies, receiving appropriations from the state. These appropriations range from $500 to $75,000 and aggregate an annual expenditure of approximately $850,000, or nearly one-fourth of the general funds annually available in the state treasury.

Governor Without Assistance to Prepare or Power to Execute the Budget

Under the present disintegrated organization of the Maryland state administration the governor has no cabinet assistance in the formulation of his financial program, and lacks the full control necessary to enforce coöperation in the expenditure of appropriations. The budget amendment seeks to bring the numerous and widely scattered administrative agencies under the control of the governor by compelling them to submit to him estimates of their needs, and by authorizing him to recommend to the legislature the maximum amounts which they may expend. While this may be effective as a means of preventing a deficit in the state treasury, it does not seem likely that it will secure coördination of work and coöperation of administration.

Furthermore, the governor is not provided with any permanent staff assistance in the preparation of his budget. He must rely almost wholly upon independent administrative officers and agencies to gather the budget data. He has no department or staff working directly under him, which is continuously engaged in gathering the information upon which he may base his budget recommendations to the legislature.

Budget Amendment and Its Provisions

The uncontrolled action of the Maryland legislature in the passage of appropriation measures had created by 1915 a deficit in the state funds of more than one million dollars. This aroused the people of the state to the need for an effective budget system. In the campaign of 1915 budget planks appeared in the platforms of the two leading parties — the Democratic party pledging itself to the appointment of a commission to prepare a report with definite budget recommendations. Upon the election of Governor Harrington a citizen commission was appointed, with Dr. Frank J. Goodnow (former member of President Taft's commission on economy and efficiency) as chairman. This commission made a report, with a proposed constitutional amendment to establish an executive budget system, which was laid before the legislature in 1916. The amendment was approved by the legislature after the defeat of a proposal to substitute for the governor the board of public works (consisting of the governor, the comptroller, and the state treasurer, the last being elected by the legislature.) It was ratified by the voters November 7th. 1916, and became section fifty-two of article three of the constitution.

The following is a summary of the provisions of the amendment:

1. Estimates are required to be made by all spending agencies and submitted to the governor at such time and in such form as he may prescribe. The estimates of the legislature are certified by the presiding officer of each house and those of judiciary by the comptroller.

2. The governor may review by public hearings all estimates and may revise all estimates, except those of the legislative and judiciary departments and those relating to public schools.

3. The governor is required to prepare two budgets, one for each of the ensuing fiscal years.

4. Each budget must be divided into two parts: I. " Governmental appropriations " for (1) General Assembly, (2) executive department, (3) judiciary department, (4) to pay and discharge principal and interest of state debt, (5) salaries payable by state under constitution and laws, (6) public schools, (7) other purposes set forth in constitution. II. " General appropriations," including all other estimates.

5. Each budget is required to contain a complete plan of proposed expenditures and estimated revenues, and to set forth the estimated surplus or deficit of revenues. An accompanying statement must show: (1) Revenues and expenditures for each of two fiscal years next preceding, (2) balance sheet, (3) debts and funds, (4) estimate of state's financial condition at the ends of the fiscal years covered by budgets, (5) explanations by the governor.

6. The governor is required to deliver the budgets and a bill of proposed appropriations, clearly itemized and classified, to the presiding officer of each house within twenty days (if newly elected, thirty days) after the convening of the legislature.

7. The budget bill, or appropriation bill, must be introduced into each house immediately upon its receipt by the presiding officer. The governor may amend or supplement the bill while in the legislature.

8. The governor and administrative officers designated by him have the right, and when requested by the legislature are required, to appear before the legislature to defend the budget bill.

9. The legislature may not amend the budget bill to change the public school funds, or salaries and obligations required by the constitution; it may increase or decrease items relating to the general assembly, or increase those relating to the judiciary, but can only reduce or strike out others.

10. The legislature may not consider other appropriations until the budget bill has been finally acted upon.

11. If the budget bill is not enacted three days before the expiration of the regular session, the governor may by proclamation extend the session.

12. The budget bill becomes law upon passage by the legislature without signature of governor.

13. Every supplementary appropriation (1) must be embodied in a separate bill, limited to a single purpose, (2) must provide the revenues necessary to pay the appropriation by a tax, direct or indirect, to be laid and collected as directed in the bill, (3) must receive the majority vote of the elected members of each house, (4) must be presented to the governor and be subject to his veto.

Form, Preparation and Filing of Estimates

The actual work of preparing the first Maryland state budget was begun in November, 1917. The estimate forms were prepared by the department of legislative reference and approved by the governor. The budget classification, as adopted, followed objects of expenditures; namely, (1) salaries and wages, (2) expenses — maintenance other than personal service, (3) purchase of land, (4) buildings, (5) equipment, and (6) new construction. The amounts appropriated and expended for the fiscal year just ended, also the amounts appropriated for the current fiscal year, were required to be given in detail upon the estimates. The appropriations for each of the fiscal years of the next biennium were required to be clearly itemized. A few of the spending agencies at first hesitated to make itemization, since they had been so long accustomed to request lump-sum appropriations from the legislature. Each estimate sheet provided space for the governor's allowance and necessary explanatory remarks.

The estimates were required to be filed with the governor by December 10th, but many of the spending agencies were late in filing their requests, owing to the novelty of the system and to insufficient and inadequate data at hand for preparing their estimates. Many of the estimates were incorrect when submitted and had to be returned and made up the second time. Had the forms been prepared and sent out earlier, the estimates might easily have been submitted to the governor a month before they were, since the fiscal year of Maryland ends on September 30th. This would have allowed the spending agencies a month's time after the close of the fiscal year for the preparation of their estimates, and at the same time would have given the governor more time, which proved to be much needed, for review of the estimates and preparation of the budget.

Public Hearings and Revision of Estimates

Early in December Governor Harrington secured the services of a budget specialist from the New York Bureau of Municipal Research, who, with the assistance of the executive office force, compiled the estimates and other data for the budget and drafted the budget bill.   About the middle of December the governor began to hold public hearings upon the estimates and continued almost daily until the end of the month, in which time he had heard more than eighty of the state's spending agencies.   He required a number of agencies to appear before him; to others he granted hearings upon request.

After the hearings were concluded, the governor set to work to review all the estimates and make his allowance for the budget.   The total of the requests for appropriations far exceeded the total estimated revenues as calculated by the state comptroller.   In order to make the expenditures of the first state budget commensurate with the anticipated revenues, the governor asked the administrative heads of the large departments and institutions to collaborate with him in the revision of the estimates. Acting upon the governor's advice, they reduced their estimates at those points where they judged reductions would least hamper the normal growth of their work. The governor, under the provision of the budget amendment, included the legislative, judicial, and educational estimates in the budget without revision; but he had, nevertheless, been consulted as to their probable totals while they were in preparation and reserved to himself the right to make suggestions with regard to the amounts requested.

Budget Submitted to Legislature

Governor Harrington was unable to deliver his budget to the legislature within the time limit fixed in the budget amendment (twenty days after the convening of the legislature, which met on January 2d), owing to delay in printing the budget and to other contingent circumstances. The legislature, however, agreed to extend the time one week, and on January 29th the governor transmitted his budget and budget bill in printed form to the presiding officer of each house. At the same time each member of the legislature was supplied with a copy of the budget. The budget was immediately introduced by both the president of the Senate and the speaker of the House in their respective houses.

Form and Content of Budget

The general form of the budget is prescribed in the amendment. As actually made up, it contained in consecutive order the following statements and data:

1. The actual and estimated revenues and expenditures for the fiscal years of 1917 and 1918, showing the balance at the end of each fiscal period.

2. A balance sheet of the current assets and liabilities of the state.

3. A statement of the condition of state debt and sinking funds.

4. A statement of the estimated revenues for the period to be financed, *i.e.*, the fiscal years of 1919 and 1920.

5. A general summary to the financial requirements and estimates of the state's financial condition at the end of each of the years to be financed.

6. A statement from the governor relative to a possible decrease of the state tax rates.

7. A general summary of all the estimates for appropriations.

8. A complete and itemized tabulation of all estimates with the governor's allowances.

An appendix to the budget contained certain important statistics relating to the expenditures, receipts, per capita cost, etc., of more than one hundred institutions and agencies receiving state aid.

The estimates were classified in the budget by organization units, and, according to the provisions of the budget amendment, were grouped under two heads: I, " Governmental appropriations," and II, " General appropriations." Included under Part I were the legislative, executive, and judiciary departments, the various state departments, boards and commissions, the public schools, and the public debt. Under Part II were grouped the remaining estimates, namely: those of state institutions, state-aided institutions, and for miscellaneous purposes.

Form and Provisions of Budget Bill

The appropriations carried in the budget bill were arranged by organization units, following the arrangement in the budget. The appropriations to the various organization units were made in lump sums for salaries and wages and for expenses with itemized schedules following each sum so appropriated whenever more than one item was included. These schedules " represent the initial plan of distribution and apportionment of the appropriations." Each lump-sum appropriation must be paid out in accordance with the schedule which relates to it, unless and until such schedule is amended. In order to give flexibility to the expenditure of the appropriations and to provide, at the same time, for executive control over spending agencies, the governor is empowered to authorize transfers between items within any schedule, thus amending the schedule. Whenever a schedule is amended by the governor it must be transmitted with his approval to the comptroller, who thereafter is required to pay out the appropriation, or whatever balance may remain, in accordance with the amended schedule. All transfers and changes in the schedules of the original budget bill made by the governor must be reported by him to the next session of the legislature.

Standing Committee Consideration of Budget Unsatisfactory

While the budget amendment places certain definite limitations upon the action of the legislature when considering the budget, it prescribes no definite procedure. The budget and budget bill, as has been stated, were submitted simultaneously in each house of the legislature on January 29th, and were immediately referred to the finance committee of the Senate and to the ways and means committee of the House. The governor did not make any oral statement to the legislature at the time of presenting the budget. It is stated that neither committee, especially the House committee, gave sufficient time to the consideration of the budget to act upon it properly and intelligently. The work that had taken the governor three months for preparation, after an intimate acquaintance of four years with the state's business, the ways and means committee passed upon in practically two or three sittings, each of very short duration. The Senate committee, however, considered the budget somewhat more seriously. No public hearings were held by either committee on the budget bill, since it was not necessary, as formerly, for the spending agencies to appear before the committee urging their requests for appropriations. The only matter that now concerned the state agencies was to see that the allowances made to them by the governor were not reduced or eliminated by the action of the committees or the legislature. The Senate finance committee, however, found occasion to call before it a few of the department heads, for the purpose of explaining some of the budget allowances, and in one or two instances the committee desired to find out if subordinates gave full time to state work.   The governor also explained to the finance committee certain of the appropriations.

Legislative Action on the Budget Bill

On March 20th, the governor submitted to the Senate his first supplemental budget, which, under the provisions ·of the budget amendment, became part of the budget bill as amendments or supplements to the appropriations and items contained in it.   On March 22d the finance committee reported the budget bill and supplement favorably to the Senate.   A motion to defer action on the bill was voted down, and the committee's favorable report was adopted.   Immediately the president of the Senate submitted a second supplement to the budget by the governor, who asked that it might also be made a part of the budget bill.   Upon a motion the additional supplement was accepted.   The budget bill was then read the second time and ordered to be printed after a third reading.   It passed the Senate without amendment on March 26th, and was sent to the House, where it had its first reading on March 27th.   It was reported out of the House committee on March 28th and read a second time.   Among the several amendments proposed in the House, two were adopted, one eliminating the salary of the assistant chairman of the roads commission, amounting to $2,000 (the governor having reduced it from $3,000 by his first supplemental budget), and the other striking out an appropriation for the director of farm products amounting to $12,000.   The elimination of the latter item would have followed as a matter of course, since the bill creating the office had been defeated in the legislature, so that only $2,000 was really eliminated from the governor's budget for each of the two years.   When this amount is compared with the total budget of each year, aggregating about $12,000,000, the House, although the majority was politically opposed to the governor, may nevertheless be regarded as approving the governor's budget practically as he submitted it. The rules of the House were suspended and the budget bill was passed the same day it was amended.   The Senate, being of the same political faith as the governor, refused to accede to the amendments of the House, and a conference committee was appointed.   The first conference committee disagreed and another was appointed; this committee made its report on March 30th, when the Senate concurred in the amendments of the House and finally passed the budget bill as thus amended.   Since the governor had the assurance that the budget bill would be passed within three legislative days before the end of the session (April 1st), he did not issue a proclamation extending the session, as provided for in the budget amendment.

No Supplementary Appropriation Bills Enacted

During the 1916 session of the legislature between thirty-five and forty bills, appropriating money out of the state treasury, were enacted into law.   The legislature of 1918, acting under the provisions of the budget amendment, passed only seven bills making appropriations out of the state treasury, two of which were duplicates of two others and were for that reason vetoed by the governor.   Another was also vetoed, and still another was reduced by half.   The four bills approved by the governor carried appropriations totaling $19,000.   The seven appropriation bills which were passed by the legislature appropriated unexpended funds then in the state treasury and, upon a ruling of the attorney general, were not in conflict with the budget amendment which requires such bills to make provisions for their own revenue, since the budget bill which was passed in compliance with the budget amendment did not go into effect until October 1, 1918.   There was not, therefore, a single supplementary appropriation bill passed for the fiscal years 1919 and 1920.

The Serious Weaknesses of the Maryland System

The serious weaknesses of the Maryland budget system seem to be the unfortunate position of the governor with respect to the administrative departments and the lack of adequate procedure for legislative consideration of the budget. There was little review and criticism of the governor's financial program. Most of the review work was done by the two committees, which worked separately and did not coöperate at any time because of political hostility. The intent of the budget amendment seems to be that more consideration should be given to the budget upon the floors of the legislature than it actually received in 1918. While it is true that every member of the legislature was supplied with a copy of the governor's budget, and knew at once from the printed journal of each house just what supplements the governor had made, still it is not probable that many of the members scrutinized the budget very closely. Practically no attention was given by the legislature to the subject of revenues.

The fact cannot be too much emphasized that the governor of Maryland is not free and unhampered in making his budget recommendations to the legislature, since authority and responsibility for a large part of the executive and administrative acts are not centered in him. As has already been pointed out, there are several administrative agencies of the state which are independent of the governor by reason of the methods by which they obtain office, some being elective and others being appointive by the legislature. Furthermore, there are entirely too many separate administrative agencies for the governor to keep a close watch upon all expenditures without the interposition of coördinating heads responsible to the governor and an executive staff for the current review and revision of requisitions for funds under a system of executive control which would bring matters of administrative policy to the executive attention, before it was too late to correct abuses or misuses of discretion. The consolidation of the administrative agencies of Maryland into a few integrated departments directly under the governor is needed in order to fix executive responsibility before an executive budget can be made an effective part of the government.

NEW JERSEY

A Short Ballot Which Does Not Centralize Executive Responsibility

Although New Jersey has a short ballot, the governor being the only elective administrative officer (term, three years), responsibility for administration is not centered in the chief executive because of the numerous independent administrative officers, boards, and agencies over which the governor exercises only nominal control.

Beginning in 1915, the legislature enacted several laws providing for the consolidation into integrated departments of a number of independent administrative agencies. The 1915 legislature, following the recommendations of the economy and efficiency commission of 1912, enacted laws establishing the departments of conservation and development, commerce and navigation, taxes and assessments, and shell fisheries. The 1916 legislature provided for the reorganization of the departments of labor and agriculture. More than twenty separate departments, bureaus, and agencies were merged into these six consolidated departments. The 1918 legislature enacted a law creating a department of charities and corrections, which exercises control over the charitable, correctional, reformatory, and penal institutions of the state. All of these departments, except the department of labor, are administered by boards, the members of which are appointed by the governor, with the approval of the Senate, for overlapping terms, in most cases very much longer than the term of the governor.   For example, the state board of charities and corrections is composed of eight members appointed for overlapping terms of eight years, the governor being an *ex officio* member of the board. The commissioner, or chief executive officer, is appointed by this board and serves at its pleasure.

Even under the partial consolidation which has been effected more than fifty independent administrative officers and agencies still remain. A few of these, notably the state treasurer and state comptroller, are appointed by the two houses of the legislature in joint session.   The majority, however, are appointed by the governor with the advice and consent of the Senate.   A few minor officers and boards are appointed by the governor without let or hindrance.   Hence it may be seen that the legislature, particularly the Senate, shares with the governor the responsibility of administration.

In financial administration and budget making the governor does not act alone.   Such matters come before an *ex officio* board — the state house commission, composed of the governor, the state comptroller, and the state treasurer (the last two being appointed by the legislature).   This commission exercises control over the various funds of the state, such as the revolving and supplemental fund. It also has control over the transfer of items within the appropriations granted to organization units by the legislature.   The budget recommendations of the governor to the legislature are in reality the recommendations of this board and the two budget assistants.

The Edge Budget Law — Its Provisions

As early as 1895 the New Jersey legislature took steps to improve its appropriation procedure by providing that no money should be paid out of the state treasury unless appropriated by the annual appropriation act, but the initiative was allowed to remain with the joint appropriation committee. In 1907 and 1914, measures were enacted which were designed to give the comptroller better control over the receipts and disbursements of the state. However, in 1915, the comptroller made a recommendation in favor of the establishment of a budget board. At the 1916 session of the legislature a bill was introduced to create a state board of estimate to consist of the governor as chairman, the comptroller as secretary, the state treasurer, and two members to be appointed by the governor for overlapping terms of six years. The weight of opinion in the legislature, however, favored placing upon the governor the responsibility for the formulation of a financial plan to be submitted to the legislature. Support was therefore given to another bill, sponsored by Senator Edge, which became a law. This law, Chap. 15, Laws of 1916, provides for the following procedure:

1. The estimates are prepared by all spending agencies on prescribed blanks, giving itemized requests and trial balance, and presented to the governor on October 15th. (As amended by Chaps. 221 and 144, Laws of 1918.)

2. Rules 1–8 appended to law, contain a budget classification and prescribe the form of the estimate sheets in detail.

3. Each estimate must be sworn to by the administrative head or other designated officer of spending agency making same.

4. The estimated revenues are furnished the governor by the comptroller and treasurer jointly.

5. The governor must review all estimates and determine the necessity of appropriations. He may conduct hearings, summon witnesses, and make investigations. For this purpose he is allowed to name two special assistants and to call upon administrative officers.

6. The governor is required to prepare a summary of the estimates and make recommendations thereon, the total of which must not exceed the anticipated revenues of the state.

7. The budget must be in the form of a separate message to the legislature, containing a summary of the estimates and reports with recommendations thereon. The mandate of the law is that the budget must be in a form to be easily understood.

8. The governor is required to submit his budget to the legislature on the second Tuesday of January.

9. The law prescribes that the budget shall be given such publicity as is deemed wise.

10. The governor may transmit special messages to the legislature requesting additional appropriations after the budget has been submitted.

11. It is the evident intent of the budget law that there shall be no supplemental, deficiency, or incidental bills.

12. No money may be drawn from the state treasury except by the general appropriation act.

13. Transfers within the appropriation of any organization unit may be secured by application to the state house commission, composed of the governor, comptroller, and treasurer. (As amended by Chap. 290, Laws of 1918.)

14. The governor has the power to investigate the revenues and income of spending agencies, which are not derived directly from the state treasury.

Form and Preparation of Estimates

The estimate blanks employed in preparation of the first budget (1917) were modeled directly after the forms suggested in the rules appended to the budget law. These blanks were found in practice to be indefinite and confusing in their classification; they did not provide for the reporting of sufficient information, and they did not attempt to coördinate the budget with the work of the civil service commission and the central purchasing office.   In the preparation of the budgets for 1918 and 1919 the estimate blanks previously used were supplemented by other forms calling for a detailed estimate of farm, shop, and industrial activities, a complete summary of requests for appropriations to accompany the estimates of schools, and a similar summary to accompany the estimates of institutions.   The institutions were required to give their per capita cost for each division of budget classification. The budget classification is prescribed in the law as follows: (1) maintenance (other than salaries); (2) salaries; (3) repairs and replacements; (4) miscellaneous, and (5) new buildings.   It has been used so far without modification.

The estimate forms were prepared by the continuing budget assistant and sent out to the spending agencies about September 30th.

Under the budget law, as amended in 1918, the estimates are to be prepared and submitted to the governor by October 15th.   It is reported that most of the estimates came in on time with one exception.   The department of charities and correction (controlling all charitable and penal institutions of the state) did not get its estimates prepared and submitted until about December 25th.   This delay was attributed to the fact that the department was newly organized, having been created by a law passed in 1918.   The institutions (charitable and penal) prepared their estimates and submitted them to the department of charities and correction, which revised them before submitting them to the governor.

Two Budget Assistants

The budget staff of the governor was composed of two budget assistants, one clerk, and one stenographer.   One budget assistant worked about four months, beginning about October 15th.   He is by profession an accountant, with business connections in New York City.   The other budget assistant worked the year around at an annual salary of $2,500.   Formerly he was in the newspaper business.   Both assistants were appointed by the governor.   The sum of $10,000 is appropriated to carry on the expenses of budget making.   The continuing budget assistant has an office in the statehouse, and wants for next year a statistical clerk attached to his office, whose duty it will be to compile certain budget data during the year.   At the present time he receives bi-monthly a copy of all pay rolls as filed with the civil service commission and the comptroller.

The " Budget Commission "

While New Jersey's device is styled an executive budget and was so considered when the act was passed; under a section of the budget law which permitted the governor to name a permanent budget committee, he has appointed a body which is styled the " Budget Commission."   It is composed of the state house commission (*i.e.,* governor, state treasurer, and state comptroller) and the two budget assistants.   While it may be inferred from the reading of the budget law that the governor is solely responsible for the recommendations for appropriations to the legislature, as a matter of practice two members of the commission are not his agents and the judgment of all five of the members of the budget commission enter into the recommendations as finally submitted to the legislature. The last year of his official term, it is said, Governor Edge was inclined to trust largely to the judgment of his budget assistants.   He was running for United States senator, and was therefore busy with his campaign and other duties.   Under such circumstances it may be fairly questioned whether the executive budget idea was not abandoned by its sponsor.

Review and Revision of Estimates

From October 15th to about November 20th the two budget assistants examined the estimates as filed and investigated many of the items by visits to the departments or institutions. In fact, it is reported that during this period they visited all of the state institutions and looked into the need of their requests. The budget assistants were permitted to call upon any department for assistance. Following these investigations, the budget assistants made tentative recommendations for appropriations to the governor. Upon receipt of the tentative recommendations of the budget assistants the governor began consideration of the estimates. The budget assistants had arranged all budget data under organization units and presented them to the governor at the time of making tentative recommendations.

Public Hearings

The governor called public hearings, beginning on November 20th, for a period of about one month. During this time most of the state spending agencies appeared before him as he sat with other members of the budget commission. The prospective members of the joint appropriation committee of the 1919 legislature were invited to sit at these hearings. Two or three of the nine prospective members attended several of the hearings. It is said that the policy will be to invite the governor-elect to sit at these hearings preceding a change of administration. Just how far his suggestions will be considered by the retiring governor in making recommendations is a question.

The Budget Message

A summary of the estimates, together with the governor's recommendations, was published in the form of a budget message to the legislature and was transmitted to it on the second Tuesday of January, 1919. This document of about one hundred and fifty pages contains the following:

(1) A brief and general budget statement by the governor.

(2) A statement of the actual and estimated condition of the state treasury at the ends of the last fiscal year, the current year, and the year to be financed prepared by the comptroller and treasurer jointly.

(3) A summary of proposed appropriations by organization units under functional grouping.

(4) Detailed supporting schedules.

Each member of the legislature was furnished a copy of this message, and it was referred to the joint appropriation committee.

The Joint Appropriation Committee and Its Work

The joint appropriation committee of 1919 was organized immediately after the fight over the choice of a Speaker for the House ended. The committee is composed of nine members — four from the Senate and five from the House. The chairman of the joint committee is always a senator — this year it was Senator Whitney, who had for three years been a member of the appropriation committee. Usually there is only one member from each house on the committee representing the minority party — this time the Democratic party.

At the time the estimates were made up by the spending agencies enough copies were made to furnish each of the nine members of the committee with a copy. With these copies of the estimates and the governor's recommendations in his budget message the committee began its work.

In a number of cases new estimates were prepared by the spending agencies for presentation to the committee or additional appropriations other than those recommended by the governor were requested by letter. In its consideration of the requests this year the committee permitted the two budget assistants to sit in at the hearings and to accompany it on its visits to the institutions.

The procedure of the committee was practically the same as that of previous years. Hearings were held, junkets were taken, and increases were made in the governor's recommendations. The junkets took a somewhat different turn, since the budget assistants accompanied the committee and pointed out things to substantiate their own and the governor's recommendations for appropriations. In other words, it was an attempt to justify the governor's stand over against the spending agency's request in some instances. One day a week during February and part of March was set aside for junkets by the committee. All the state institutions were visited. Sometimes as high as three or four were visited in one day, spending an hour or two at a place. In order to justify this second round of visits, when the institutions had been visited in October and November by the budget assistants, one of the governor's budget assistants took the position that it was considered a desirable check or verification of the governor's budget recommendations.

The joint appropriation committee spent the latter half of March hearing again the needs of the various spending agencies as the governor and the other members of the budget commission had done during the preceding November and December. The committee then set to work with the aid of one or two assistants to draft the general appropriation bill, which was finished and ready for introduction on April 8th.

Legislative Action on the General Appropriation Bill

The general appropriation bill was introduced into the Senate by Senator Whitney, following the usual procedure, on April 8th (S. B. No. 244). It was immediately referred to the committee on appropriations from whence it had come. An " official copy reprint " was made and introduced in the Senate on April 9th. This likewise went to the committee on appropriations. On April 10th Senator Whitney, chairman of the committee on appropriations, reported the appropriation bill out. It was taken up, read a second time and ordered to be printed. On April 11th it was taken up and read a third time and passed on a vote of fifteen for and none against. There was little discussion of the bill and no amendments offered. Immediately after its passage the president of the Senate directed the secretary to carry the bill to the House and to inform that body that the Senate had passed it, and to request concurrence. The House received this message from the Senate and after adoption referred it to the committee on appropriations. On the same day (April 11th) Mr. Glover, chairman of the House committee on appropriations, reported the bill favorably without amendment to the House. It was immediately taken up and read a second time, whereupon Mr. Kellam moved that the rules be suspended and the bill be taken up for a third reading and final passage. The motion carried. Mr. De Voe then offered an amendment providing for the appropriation of $500,000 for the purchase of the rights of way of the New Jersey Intercostal Ship Canal. This amendment was lost by a vote of twenty-four to thirty-three. The appropriation bill was then taken up on motion of Mr. Kellam under suspended rules and passed by a vote of fifty-eight in the affirmative and none in the negative. There was little discussion in the House, April 11th being the last day of the session. Thus it appears that the general appropriation bill was introduced in the

Senate three days before the end of the session, and passed both the Senate and House on the last day of the session.

Effect of the Governor's Veto

The general appropriation bill was approved by Governor Edge on April 17th, and became Chapter 261 of the Laws of 1919. At the time of approving the bill the governor vetoed seventeen items amounting to $69,207. The veto message, it is stated, was written by the governor's continuing budget assistant. The items vetoed were, in most instances, additions which the joint appropriation committee had made to the governor's budget. In fact, very few reductions were made by this committee in the budget recommendations as submitted by the governor to the legislature. Numerous increases were made in the items of the personal service schedules, many of which were lumped together in such a manner as to prevent the governor from vetoing the items.

Form and Provisions of the General Appropriation Act

The appropriations in the general appropriation bill are made to organization units. Each unit is given a number to be used in setting up and keeping the expenditure and control accounts. The items of appropriation under the organization units are usually lumped together under a few main heads. Only in a few cases are the appropriations for personal service itemized. The appropriation act gives the comptroller the power to interpret the purpose of all appropriations; the intention being to give flexibility to the expenditure of the state's money. Transfers may also be made by permission of the state house commission between the items of appropriations granted to an organization unit.

The provision of the budget law providing for transfers within appropriations of any organization unit by application to the state house commission does not seem to be working with the greatest degree of satisfaction. The experience of the last two years has shown that large numbers of transfers were requested and made during the closing months of the fiscal year. As soon as the spending agencies found there was going to be a balance in some items of their appropriation they immediately requested a transfer to other items, usually personal service, so they could expend all their appropriations.

The general appropriation act contains all of the appropriations for the fiscal year beginning July 1, 1919, and ending June 30, 1920. Hence, it seems that the provision of the budget law prohibiting the passage of supplemental, deficiency, or incidental bills has operated effectively. The general appropriation bill, however, carries an " emergency fund " of $10,000, and a " revolving and supplemental fund " of $250,000, the former to be administered by the governor for contingent purposes, the latter to be under the control of the state house commission and to be used in its discretion to supplement other appropriations, to meet deficiencies, and to supply the purchasing department with a revolving fund for the purchase of supplies. In this way, it is claimed, the passage of supplementary appropriation bills is avoided and all appropriations are included in one bill.

Use of Civil Service and Central Purchasing Records in Budget Making

The civil service commission of New Jersey is attempting gradually to classify and standardize the personal-service end of the budget. An attempt was made in preparing the budget for 1919–1920 to apply a scale of increases to the lower grades of personal service. Both the governor's budget officers and the joint appropriation committee took into consideration the recommendations of the civil service commission in nearly every instance with reference to compensation for personal service. The joint appropriation committee in many cases referred the department heads to the civil service commission for agreement upon salary increases before passing upon their appropriation requests. This plan seems to have given the civil service commission a rather definite voice in the matter of compensation control. Such coöperation seems necessary to proper budget procedure.

In the case of the central purchasing office, which controls the supply end of the budget through its power to purchase all supplies for the state, there was an apparent lack of coöperation with the budget-making authorities. It is stated that the purchasing office was not consulted in the preparation of the estimates for supplies by any of the departments or institutions, except to a limited extent by the department of charities and corrections. Neither did the budget commission nor the budget assistants consult the purchasing agent about the probable prices of supplies for the coming year before making up the budget recommendations. There was no coöperation between the work of the joint appropriation committee and the purchasing office. It seems that the data of the purchasing office with respect to the trend of prices and the prospective needs of the several state agencies should be made use of in the preparation of the budget.

New Jersey Budget a Hybrid Type

The New Jersey budget, instead of being an executive budget, is in reality the work of a budget commission, consisting of the governor, comptroller, treasurer, and the two budget assistants. Members of the joint appropriation committee of the previous legislature are also permitted to sit with this commission and to make recommendations with reference to the proposed appropriations. The budget recommendations, as finally submitted by the governor to the legislature, are the result of the composite judgment of both administrative and legislative officers.

The New Jersey budgetary procedure has another serious defect which some states, as Maryland and Nebraska, have foreseen and made provisions against. Under the budget law the retiring governor is required to prepare the budget and immediately upon submitting it to the legislature goes out of office. Thereupon the governor-elect comes into the office and assumes responsibility for budget recommendations which he did not make.

For constitutional reasons the budget law of New Jersey contains no provisions governing the legislative procedure upon the governor's proposals. It has been the practice of the joint appropriation committee, after having received the governor's budget, to do whatever investigating it deemed necessary and then proceed to draft the general appropriation bill, disregarding, if it chose to do so, the governor's recommendations. As a result, the legislature has followed practically the same procedure since the adoption of the budget law as it did before in making appropriations. Governor Edge, the author of the law, admitted this to be a serious defect in the law, but one which could not be avoided without constitutional change.

PART IV. PROPOSED NATIONAL BUDGET LEGISLATION

CHAPTER XVIII

Specific Recommendations of Commission

In the report of the commission on economy and efficiency sent to Congress June 27, 1912, by the President with his approval the commission said:

" The development of a budget necessarily carries with it means for developing a definite administrative program; and means for presenting and defending it before the legislative branch of the Government and the country."

The recommendations of the commission were these:

1. That the President, as the constitutional head of the executive branch of the government, shall each year submit to the Congress, not later than the first Monday after the beginning of the regular session, a budget.[1]

2. That the budget so submitted shall contain:[2]

    (a) *A budgetary message* setting forth in brief the significance of the proposals to which attention is invited.

    (b) *A summary financial statement* setting forth in concise form:

    (1) the financial condition (a statement of resources and liabilities.)

    (2) the condition of appropriations.

---

[1] The Need for a National Budget — House Document 854, Sixty-second Congress, Second session.

[2] *Ibid.*, pp. 3 and 4.

(3) revenues and expenditures for the last completed fiscal year, and

(4) the effect of past financial policy as well as of budget proposals on the general-fund surplus.

(c) *A summary of expenditures* classified by objects (things bought) setting forth the contracting and purchasing relations of the Government.

(d) *Summaries of estimates* setting forth:

(1) the estimated revenues compared with the actual revenues for a period of years.

(2) estimated expenditures (by departments) compared with actual expenditures for a period of years.

(e) *A summary of changes in law* setting forth what legislation it is thought should be enacted in order to enable the administration to transact business with greater economy and efficiency, *i.e.* changes of organic law which, if enacted, would affect appropriations as well as the character of work to be done.

3. That the Secretary of the Treasury be required to to submit to the Congress the following reports supporting the general summaries and executive conclusions or recommendations contained in the budget as follows:

(a) *A book of estimates* containing the supporting details to the summaries of estimates of expenditures contained in the budget.

(b) *A consolidated financial report* containing a detailed statement of revenues and a consolidated statement of expenditures by de-

partments and establishments for the last
five years, with such explanatory matter
as is necessary to give information with
respect to increases and decreases in revenues and expenditures or other relations
to which it is thought the attention of the
executive and legislative branches is to be
given.

4. That the head of each department and independent
establishment should be required to submit to the
secretary of the treasury and to Congress annual
reports which, among other things, would contain detailed accounts of expenditures so classified as to show amounts expended by appropriations, as well as by classes of work, together with
the amounts of increases or decreases in stores,
equipment, property, etc., including lands, buildings, and other improvements as well as such
other data or operative statistics and comment in
relation thereto as may be necessary to show results obtained and the economy and efficiency of
doing government work, as well as of contracting
and purchasing.

5. That the President and heads of departments issue
orders which will require such accounts to be
kept, such reports to be made, and such estimates
to be prepared as will enable them to obtain the
information needed to consider the different conditions, relations, and results above enumerated
before the estimates are submitted; that the President recommend to the Congress the enactment
of such laws as will enable the administration to
comply with the requirements of Congress.

6. That the President recommend for the consideration of the Congress such changes in the form of
appropriation bills as will enable the Government

to avail itself of the benefits of the exercise of discretion on the part of the executive in the transaction of current business in order that the Government may do work and accomplish results with economy and efficiency and as will definitely fix responsibility for failure to exercise such discretion.

Discussing the " reasons urged for the submission of an annual budget with special message by the President," the commission said: [1]

" The adoption of the recommendations . . . would have for its effect to make him [the President] responsible for knowing what the estimates contained before submission; to make him aware of financial conditions; to bring before him for consideration the changes desired. The recommendation that the secretary of the treasury shall prepare the book of estimates containing the detail items in support of the summaries contained in the budget would have for its effect to make the secretary of the treasury not only the official editor of estimates prepared in departments (which he now is) and the ministerial agent for their transmission to the Congress, but also an effective assistant to the President in bringing together the data and in presenting them in such form that their significance can be readily understood and considered, thereby enabling the President and his cabinet to act intelligently. To this end there would be worked out as a result of conference, and stated in summary form, a definite administrative program to be presented by the President as the head of the administration in the consideration of which each member of the cabinet would arrange the details of his estimates in such manner as to support this program. . . .

" In other words, it is assumed that the President as the

[1] *Ibid.,* p. 144.

one officer of government who represents the people as a whole is in a better position to lay before the Congress and to state to the people what the Government is doing and what it proposes to do; that the President, under the powers given to him by the Constitution, is in a better position than any one else to dramatize the work of the government — to so impress this upon the attention of the people, through the public press, by means of a budgetary message as to arouse discussion and elicit comment such as will keep Congress as well as the administration in touch with public opinion when deciding whether or not the proposals are such as will best meet welfare demands."

Submission of Budget by President Taft

Not only were these recommendations commended to the favorable attention of Congress in a special message asking for its coöperation, in a revision of laws and practices to make their adoption practicable, but the thought was further enlarged upon in a subsequent message submitting a budget to the next regular session.

" The recommendation of such measures as may be thought to be necessary and expedient and requests for support, in the form of estimates for further expenditures," the President said, " should be premised on a knowledge of service needs. The needs of the service can only be known to those who are in charge of administrative detail. Representation of what has been done as well as what should be undertaken in the future must come from those who are acquainted with technical requirements. A sense of proportion, however, can come only from those who must assume responsibility for the administration as a whole. . . .

" The advantage to the Congress of having placed before it a definite statement and proposal, one which is submitted by the responsible head of the administration, must also be apparent. Such a statement will greatly facilitate

the adoption of a procedure whereby the deliberative
branch of the Government may determine the gross
amount to be appropriated in advance of decision as to
what amount shall be allowed for each detail of the Government's business, rather than leave the relations of income and outgo to be computed after the action has been
taken on the many matters which are brought before the
Congress for determination.

" Size and complexity of the problem make it necessary
for officers to have the advantage of seeing the business of
the Government in perspective.   But judgment with respect to the requirements of particular services requires
that exact information be made available for the consideration of detail.   This budget is submitted, therefore,
not only as an instrument through which a perspective
may be gained, but as an index through which members of
Congress and the public may obtain ready references to
supporting reports and detailed records of account.

" The need for such an index through which exact information may be obtained as a basis for judgment about
problems of public business is evident to one familiar with
the governmental problems.

" The highly complex and technical character of questions that must be decided by executive heads of departments is suggested by the complexity of departmental organization.   In the department of the navy, for example,
there exist at present thirty-four navy yards and stations,
thirty-one naval coaling plants, forty-three naval wire-
less stations, twelve naval magazines, fourteen purchasing,
pay, and disbursing offices, nine inspection districts, sixteen hydrographic offices, twenty hospitals, twenty dispen-
saries, fourteen naval schools, three schools for the marine
corps, seven naval medical schools, four naval training
stations, thirteen target ranges (naval), one target range
and permanent camp of instruction for the marine corps,
three medical supply depots, thirteen recruiting stations,

forty-eight marine posts and stations, and a naval militia, besides the fleet, which is the actual fighting machine of this branch of the military establishment. More concretely, the administrative requirements may be shown by reference to a single station (one of the thirty-one above mentioned), such as the proving grounds at Indian Head. Here under the jurisdiction of an officer known as the senior assistant are a police force, office buildings and grounds, living quarters, a water-supply system, boats and wharves, a railroad, a power plant, a carpenter shop, an electrical shop, a tin shop, a repair and pipe-fitting shop, a storehouse; and under the jurisdiction of an officer known as a powder expert is a chemical laboratory, a sulphuric-acid factory, ether factory, dry house, boiling tubs, dehydrating house, an intensifier house, a solvent recovery house, a reworking house, a nitric-acid factory, a roaching and pulping house, a mixing house, a press house, a blending and packing house, a powder factory and magazines, a signal house, a rocket house, and a storehouse. These may be taken as illustrative of the character of the administrative attention required in directing and controlling the activities of one of the many institutional subdivisions of one department of the Government."

Why Commission's Recommendations Were Limited

The conclusion drawn from this is that a requirement laid on the executive to prepare information in advance of the meeting of Congress needed information of a plan or program of service which will include all the varied activities of the Government, to put upon the department heads the necessity of preparing their information in such form that they can explain and defend their expenditures and estimates to an executive staff engaged in the preparation of a budget, and then to justify their claims in the course of a cabinet inquiry before the budget is made official, is desirable both from the viewpoint of executive management and for purposes of review criticism and discussion before Congress.

With respect to the development of a procedure or means whereby five hundred members of Congress and the country at large may be informed of the service and financial needs before money is voted for support, the temper of Congress at the time was such that the subject was purposely avoided, except as indicated by the general principles laid down: (1) that the executive should be made responsible for preparing and submitting a plan which would include the needs of every department and establishment which the executive would be prepared to explain and defend, and (2) that opportunity be given " for presenting it and defending it before the legislative branch of the Government and the country." Whatever may be the use made by Congress of committees for purpose of inquiry and by way of preparedness of its leadership for criticism and discussion, it is obvious that the desired end could be achieved only by bringing inquiry, criticism, and discussion of budget proposals out into the open, and having the proceedings conducted in such a way that the whole membership may be brought face to face with officers in charge of the activities which are made the subject of review. And under our constitutional form in which the heads of departments are not given a seat in the deliberative body while in formal session, this may be done only by having the inquiry, criticism, and discussion take place in committee of the whole with the executive present, instead of in the recesses of the standing-committee room where, if other members and the press were permitted to attend, they would be required to follow the performances of a twenty-nine ring circus with nothing definite or authentic as a measure to be acted on before them for discussion.

CHAPTER XIX

In the states, opposition to boss rule had carried with it a prevailing public opinion hostile to legislative committee domination. Because of this hostility the defenders of the standing-committee system (the advocates of the "legislative budget" idea) had won out in only two of the forty-four legislatures where new budget procedures had been passed. In the other forty-two states honors were about evenly divided between the advocates of the "executive budget" idea and the advocates of the "commission budget" idea. The latter were made up of advocates of "government by commission," who had succeeded in all of the states in making the government more serviceable; but it finally came to be recognized that they had done this in a way to weaken instead of strengthen the processes of popular control. The advocates of the executive budget idea had won out against the advocates of the commission government in twenty-two states; they undertook to preserve the advantage gained by the "government-by-commission" advocates by way of improved service; in fact, to make the public service more efficient, and at the same time to make the administration responsive to public opinion by making the head of it responsible directly to the electorate.

These two forces had been opposed to each other as to method, in controversy over the budget; but they were united in opposition to the boss, and to the irresponsible party machine — *i.e.* in all the states except New York

341

and Arkansas, where " government-by-commission " advocates had joined with " the old guard," with the result above described (Chapter XVI).

Opposition to Executive Budget Idea in Congress

In the Federal Government quite a different situation was present. The " government-by-commission " advocates were specialized, and their leadership was local. The " commission " idea made little headway there — the effort to make the government more serviceable coming from the executive; and the executive took the lead in bringing forward a budget proposal. So that the controversy which arose over methods and procedure was between these forces: on the one hand were those who advocated changes to make the President responsible for leadership in matters of administration and finance; on the other hand were those who sought to protect the existing system of " government-by-chairmen-of-standing-Committees-of-Congress."

When President Taft proposed an " executive budget," all the " chairmen " in Congress were of the opposition party, and his measure was humanely disposed of under the rules without being rough-handled on the floor — in fact, without being discussed at all on its merits. As has been said, the President sent to Congress his recommendation, June 27, 1912, " to suggest a method whereby the President, as the constitutional head of the administration, may lay before the Congress, and the Congress may consider and act on a definite business and financial program; to have the expenditures, appropriations, and estimates so classified and summarized that their broad significance may be readily understood; to provide each member of Congress as well as each citizen who is interested, with such data pertaining to each subject of interest that it may be considered in relation to each question of policy which should be gone into before an appropriation for expenditures is made; to have these general summaries supported by such detail information as is necessary to consider the economy and efficiency with which business has been transacted; in short, to suggest a plan whereby the President and the Congress may coöperate," etc.

Recognition of Need for Change of Rules

While the only legal enactment resulting was a " rider," the purpose of which was to prevent the preparation of a budget by the President, there were evidences that the many and frequent attacks on the standing-committee system as a device which fostered " pork-barrel politics " had opened the eyes of many of the members to its unpopularity. As far back as 1864 a resolution had been introduced " to provide that the heads of the executive departments may occupy seats on the floor of the House of Representatives "; and in 1881 a bill was introduced to extend the privileges of the floor to heads of departments in both houses. The report made by the committee, to which the bill was referred, had described the irresponsibility of the executive, and ascribed it to the rules of Congress. This was done with a frankness that entitles the picture drawn in the report to be preserved as a companion piece to the one drawn by Senator Root when he described " the system " before the New York Constitutional Convention in 1915.

" It has been notorious for years," said the committee, " that by personal interview with members, by private conversation at the office, in social intercourse at casual meetings on the floor of the two houses, by verbal statements to the chairmen of committees — liable always to be misunderstood or even misrepresented — by unofficial communications to the committees themselves, these officers originate, press forward, modify, or entirely defeat legislation; and it has often happened that the rules of the House have been violated by stating what occurred in committee, in order to convey to members the opinions or wishes of a secretary. . . ."

" Their secret, silent, omnipresent influence is felt, yet they are without responsibility. It is not necessarily corrupt because it is secret and silent; but it may be; and wherever opportunity for corruption exists there will be, there ought to be, suspicion and distrust."

A Proposal Which Would Have Given to the Nation an Executive Budget

The proposal to give the cabinet the privilege of the floor was made with a view to protect Congress from the imputations of conspiracy, at a time when the whole public service was honeycombed with placemen, two years before the civil service reform act was passed, and two years before Cleveland was elected in a campaign the slogan of which was " a public office is a public trust." Had this bill been passed, it seems beyond question that, long since, we would have had a budget and would have developed responsible government.

" Would it not be better," said the committee, " that their opinions should be expressed, their facts stated, their policy enforced, their acts defended in open day on the floor of the House, in the face of the nation, in public speech, in official, recorded statement, where there can be no hidden purpose, no misconception, no misrepresentation?

"This would enlighten the House, inform the country, and be just to the officer. It would substitute legitimate for illegitimate power. It would establish an open, official, honorable mode of exercising that power instead of a secret, unrecognized mode, liable to abuse, and therefore always subject to the suspicion that it has been abused. It would establish authorized and accurate, instead of unauthorized, and therefore uncertain and inaccurate, communication with the House." (Privilege of the

Floor to Cabinet Officers, Reports to Congress, 1913,
p. 19.)

This was a proposal that came from the opposition in
Congress at a time when the executive was à Republican.
When President Taft came forward in 1912 and urged
upon Congress an executive budget, although he did not
include any specific proposal with respect to changes in
rules and organization of Congress to make " coöperation " between the two branches effective, the measure itself carried with it the same implications and the same
arguments as were employed by the committee that reported in 1881; and the old question was again revived.
But there was this difference: The attitude of the people
toward the executive had changed; the influence of President Cleveland, the leadership of President Roosevelt,
the frequent attacks on Congress and state legislatures
as dispensers of " patronage " and " pork," the confusion
which resulted from the unrelated and irresponsible leaderships of standing committees, all helped to carry conviction that the proposal of President Taft was sound, although he himself was politically discredited; President
Taft's proposal was taken seriously by the people, and
therefore it was a matter which could not be entirely
passed by in Congress. It called for a counter-proposal
by the friends of the existing system.

Mr. Fitzgerald's Proposal to Return to the Old Practice

It is an observation which carries with it the full weight
of experience, that, once power is given, those who possess it are loath to give it up. And this finds exemplification not alone in executives; it has proved to be equally
true of the " chairmen " of legislative committees on whom
the representative branch has bestowed leadership — the
leadership which customarily goes with executive responsibility. This fact finds illustration in the proposal of
Congressman John J. Fitzgerald, chairman of the com-

mittee on appropriations, who came forward in a speech
with a counter-proposal.   We need no executive budget,
said he; all we need is to return to the committee organization and procedure in use in Congress from 1865 till
the Cleveland administration.   The organization and procedure recommended by Mr. Fitzgerald, it is to be observed, was brought into use the year following the resolution to give to the cabinet the privilege of the floor.
Up to that time all finance measures both for revenues
and expenditures had been handled by one committee with
results that were appalling.   The remedy for the chaos
that obtained in disintegrate, financial and administrative
measures passed during the war was to put the raising of
revenues in the hands of one committee and the authorization of expenditures into the hands of another.   Following this act, some twenty years later, in a quarrel between the chairmen of the two committees, the leader in
charge of the ways and means committee sought to detract from the influence of the chairman of the appropriation committee by breaking up and distributing its powers.   Now Mr. Fitzgerald proposed to return again to
the system in existence during the time that so much dissatisfaction had been shown.

> "Enlarge the committee on appropriations suffi-
> ciently to enable its work to be properly done," said
> Mr. Fitzgerald.   His proposal was to " place on that
> committee the chairmen of the committees which now
> have annual supply bills, so that they could continue
> in touch with the respective bills now committed to
> legislative committees over which they preside.   This
> would largely reintroduce a practice which was fol-
> lowed from the creation of the committee on appro-
> priations in 1865 till the end of the forty-fourth Con-
> gress, of having as conferees on the respective supply
> bills two members of the committee on appropriations

and one member of the legislative committee having jurisdiction of the legislation affected by the bill."

Evidence of the fact that this was not a question of principle but one of power is found in the approval of Mr. Fitzgerald's proposal by Mr. Cannon of Illinois, who, perhaps more fully than any other man now living, stands for the autocracy exercised through the committee system. In urging a return to a single appropriation committee, such as we had from 1865 down to the time of the Cleveland administration when, in a fight between Mr. Randall and Mr. Morrison, its powers were dissipated among a number of departmental committees—in urging this as a means of preventing extravagance and waste, both Mr. Fitzgerald and Mr. Cannon seem to overlook the fact that this was the outstanding period of our history during which patronage, spoils, and pork-barrel politics ran rampant; and that the history of congressional appropriations during this period is one which caused every disinterested patriotic American to blush for shame. If there are good reasons for a return to the methods and practices under which the public treasury was made the football of " party " politics they must be found in the operation of principles of representative government not then invoked, for there can be no doubt of the shamelessness with which the treasury was legally looted, and patronage and special privileges were distributed to the faithful.

Mr. Sherley, ranking majority member of Mr. Fitzgerald's committee, who later succeeded him as chairman, supported the proposal which had such worthy parentage and sponsorship, but broadened it to include the preparation and advocacy of revenue bills as well — so that Congress might have brought before it a well-considered financial plan in the form of a " legislative budget." His proposal was a modification of the legislative practice carrying it still farther back, before 1865 — the avowed purpose of the modification being to adapt it to the much more highly elaborated standing-committee system. He introduced the following:

"Resolved, That the following rule be added to the rules of the House, and to be known as section 6 of Rule X:

"6. There shall be a committee on estimates and expenditures, whose personnel shall consist of the following members: the chairmen and three ranking majority members, and the ranking minority member of the Committees on Ways and Means and Appropriations, and the chairmen and ranking minority member of the committees on Rules, Agriculture, Foreign Affairs, Military Affairs, Naval Affairs, Post Offices and Post Roads, Rivers and Harbors, and Indian Affairs. The chairman of said committee shall be selected by the members thereof. Said committee shall, as soon after the convening of each regular session of Congress as may be, report to the House the amount of revenue probably available for appropriation for the next fiscal year, and apportion the amount to the several appropriation bills within the jurisdiction of the committees empowered by the rules and practice of the House to report appropriations from the Treasury. This report, or supplementary reports to meet the exigencies of the public service, may be made on any legislative day after the reading of the Journal, and when agreed to by the House shall limit the totals of the appropriations reported by the several committees."

Mr. Sherley's Proposal

While the change in rules proposed by Mr. Sherley is better designed to bring order out of the chaos that has existed in American financial legislation for a century, and better adapted for a businesslike handling of finance

than is the proposal of Mr. Fitzgerald, it would not reach
any of the fundamental defects which have been so frequently described: it would not bring before Congress at
the beginning of the session, as the chief business to be
transacted, a plan or program of service to be financed;
but in the nature of things it would delay finance bills
till near the close of the session; it would not leave Congress free to exercise its most important function of inquest and criticism; it still assumes that leaders of Congress, with the aid of their respective committees, should
prepare and submit proposals for administration and
finance, thereby putting responsibility where it stands in
the way of open, free discussion. It did not provide for
having the estimates prepared and submitted by responsible executive heads — but made them simply ministerial
agents to collect information for the committees; it did
not provide for giving adequate information to members
and to the electorate to guide them in their voting; it did
not adequately provide for accountability by requiring
the heads of departments to stand up like men before Congress and the country, openly and publicly to explain and
defend their acts and proposals — and to meet criticism
when offered. It was not a device to determine and enforce executive responsibility, but was a device to secure
and enforce secret committee domination of both branches
of the government. It was frankly a measure to preserve the standing-committee system. In his remarks
supporting his proposal it was admitted that all inquiries
would still be made and all conclusions would still be
reached in secret. Speaking on the size of the committee,
he said:

"This committee would consist of sixteen majority
members and ten minority members. It is urged that
that is too large a number, but I desire to suggest to the
House that it is really two committees, because the majority members would necessarily come to their conclusions

in private, just as the majority members of the Committee on Ways and Means now do."

Mr. Fitzgerald and Mr. Sherley both give us the very "practical" reason for urging a legislative budget as against the executive budget proposed by Mr. Taft, viz.: that members of Congress will not consent to giving up the powers which under the old system of standing-committee leadership they have come to enjoy. This was before sides had been taken in the states and opinion had come to register itself when opportunity was given to choose between irresponsible and responsible leadership. But whatever may be the effect of six years of discussion outside of Congress on the minds of individual members, it seems that they still hold to the opinions then expressed. And this view is shared by Mr. Cannon of Illinois.

Support Given by Mr. Cannon

Mr. Cannon not only supported Mr. Fitzgerald in his opposition to Mr. Taft. but he still continues to hold his views even in opposition to the platform policy of his "party" which declared for the executive budget in their platform on which candidates went before the people for election to Congress. In a recent article on " The National Budget " he has more fully elaborated his views:

" When we [*i.e.* members of Congress] create a budget commission we will keep it in Congress, and as far as possible in the House of Representatives. . . . I believe that the House of Representatives should have one committee with jurisdiction over appropriations."

In this last assertion, Mr. Cannon evidently has in mind the proposal of Mr. Fitzgerald — to return to the practice from 1865 to the first Cleveland administration, notwithstanding the fact that the public scandals of that period came near landing Mr. Tilden in the presidential chair. Mr. Cannon also seems to think well of Mr. Sherley's proposal. Discussing the desirability of keeping the leadership in matters of administrative policy in the hands of committee chairmen, he says:

" For the first seventy-five years of its existence the House had a budget committee — the Committee on Ways and Means. That committee reported both revenue bills and appropriation bills."

The implication is that such an organization and procedure for leadership and accountability would solve our difficulties. But he makes no mention of the fact that during all this seventy-five years when " the House had a budget committee," the nation never had a budget; nor is mention made of the fact that it was during this period that the whole " American " system of government-by-chairmen-of-irresponsible-standing-committees, and the " American " system of patronage and spoils became firmly rooted in a soil made fertile by democratic ideals — a soil in which the Constitution had been planted in the hope that it would give to the people a fruitage in the form of responsible government.

Constitutional Objections Urged to Executive Budget

In the controversy over a national budget the defenders of the system of " government by standing-committees " are for some form of " legislative budget " or by second choice for a " commission budget "; they have never been for an " executive budget " procedure which squarely recognizes the right and the need of the executive (as the one responsible to the people for the manner in which the public business is done) to stand up before the representatives of the people who control the purse, and give an account of executive stewardship. They are squarely against giving to the executive a chance to stand up before the appropriating body to explain and defend requests; and they are just as squarely against giving to the people a chance to take sides with leaders for and against policies and measures thus openly discussed when issues are joined.

Mr. Cannon assumes that to permit the executive to prepare and present and publicly explain and defend a plan for which he is asking support, to permit the executive to go before the whole membership, submit himself to questioning, and be accorded only the privilege to participate in discussion without a right to vote, and without the right of immunity for his statements, would be " away from the budget plans of those who prepared the Constitution, and when Congress consents to the executive making a budget it will have surrendered the most important part of a representative government. . . .

" I think," says he, " that we had better stick pretty close to the Constitution with its division of powers well defined and the taxing power close to the people."

These Objections Answered by Members of Congress

It is not necessary to go to the opinions of men who have occupied both judicial and executive positions to refute that idea. Mr. Taft held that the power of the President to prepare and submit a budget was amply provided for in the Constitution — that the only thing which stood in the way now, without change of law, was the attitude of Congress. Justice Hughes held to the view that an executive budget is not only consistent with the Constitution, but is necessary to the fixing of executive responsibility — the very reason for the separation of powers. Governor Lowden and some twenty other state governors of both parties, most of them lawyers of repute, have urged that if they are to be made responsible to the people they should be given a hearing. They saw nothing unconstitutional in these proposals. Only those who are seeking to defend a present practice raise the issue. But let us accept the view that all persons who have been in executive positions are interested parties. Let us return

to the report of the committee of congress to which was
referred the question as to whether members of the cabinet should not be given the privileges of the floor. These
were all congressmen. They point to the fact that two
constitutional objections have been urged to giving the
privilege of the floor to the cabinet: (1) that it is inhibited by the provision that no person holding office shall be
a member of either house; (2) that it violates the principle of the separation of powers.

With respect to the first, they have this to say:

" The provision of the Constitution that ' no person
holding any office under the United States shall be a
member of either house during his continuance in office '
is in no wise violated. The head of a department, reporting in person and orally, or participating in debate,
becomes no more a member of either house than does the
chaplain, or the contestant, or his counsel, or the delegate.
He has no official term; he is neither elected nor appointed
to either house; he has no participation in the power of
impeachment, either in the institution or trial; he has no
privilege from arrest; he has no power to vote."

With respect to the second objection — that it was a
violation of the principle of separation of powers — they
make this answer:

" Your committee is not unmindful of the maxim that
in a constitutional government the great powers are divided into legislative, executive, and judicial, and that
they should be conferred on distinct departments. These
departments should be defined and maintained, and it is a
sufficiently accurate expression to say that they should be
independent of each other. But this independence in no
just or practical sense means an entire separation, either
in their organization or their functions — isolation, either
in the scope or the exercise of their powers. Such isolation would produce either conflict or paralysis, either
inevitable collision or inaction, and either the one or the

other would be in derogation of the efficiency of the government. Such independence of coequal and coördinate departments has never existed in any civilized government, and never can exist. . . .

"If there is anything perfectly plain in the Constitution and organization of the government of the United States, it is that the great departments [the legislative, executive, and judicial branches] were not intended to be independent and isolated in the strict meaning of these terms; but that although having a separate existence, they were to coöperate, each with the other, as the different members of the human body must coöperate with each other in order to form the figure and perform the functions of a perfect man."

A Question of Responsible Government

Point is made by Mr. Cannon and others that " The representatives are the men who have to bear the responsibility for unpopular taxes, and are first to feel the weight of the voters' dissatisfaction.   They get kicked out whenever the people think too much has been taken out of their pockets for a government budget."

Whereas, " none of these executive officials are responsible to the people or can be called to account by the voters."

This is a view that is very much overworked.   It neither bears analysis nor squares with the facts.   Suppose that the people of the United States are dissatisfied with appropriations made, recommended, and pushed through by the committee of which Mr. Cannon is a member.   How can they reach him so long as he gets enough appropriated for his own district to keep up his fences there?   How can any member of Congress be reached by the people of the United States so long as he keeps his own district behind him?

CHAPTER XX

Attempt to Preserve the Status Quo

FROM a careful study of the organic laws of the American states it is apparent that the function and purpose of a budget has not been clearly understood. In many cases it seems to have been assumed that a budget is something to be adopted and used with little or no thought given to the administrative and deliberative machinery to which it is to be attached. It is assumed that it is something that is complete in itself — instead of being a procedure or technique to be learned and used to make the two great political branches of the government more coöperative and serviceable to democracy. Of the forty-four states which passed budget laws from 1911 to 1919, only about one fourth of them took any steps to make readjustments in organization and practice looking toward the achievement of the desired end. In the two states which adopted a " legislative budget " and the nineteen states which adopted one form or another of a " commission budget " this might, perhaps, be defended, since both of these methods of review and control of administration and finance are designed not to disturb the *status quo ante:* the one being applied to protect the *status quo ante* of the " government-by-chairmen-of-standing-committee " form of legislative organization; the other being applied to protect the *status quo ante* of the " government-by-commission " form of administrative organization. And while the executive budget proposal is based on a desire to get away from the results of the *status quo ante* in both

355

branches of the government, nevertheless institutional inertia and the desire of persons in power to stick to and protect what they have has been an obstacle difficult to overcome in the twenty-three states which have adopted the executive-budget principle.

The fact is that although a majority of the states have adopted the executive budget idea, there are only three of the twenty-three states that attempted to make a complete readjustment of the administrative machinery to insure the effectiveness of this method or technique of control; and none of these revised the deliberative practice to make it consistent with an underlying purpose, viz., to make the administration accountable to the membership of the constitutional appropriating body; none of them even considered the question as to what procedure was needed to make the government responsible to the people. After the administrative codes of Illinois, Idaho, and Nebraska had become law the several governors of these states were in no better position to make an executive budget operative than was the Federal Government at the time that President Taft prepared and submitted his budget under the powers given to him by the Constitution with the assistance of the staff provided by special appropriation. The rules of the deliberative, appropriating body, as they stood, made it possible for an opposition majority in Congress completely to ignore the measure submitted by the President. The rules of the deliberative appropriating bodies in the states make it possible for them completely to ignore the recommendations of the respective governors — and in the standing-committee rooms of the legislature to proceed as if no such laws were on the statute books. Assuming that the existing rules of legislative procedure are continued, and public opinion lies dormant on the subject, the legislatures of the " reorganized " states may do exactly what Congress did after the National Government had been organized

in 1789 — exactly what the standing-committee system
has done to the Federal administration for one hundred
and thirty years — exactly what the New York legislature did to Governor Whitman's budget measures in
1916 and 1917.

Reorganization of Legislature and Revision of Rules Needed

The one conclusion which may be drawn from state
experience that will be helpful in the consideration of
the budget measures now before Congress is that it is
not administrative reorganization but a reorganization
or readjustment of working parts of the deliberative body,
a revision of rules, that is necessary. All the most progressive of the states have sought to do, in their efforts
to make the executive responsible, is to adopt the Federal
Government plan of administrative organization: — to do
what our forefathers, who sat in the Constitutional Convention at Philadelphia, did in 1787. The whole history
of the Federal Government stands as evidence that this
alone is not enough; that budget making involves the
working relations of all branches of the Government; that
with the power to control the purse in the hands of the
representative body Congress may so conduct itself as to
defeat its very purpose by adopting rules which bar the
administrative leaders who are to be made accountable
from a hearing, and convert the public forum of the nation
into a lot of secret conferences for inquest and determination of questions of public policy, the information thus
obtained to be used for personal and party ends.

Party Interest in a National Budget System

There is at this time a favoring circumstance, however,
in a new public opinion. A new national consciousness
has been aroused. And party managers have begun to
set their sails to catch the favoring wind in the hope that

it will waft their chosen candidates into office. While
in the states there has been no uniformity in party align-
ment on the subject — the Democratic party demanding
the "executive budget" in one state, and the Republican
party demanding it in another — the National Republican
party, in 1916, adopted a resolution and made an appeal
to the people on a platform favoring the adoption of
the executive budget. In the election which followed
they did not succeed in gaining control of either branch
of the government, but in the by-election of 1918, a
working majority of this party was elected to Congress
and presumably had a moral obligation to the people.

All the political writings of President Wilson also
seem to indicate that he favors a political system that
provides for responsible executive leadership — in fact
President Wilson as student and teacher of politics has
done more than any American to call attention to the
essentially irresponsible quality of our leadership; all of
his political writings seem to condemn the decentralized,
irresponsible, headless, planless, spineless leadership of
a multitude of standing committees in Congress, all of
them seem to point toward favorable consideration of a
plan which would give us some form of responsible executive leadership — a leadership at least responsible to
the representative body and not merely a "supervisory"
executive.

Bills before Congress:

The Republican members of the present Congress are
pledged to the executive budget as a method of handling
questions of public policy so far as these are reflected
in problems of administrative organization and public
finance. It is therefore from the viewpoint of this
assumption that the measures brought before the Republican Congress will be judged. Shortly after the incoming
of the new Congress, a number of bills were introduced

in the House and the Senate to effect this change. Because revenue and appropriation bills originate in the House of Representatives, the budget procedures proposed by members of that body will be stressed. The budget bills as proposed in the House during the last session may be classified as follows:

(1) The *Frear* bills (H. R. 4061; H. R. 3738; and H. J. Res. 83) the evident purpose of which is to provide for an out-and-out *executive budget.*

(2) The *Green* joint resolution (H. J. Res. 168) the evident purpose of which is to provide for an out-and-out *legislative budget.*

(3) The *Good* bill (H. R. 1201) the evident purpose of which is to provide for a legislative budget, *camouflaged* to look like an executive budget, or a *commission budget.*

(4) The *Andrews* bill (H. R. 551), a part-way measure dealing only with the audit function.

(5) The *Tinkham* resolution (H. R. 107), a part-way measure dealing only with the organization and procedure of Congress.

(6) Various initial measures to provide for the study of budget systems and to report recommendations (the Mann Resolution, H. J. Res. 29; the Goodwin Resolution, H. J. Res. 59; and the Tinkham Resolution, H. R. 1017).

The Frear Bills

Taking these up in the order above listed, Mr. Frear presents his concept of a needed budget plan in three separate measures. The first bill listed above (H. R. 4061) is a clear-cut proposal to put the responsibility on the President, as the constitutional head of the administration, for the preparation each year of a plan of public service to be financed. This would be done by making the Secretary of the Treasury the finance minister of the President with a budget bureau under him, the head of which would be appointed by the President. Thus the Secretary of the Treasury would be given both the power and the staff facilities to perform the function of initial review and revision of estimates both of revenues and expenditures. But this is only a first step. They must then be brought before the President not later than November 15th, so that the issues raised may be threshed out with the cabinet and an executive decision reached before Congress assembles. Thus a well-considered administrative plan could be presented to Congress when it assembled. The second bill listed (H. R. 3738) provides for the exercise of the critical or audit function by Congress. Mr. Frear would furnish Congress with the necessary staff by transfer of the audit organization from the Treasury to an independent office of Auditor General, the head of which would be appointed by the speaker, the majority leader and the minority leader of the House, to hold office during good behavior, removable for cause by a two-thirds vote. The office would report the results of critical examination to a "joint budget committee." The third proposal of Mr. Frear, as a complement to the other two described (H. J. Res. 83), is for the creation of "a joint budget committee" of Congress, with power to inquire into the acts and proposals of the administration, and to report out amendments to the administration revenue and appropriation plan — with no power to amend requests, except to reduce items, unless upon a two-thirds vote favorable to the amendment.

With one possible exception noted below these bills are straightforward and consistent throughout. If there is to be an executive budget, three things must happen: (1) the executive must be made responsible for preparing an account of past acts and a plan of service needs to be financed — and he must be provided with adequate machinery for doing it; (2) Congress must exercise the critical reviewing and the approving function — and must be provided with adequate machinery for this; (3) the procedure must be such as to enable the people through the electorate and the representative body to enforce executive and representative responsibilities — to which end these essentials must be provided: (*a*) the executive must be provided with the means of controlling expenditures after appropriations have been made so that he can defend his acts and give a good account of his stewardship; (*b*) the executive must be given a chance to come openly and publicly before the representative body to present his report and proposals so that he may defend his proposals and make every member of Congress responsible as well for the manner in which he votes; (*c*) both the executive and members of the representative body are entitled to a procedure by means of which responsibility may be kept clear — so that no action can be taken which will shift or confuse responsibilities.

Reasons *pro* and *con* may determine that it would be better to organize an executive staff in some other manner than provided by the Frear bills; likewise provisions for current allotment and executive control of funds appropriated may be needful; some other or further elaboration of audit and reviewing organization and procedure might be desired. But the underlying principles are sound — *if the people want to have a responsible executive and representative body, and if the people want to provide themselves with the means of intelligent enforcement.*

There is one point in the Frear plan on which there may be misunderstanding, viz.: Section 7 of the accompanying resolution (H. J. Res. 83) provides, " That for the purpose of giving the House immediate and direct information as to the said estimates and of offering explanations in regard to the proposed expenditures of the said budget bill, the heads of the several executive departments may be required to appear in the House and Senate during the time said bill is under consideration, to answer questions relating to the provisions of said bill." Section 2 provides for initial hearing in a joint committee of the House and Senate. Section 3 gives to this committee the power to call executive officers before it, and go over the estimates item by item in hearings. These two provisions are antagonistic. If the initial hearings are in a small committee made up of leaders, party discipline will prevent a real effective hearing on the floor or in committee of the whole. A number of states have made similar provision and the result has not been encouraging. The whole process of appropriation has been just as " invisible " as before; there has not been developed an open-forum-method of handling questions of finance, and it may be safely predicted that there never will be until the executive is required to come before the whole body to make good his request for funds. In other words, the committee work must be in the nature of preparation for the trial and not the trial itself. If the Frear bills had been pushed forward for enactment this is a point that should have been made clear.

The Green Resolution

The Green Resolution (H. J. Res. 168) has the merit of being a straight out-and-out measure for the establishment of a *legislative budget*. It provides for a " budget committee " to be made up of five members selected by the ways and means committee of the Senate. And it is made " the duty of the Secretary of the Treasury, immediately upon receipt of the regular annual estimates . . . or as soon as practical to transmit a detailed statement of all estimates to said budget committee." From this point on, everything would proceed according to the Sherley model. There would be no executive responsibility for anything except to see to it that the clerks prepared the information called for. It is simple. There is no need for reorganization anywhere, because the whole past development, both legislative and bureaucratic, has been one that is suited to such a planning agency. The Green measure would simply glorify " government-by-chairmen-of-standing-committees " by organizing a " super-committee." With this the whole problem of budget making would be solved — *unless perchance it might develop that the people of the United States might continue in the future, as in the past, to find fault with the " invisible " and " irresponsible " government.* In that event, the Green bill, or the Fitzgerald proposal, or the Sherley proposal, or the Cannon proposal, or any other proposal for a " legislative budget " if adopted, would in time be relegated to the political scrap heap that is already piled high with time serving palliatives and ill adapted efforts at reform sought and achieved without disturbing the *status quo ante.*

The Good Bill

The Good bill (H. R. 1201) has not the merit of clarity possessed by the Frear Bills and the Green Resolution described above. One may read it time and again and still be in doubt as to what it does aim to accomplish. But of one thing the reader feels certain; that there is an attempt to capitalize the popular clamor for responsible government through the institution of a budget procedure. The framers of the bill have evidently tried to be nice to every one. The bill holds out the appearance of an *executive budget* measure; but on analysis it is found to lack the essentials, and one is left with the conviction that it is a complete surrender to the " chairmen " who would protect their great powers by insisting on the Congressional *status quo;* that it is essentially a well-camouflaged *legislative budget* device — a Republican measure well designed to fulfill the prophecy of Mr.

Cannon, which in fact is a redemption of the party pledge by the Fitzgerald-Sherley route.   Or it might turn out to be a " commission budget plan "— a thing not suited to the Federal Government and therefore in effect under the domination of the chairmen of standing committees because opposed to executive responsibility.

The apparent executive character of the proposal is given by clauses like these:

" There is created in the office of the President a bureau of the budget."

" There shall be in the bureau a director and an assistant director, who shall be appointed by the President, with the advice and consent of the Senate."

" The bureau of the budget shall assist the President in the performance of the powers conferred upon him by this act."

But none of these deal with essentials.   The location of the bureau " in the office of the President " is a figure of speech unless the bureau is in fact his staff agency. Appointment " with the advice and consent of the Senate " does not fix responsibility.   The requirement to " assist the President in the performance of the powers conferred " depends entirely on other clauses to make it vital.   These are discussed below.

The Andrews Resolution

The Andrews Bill (H. R. 551) does not assume to be more than a part-way measure.   It has for its purpose to transfer the audit function to Congress.   This is entirely consistent with an executive budget — in fact a complementary part.   But the audit function should never be confused with accounting.   The accounting must be performed by those who are held accountable. And there is much more to accounting than simply keeping within or recording charges against appropriations. There must be accounts with properties and indebtedness;

account showing unit costs; accounts showing operations by functions or kinds of public services rendered; accounts by organization units or officials to be held responsible. There are various subjects concerning which information is needed for purposes of administration that have no relation whatever to the question of "authority" to spend. These accounting functions must be left with the responsible officer as a means of keeping in touch. The audit function is one of review of accounts and official acts and should be in the hands of the critical agency. But if the leadership in the matter of administrative planning and finance is in the hands of chairmen of congressional committees, then the audit function is at once impaired. Only in case of an executive budget should the Auditor General be put under the committee that takes leadership before Congress.

The Tinkham Resolution

One of the measures which by its terms seems to recognize a need for revision of rules of Congress is the Tinkham Resolution (H. R. 107). The preamble of this resolution recites:

"Whereas there are now pending before Congress a number of bills providing for the establishment of what is known as a national budget system; and,

"Whereas an essential feature of this system is that the President shall annually transmit to Congress, upon its assembling in ordinary session, a document known as a budget which, among other things, shall present in one place a complete coördinated statement of the provision which, in the opinion of the President, should be made for meeting the revenue and expenditure needs of the government for the next ensuing fiscal year, to the end that the problem of financing the government may be considered as a whole at one time, and especially that a proper balance may be maintained between prospective revenues and expenditures; and,

" Whereas it is essential, if this unity of financial program is to be maintained, that the rules of the House of Representatives shall be so framed that the budget, when received, will be considered as a whole, instead of being split up and the several parts being considered by separate committees acting independently of each other as is necessary under the existing rules of the House; and

" Whereas it is further essential that safeguards shall be thrown around the budget bill . . . to prevent its undue change by individual members."

These whereases speak of the necessity for change in rules, and the resolution speaks of nothing else, except to suggest the character of changes to be made.   It is a question, therefore, whether the proposed change in rules would be ill or well adapted to the institution of an executive budget.   The proposed changes in rules are deserving of special consideration because it is proposed by Mr. Tinkham that the " super-committee " idea be used for the purpose of inquiry and discussion.   This is the device proposed by Mr. Sherley, for use in the preparation of a " legislative budget."   Mr. Tinkham would adopt it for use with the " executive budget."   His suggestion raises the question as to whether it is adapted to the purpose.

Critical Discussion of Executive Proposals Before the House

The purpose of bringing revenue and appropriation measures of any kind before Congress is to enable the representative body to control the administration by controlling the purse.   To achieve this result some one who has knowledge of the service needs must prepare and be sponsor for the measure to be inquired into and voted on by the members.   The past practice has been for.

Congress to divide up the work among a large number of committees. Special committees first become familiar with service needs of a particular department or office. Then in due time this committee frames a measure to be brought before Congress which measure is sponsored by the chairman. The useful function of the "super-committee," as seen by Mr. Sherley, was to enable all of the chairmen of these several committees to get together, and then through a "super-chairman" to present a consolidated bill or "legislative budget."

This device, however, was not urged as a means of making the executive responsible; nor was it urged as a means of giving publicity to the work of Congress. It was urged as a means of preventing executive leadership. The "executive budget" is based on quite another assumption. Its purpose is to force the executive, who is asking for financial support and who by reason of his everyday contact with the problem of administration has knowledge of service needs, to assume responsibility for bringing before the membership of the deliberative body a well-considered plan of service and finance at the beginning of the session, instead of leaving it to a committee to bring its proposals at the end of the session after they have had time to study the service needs.

Both the protagonists of the "legislative budget" and the protagonists of the "executive budget" assume that the best person to be sponsor for a plan is the one who prepares it and is therefore most familiar with the considerations that led to the request for funds in the form presented. The difference lies in the fact that the executive, assisted by his cabinet, would prepare and sponsor the plan in the one case; and a chairman of a legislative committee, assisted by his fellow members, would prepare and sponsor the plan in the other. But in both cases the one who proposed the plan would be expected to sponsor it. Now this, being the one principle commonly accepted by both groups of protagonists, in case an "executive-budget" plan is adopted, there is no occasion for referring the departmental requests to a committee to obtain the information needed for the preparation of a finance plan, as would be the case if a "legislative budget" is to be prepared.   This work has already been done in executive cabinet before the appropriating body meets.

With an "executive budget" the only need for a committee is to develop criticism and discussion.   And for this purpose both the Frear and the Andrews plans of audit and committee inquest are adapted.   For this purpose the congressional bill proposed by Mr. Tinkham would seem to be as illsuited as anything that could well be imagined.   The committees, whose chairman (together with a super-chairman chosen by the House) would constitute the majority of this "super-committee," would not, in the normal course of events, be men who would be disposed to criticize the executive and the departmental heads.   Normally they would all be of the same party; politically they would all be bedfellows.   If the members are to become informed through searching criticism and discussion before they are called on to vote away hundreds of millions of public money they must provide for having criticism offered by persons who are critically disposed — the organization and leadership for this purpose must come from the opposition.

Such an organization for purposes of inquiry and discussion as is suggested by Mr. Tinkham, assuming that the President were to submit a budget, would be adapted to only one purpose — to apply vigorously and use effectively the well-known principle of "gag-rule."   This is not an academic conclusion — a mere matter of logic. This result has been the uniform outworking of · such an organization — a committee of inquiry controlled by the party friendly to the administration where an "executive-budget" plan has been in operation.   On the other hand a committee whose chairman and control is taken from the opposition has proved most useful. An example of the operation of an opposition committee is found in the British Parliament — where the chairman of the "Committee on Public Accounts" as the critical committee is then called, has been taken from the opposition every year but one from 1866 until 1914, when a Coalition Cabinet was formed. This committee was made up of the best finance and administrative critics in the House. An example of the very bad results achieved by putting the critical committee under the control of the pro-administration party may be found in every province of Canada and the Dominion Government where the only function performed by them has been to whitewash the government and "gag" the opposition. The uniformity of operation of this principle is found in American practice in the "committees on expenditures" of Congress. They become actively critical only when the party in control of Congress is opposed to the administration.

This does not mean that committees in the appropriating body are less important when an "executive-budget" procedure is used than when the finance measure or plan is prepared under leadership provided in the deliberative body itself. Rather this: when an "executive budget" is laid before the appropriating body at the beginning of the session, sponsored by the head of the administration, the committee organization within the deliberative body may and should devote itself to getting the case of the administration before the membership in a manner to having it considered and determined on its merits. That is, the crying need in this country is to have decisions on matters of policy reached after deliberation; and the committee system should aid, not stand in the way of this.

This is one of the chief advantages of the "executive-budget" plan. This would bring the executive before

the money-granting body as an applicant for support and
relief of institutions and enterprises which together serve
the welfare needs of the people. Upon this application
the service needs are to be determined by a jury of 500
members, chosen by an electorate which is authorized to
speak for a hundred million people, to decide matters of
this kind. The real problem before this body at this time
is to develop a trial practice which is adapted to giving
the executive as applicant for funds a full and fair hearing, and the members of this great jury of 500 representing the American people full information and a fair
chance to know what are the service needs calling for the
action to be taken before the members of the jury are
required to vote.

Since decision involves grave questions of public policy,
in the nature of things, no matter what may be the plan
of program proposed, men will take sides " for " and
" against " and the purpose of the proceeding is to give
information so that each member may voice his judgment
when voting " for " or " against " the proposal in the exact
form presented. This means that there is need for
counsel " for " and " against " the proposal, in that
the rules should be so framed that counsel " against "
as well as counsel " for " this the greatest of all
measures that can come before Congress may have
a chance to prepare their case; that ample provision
should be made for two committees or groups of counsel
— the one to manage the case of the administration, the
other to serve the membership and the country as critics;
that these critics may serve the members by pointing out
all the social and political dangers that might follow the
adoption of the plan and bring to their attention all
the facts and arguments that should give pause before
action is taken. However desirable it may be to lay down
an organization and procedure for the conduct of the
case of the administration, this would develop in any

event; the most important consideration of all, in the development of a trial practice, is to provide for an effective organization and procedure to perform the function of critical review and discussion — the reason being that the disposition of majorities is to override minorities and not to give them a hearing.

As a matter of fact two kinds of committees now exist in Congress: one class which undertakes to represent the needs of the administration; another class which is to act as its critics. The one class is made up of the various committees which prepare and sponsor appropriation bills; the other class is made up of what are called " committees on expenditures " whose function is to bring to the attention of members things which call for censure or opposition. If the functions of advocacy on the one hand and opposition on the other are recognized as the two essentials of group deliberation, and it seems best to provide departmental specialists in Congress for each of these purposes (or committees and super-committees as suggested by Mr. Tinkham), then there should be two leaderships: the one should be organized and controlled by those who are " for " the administration; and the other should be organized and controlled by those who are " against " the administration. If the committees are so constituted, instead of having Congress having no organic means of criticism except in case a majority is " against " the President, and no organic means of advocacy except when a majority is " for " the President, as is now the case under the rules as they stand, there would be at all times a way provided for making Congress an effective court of inquest and decision — at once a public forum and a grand jury for the nation.

Appointment of a " Select Committee on the Budget "

In the contact developed, the exchange of ideas on budget proposals, the conferences growing out of the several

bills introduced looking toward the introduction of an
" executive-budget " procedure for the preparation and
consideration of service needs and requirements in financial support, it became evident that there were many facts
still to be developed before the proponents of the system
would be ready to go before Congress with a plan that they
could defend.   Therefore all the moving parties joined in
advocacy of a special committee to collect data and prepare a well-considered plan to be laid before the next
Congress.   Mr. Tinkham had proposed that the Standing
Committee on Rules report on the subject.   But this
would be a committee that had little interest in a new
budget procedure; its instinctive reaction would be to
perpetuate the rules as they have developed around
standing-committee leadership — the old system.   Mr.
Mann and Mr. Goodwin introduced resolutions for a
special committee to report on a plan.   Congressman
Good proposed a " Select Committee on the Budgets," to
which was referred for consideration and report all bills,
resolutions, and documents for the establishment of a
national budget system or proposing changes in the present
methods of dealing with appropriations, estimates, and
expenditures.   This committee held many long sessions,
called before it many persons in and out of public life,
and then reported recommending the passage of the
Good Bill.

The Amended Good Bill (H. R. 9783) Recommended by the Committee

That the Good Bill is not intended as a straight out-
and-out " executive budget " measure appears both from
analysis and by admission of its sponsors.   For purposes
of analysis let us consider each of the three phases of a
budget procedure laid down by the committee itself.   In
its report this formula is found:

" Broadly speaking a budget system has three distinct phases, namely:

(1) The formation of the budget;
(2) Action on the budget by Congress;
(3) Supervision and control of the executive of the budget."

In making critical appraisal of the bill as it came from the committee let us also consider the admitted purpose. The purpose as stated is to make the administration responsible to the people. Enlarging on this, the committee said:

" In the national government there can be no question that the officer upon whom should be placed this responsibility is the President of the United States. He is the only officer who is superior to the heads of departments and independent establishments. He is the only officer of the administration who is interested in the administration, who is interested in the government as a whole, rather than one particular part. He is the only administrative officer who is selected by the people and thus can be held politically responsible for his actions. Furthermore, as the head of the administration, it is to him that Congress and the people should look for a clear and definite statement of what provision in his opinion should be made for revenue and expenditure needs of the Government."

Only One of Three Essentials to an Executive Budget Provided For

Now with these propositions before us let us consider what provision is made for placing and keeping responsibility on the shoulders of the President. If the President is to be held accountable to the people there can be no question about this proposition: That members of the

representative body when they are called on to vote for or
against an executive proposal, and the people must know
what it is that the President stands for.   That is to say:
It is not enough to know what the original or initial request was.   A procedure must be adopted which will
enable members of Congress and the people to follow executive responsibility through each phase from the initial
request to execution: (1) What the plan was as originally prepared; (2) what propositions are made for modification before enactment, and the reasons therefor; and
(3) what was done in the conduct of the business authorized.   The Good Bill makes provision for only one of
these three essentials.

With respect to the formation of the plan of work and
finance to be laid before Congress, the Good bill is very
explicit.   On this point the report of the committee offers
a convincing argument and clear exposé:

" In order that the President may be in a position intelligently to formulate such a plan he must be given a
machinery through which he can keep in intimate and
immediate touch with all the work of the government and
be able intelligently to criticize, revise, and correlate the
requests for authorizations to engage in work or for
funds with which to pay for their several activities.   The
bill that has been prepared by the committee provides for
such machinery by the creation of a service known as the
Bureau of the Budget.   This service is placed under the
immediate direction of the President.   Its duties are to
assist the President in the performance of the powers conferred on him by the proposed act."

So much for clarity in fixing responsibility for preparing a plan or program to be submitted to Congress.   But
look as one may no provision can be found either in the
bill or in the accompanying resolution for like definition

of responsibility through the other two phases.   On the
contrary, the provisions made are no other than those
which in the past have brought to pass results that every
true American abhors —" invisible " and " irresponsible "
government.

The President Already Has All the Powers Provided For

With respect to the various changes that must necessarily be made in a measure prepared weeks or months in
advance of enactment, there is no method provided for
fixing responsibility.   Neither the President nor the
members of his cabinet are expected or permitted to come
before the representatives of the people in Congress assembled to explain, defend, and discuss the proposals as originally urged or in amended form.   And no provision
is made to enable the President to direct, control, or supervise the execution of the activities of the government after
appropriations have been granted.   Both of these are essentials to fixing responsibility.   Without them there can
be no " executive budget "— there can be no clear vision
of what the executive really stands for; there is no way
of preventing misrepresentation of the acts and proposals
of the administration on the floor of the House; there
can be no clear issues joined; there can be no publicity
given to the moving considerations that affect decisions
reached; there can be nothing to guide the judgment of
members or the people in voting except " party " loyalty.

Under the Good bill there would be almost no gain in
furtherance of efforts to establish " visible " and " responsible " government.   As was stated by President Taft,
the constitution gives to the executive the right to propose and submit a budget and this is recognized by the
committee when it says in its report:

" It thus makes more definite the constitutional obligation that rests on the President ' from time to time to

give to Congress information of the state of the Union and recommend to their consideration such measures as he shall judge necessary and expedient.' "

The committee might also have pointed to the constitutional provision quoted by President Taft in support of his proposal: The right of the chief executive to call on " the principal officers of each of the executive departments " for such information as he may desire " upon any subject relating to the duties of their respective offices." Further than this, by Act of March 4, 1909, known as the Smith law, Congress has already made it the duty of the Secretary of the Treasury, whenever the estimated expenditures exceed the estimated revenues, to transmit the estimates to the President " to the end that he may, in giving Congress information of the state of the Union, and in recommending to their consideration such measures as he may judge necessary, advise the Congress how in his judgment the estimated appropriations could with least injury to the public service be reduced . . . or if such reduction be not in his judgment practicable without undue injury to the public service, that he may recommend to Congress such loans or new taxes as may be necessary to cover the deficiencies." So far as the President is concerned, therefore, the Good bill has done nothing except to set up a new bureau to do what he already could do if he had wished to use the machinery and powers already provided. There is no reason why we have not had an executive budget except the dominance of irresponsible standing committees, and this the Good bill does not propose to change.

Intent of the Committee not to Provide for an Executive Budget

Finally, the committee in support of the Good bill frankly admits that it does not intend that the country shall have an executive budget. On this point the report says:

"It will doubtless be claimed by some that this is an executive budget. . . . The plan outlined does provide for an executive initiation of the budget, but the President's responsibility ends when he has prepared the budget and transmitted it to Congress. To that extent, and to that extent alone does the plan provide for an executive budget. . . ."

The committee in all frankness might have said: It is in fact to be made a Congressional measure before it will be considered by the membership; the executive proposal is for the information of the standing committees; the super-committee made up of irresponsible leaders will undertake to prepare the instrument that comes before the members for inquiry, discussion and action; what we propose is a "legislative budget." In other words, it is simply a plan to do exactly what the Smith law contemplates. It is a plan to induce the President to assume personal responsibility for the details of the estimates as well as a financial plan to be mulled over in the secrecy of the committee room, amended, changed, and buffeted about in any manner that a group of irresponsible "leaders" may see fit, and then give to these leaders a chance to play ducks and drakes with the President on the floor with no opportunity given to him or to his cabinet, openly and publicly to explain or defend the executive proposal as submitted, to meet irresponsible criticism or to challenge the independent proposals and the log-rolling measures worked out and agreed to by "chairmen" of standing committees who hold their positions and exercise their powers by reason of length of service, loyalty and subservience to an oligarchy which controls an organization that exists outside of the Government, responsible to no one, and which controls the Government through these standing committees.

Action in the Senate

In the Senate other measures were introduced and a similar select committee was finally appointed. This committee has done very little owing to the preoccupation of the Senate with discussion of the League of Nations. One proposal before the Senate deserves special mention, as bearing on the *executive-budget* commitments of the Republican party — Senate Bill Nos. 450 and 456, introduced by Mr. McCormick. They cover much the same ground as the Frear Bills.

The McCormick Budget Bills

Senate Bill No. 450 has for its purpose the creation of an independent audit office. By its terms, Congress for the first time in American history would have a permanent staff possessing the necessary powers and charged with the duties of currently reviewing all acts of the administration involving the receipt and expenditure of public money. Heretofore, the functions of audit and review and approval of transactions have been under the Treasury — a branch of the administration responsible to the President. But Mr. McCormick would make the President responsible for leadership in planning. Therefore the critical faculty would be in Congress. And when leadership is exercised by Congress and the President exercises the critical and veto function this is consistent. The new comptroller-auditor general, and his assistants would be independent of the administration whose acts are to be reviewed and reported on; and to make the office free from partisan influence, to give it the character of political disinterestedness, the comptroller-auditor general, the assistant comptroller-auditor general, and the solicitor of the audit office are to be given the same tenure and freedom in the exercise of discretion as judges of the Supreme Court. The bill provides that "every department account shall be examined by the comptroller-auditor general on behalf of Congress and such examination shall determine whether the payments which are charged in the accounts to the sums appropriated are supported by vouchers and proofs of payment, and whether the money expended has been applied to the purpose or purposes for which such appropriation was intended to provide. That in order that such examination may, as far as possible, proceed *pari passu* with the cash transactions of the several disbursing offices of the executive departments, the comptroller-auditor general shall have free access at all convenient times to the books of account and other documents relating to the accounts of such departments and may require the several departments concerned to furnish him from time to time, or at regular periods, with accounts of the cash transactions of such departments respectively up to such times or periods." On the fifteenth days of January of each year the comptroller-auditor general would be required to lay before Congress the accounts of the preceding fiscal year as certified and reported on by him, and to call the attention of Congress to every case in which payments exceed or are not properly charged to an appropriation, are not supported by proof, or any other fact or information which may show irregularity; and power is also given to make interim reports when the circumstances may seem to warrant. The office is also charged with the duty of critically reviewing estimates for expenditures for the information of Congress.

Senate Bill No. 456, introduced by Mr. McCormick, by its terms would create in the Treasury Department an office to be known as the Budget Bureau, charged with the duty of collecting the data needed to enable the Secretary of the Treasury to prepare a budget for the Pres-

ident to submit to Congress " in giving information of
the state of the Union " and to " recommend for their
consideration as a measure of law the annual estimates
of expenditures of the several branches of the government, and also such changes or adjustments in the revenue laws as may in his judgment be necessary to meet
such expenditures "; for which purpose it would be
made the duty of the Secretary of the Treasury before
submitting them to the President " to revise, to consolidate,
to unify, to coördinate, to reduce, diminish, or otherwise
change any item or items in the annual estimates, or in
any deficiency, supplemental, or other estimates of expenditures for the various branches of the government
in such manner as may be necessary to effect economies
and to prevent waste, extravagance, loss, duplication, and
the like "— an exception being made of the technical
branches of the War and Navy Departments which are
to be submitted to the President without change.   The
budget so made would be required to be in the hands of
the President on or before November 15th, thereby giving
to the President time to make his budget a matter of
cabinet consideration before putting it in final form for
submission to Congress.   Thus the McCormick Bills
would give to the President, under the Secretary of the
Treasury, a budget bureau, and, by operation of existing
law not repealed, the power to prescribe and install an
effective system of administrative accounts; they would
give to Congress an independent audit office for the
review and report on all past acts involving money transactions, and a means of staff review and criticism of
the estimates, for the information of members at the
time that the budget is taken up for consideration.

The McCormick Bills are more complete in certain re-
spects than are the Frear Bills, but they lack one essential
taken up by Mr. Frear.   There is nothing in the
McCormick Bills, nor in any accompanying resolution,

which provides for or suggests a modification of the rules of Congress to provide for a fair, open, and adequate consideration of the budget after it has been received by Congress.   The President has the constitutional right to present the budget in person or by letter.   But there is no suggestion of need for provision for explanation, criticism, or defense when it is taken up in detail for the information of members.   Assuming that the majority in Congress is favorable to the administration, there is no way that criticism can be effectively organized except by the members of the opposition; and to effect this the rules must be radically changed.   Assuming that the majority is hostile to the administration, there is no way to insure that the budget will be considered at all — the whole thing may be ignored and resort may be had to the same practice as now obtains.[1]

[1] This was written during the last session of Congress. During the 2nd session of the Sixty-sixth Congress the Senate Committee began hearings, with a view to making an early report. It is understood that some of those giving testimony urged that the cabinet be given the privileges of the floor on finance and administration matters and that Senator McCormick is not averse to the proposal. If he is not, or a majority of his committee is not, then it would seem that a resolution should be drawn and made part of the report. For this is the essence of the whole thing. With a change of rules giving the privileges of the floor to members of the cabinet, there can be no other than an " executive budget " procedure. Without it a visible and responsible government is impossible.

PART V. CONCLUSION

CHAPTER XXI

In writing of the progress made and of results obtained in the struggle for responsible government, we are not dealing with democracy as such. There is no question raised as to whether or not democracy is desirable. For this purpose its desirability is assumed. We are dealing with fundamentals of the organization and the procedure through which and in which democracy must express itself — the mechanism by means of which "government of the people, by the people, and for the people" must be realized.

A Question of Machinery for Making Popular Control Effective

This is the reason that our forefathers undertook to establish here a representative system. A representative system is a type of organization, a kind of machine. The purpose of its adoption was to make democracy possible to a numerous and widely scattered people. It was to provide a great and growing nation with the instruments whereby the will of the people might control their institutions of public service — to provide an effective mechanism of popular control.

Fundamentally, all processes and methods of popular control rest on the recognition of the need for leadership — the purpose of the control being to make the organization subservient by providing practical ways of holding the leader accountable to those for whose benefit an institution is established and maintained. And the exercise of this function of *control* is the only end or aim of adopting the representative principle.

Every device of popular control rests on the principle that control over the organization must be exercised through its leadership.   In a small local democracy popular control is made effective by bringing the head of the service to be controlled before an assembly composed of the whole democratic "electorate."   In a populous, widely scattered democracy, it is conceived that popular control may still be made effective; that this may be done by interposing a body of representatives — bringing the head of a service to be controlled before an " Assembly " or " Congress " made up of persons chosen by the broad democratic " electorate " to represent them, and in a manner to give the process news value, and then make their acts and decisions reviewable by the people.   In order to achieve this result the vicarious town meeting has to pursue the same method of inquiry and deliberation and initial decision as is used in the real town-meeting of the small democracy.   The success of the representative principle, however, depends on having the proceedings conducted openly and publicly and in a manner to make news of them.   In a great democracy it is only through " news " that the people may be kept as well informed as if each voter attended the meeting.   By means of such a procedure popular control may be made quite as effective through a plebiscite as if the people in fact came together in one great meeting.

In a large, populous, widely extended democracy both the representative " assembly " or " congress " and a " democratic electorate " are necessary to the exercise of popular control; the " electorate " is helpless unless the representative " assembly " or " congress " performs the inquisitorial and deliberative function, and does it in an open public, news-making manner — serving as the organ by means of which the acts and proposals of officers who are to be held accountable are made known to the people. This done, then the electorate may act with intelligence.

Adequacy of the Instruments Provided

In our political institutions, both of these instruments or organs of control have been provided. The first essential of the mechanism of control, the representative " assembly " or " congress," was provided in our early constitutions; in fact, insistence on this essential as a means of controlling the executive led to our war for independence. But its establishment did not give us responsible government. Then the second essential, a democratic electorate, broad enough to include all classes, was added by statute. But still we did not have responsible government. And if we may accept the statements of such men as President Roosevelt, President Wilson, and Senator Root, or even rely on our own much narrower knowledge, the everyday experience and observation of citizens, and the everyday comments of the press, we must conclude that we do not now have either " visible " or responsible government.

The Purpose of the Mechanism of Control

The two essential parts of the mechanism of control are both here. But the mechanism as a whole has not worked. What is the matter? When we think of the outworking of our organs of popular control, it is evident that something has gone wrong from the beginning. In looking for cause, in matters of performance, we have therefore taken a long-range view. In looking for cause, in contemplation of the working mechanism itself, we have asked ourselves these questions:

(1) On what is the mechanism of control to operate? That is, whose action is to be made subservient to the people through its use? Who is it that is to be made responsive and responsible?

(2) Why — with our system of elections which provides for freedom of choice of officers, secret ballot, ac-

curate count, etc.— has our broad democratic electorate failed in its controlling purpose?

(3) Why have our Congress and Assemblies, with their unlimited powers of inquest and discussion, still left the electorate without the information needed to enable them to act wisely and effectively? Why have the doings of those who are to be held accountable been " invisible"?

(4) Why has our leadership been irresponsible?

We ask ourselves the first question to make sure that there is no disagreement with respect to the end to be achieved by use of the controlling mechanism. The other three questions call for critical judgment. There is no difference of opinion as to what is the end to be achieved. The purpose of the controlling mechanism is to render the public service, the administration, subservient to the popular will.

In a monarchical system the king both made the laws and executed them; he decided what should be done by the government as an organ of public service, and headed the organization for doing it. In a democracy the *determining* and the *doing* functions are divided — the first being used to control the second. In a simple democracy those who come together in a meeting or moot (*i.e.* the voting members of the community) made the laws and the executive officer chosen by them looked after their enforcement; the meeting or moot decided what should be done and the chosen head of the doing organization was made responsible to the membership by being brought before the assembly to give an account of himself. When the representative principle was adopted the meeting or assembly had the same determining function to perform, and the electorate reviewed their determination and enforced their decisions by retaining to themselves the right to elect the representative reviewing body as well as the executive. Thus the objective of the controlling mechanism unquestionably has been to adapt it to using the *determining* function in such manner as to control the *doing* organization — the administration. It is primarily the executive who is to be held accountable.

The Mechanism Not Properly Used

Starting from this, the cause of the trouble has not been hard to find. We have not been using our representative assemblies or congress with a view to locating executive responsibility and helping the electorate to enforce it; we have not used them as a means of inquest and discussion of the acts and proposals of the administration having in mind giving publicity to what has been going on and raising issues with the executive — the elected head of the administration; consequently, the " electorate " could not intelligently perform its function either in choice of an executive or in choice of the representative body.

In all the constitutional discussion of democratic organization this fact seems to have been missed: That the thing to be controlled is the administration; and that the only effective way to control the administration is through its leadership. Or to put it in another way: Responsible government depends on holding executive leadership responsible. In this country we have not had responsible government because the head of the public service over which control is to be exercised has not been brought before the vicarious town meeting provided for in our Constitution. Why?

Question of Leadership

Going over our history, there are a number of things that are significant. We find that the people are still accepting and using a type of political reasoning developed at a time when they were trying to get rid of their executive because they preferred no executive to an irresponsible one — a type of reasoning developed in appeals to the people to accept the lesser of two evils.   We find that during the pre-revolutionary conflict for responsible government our foreign executive refused to submit himself to the will of the American people as expressed in their representative bodies and by the electorate, and the people rose up and overthrew the executive branch of the government.   And in this emergency a revolutionary leadership was developed in the representative body itself to run the government.   Thus the representative bodies temporarily absorbed the function of executive leadership and forsook their function of inquest and discussion of executive acts and proposals, because there were no such acts to inquire into and no such proposals to discuss.   Having developed a leadership of their own in their committees, true to all human experience, powers once acquired have not been willingly surrendered.   So that we still have an organization in the representative body as if the executive did not exist.

Refusal of Constitutional Reviewing and Controlling Bodies to Surrender Leadership

After we had gained our independence the people decided to adopt new constitutions reëstablishing the executive branch of the government — making this separate and distinct from the representative body.   But we find that the representative body did not readapt their organization and procedure; they did not surrender the type of leadership which had been set up immediately before and during the revolutionary period.

Leadership and Responsibility Part Company

During the Revolutionary War legislatures had executive responsibilities; when our constitutions were set up providing for the separation of powers, legislative leadership had taken away administrative responsibility.   Thus when the representative bodies refused to surrender the leadership that goes with executive responsibility, leadership and responsibility parted company. And they have remained parted to this day, with the results all too well known.

Our Congress and our assemblies refused to accept our executives as our chosen leaders to take the initiative in matters of finance and administration; by so doing they abdicated their function of serving the people as a part of the mechanism of popular control, for they cannot investigate their own leadership unless the leadership developed by them is also made responsible for administration, as is done in the English cabinet system.

Continuing to assert for themselves and their own organization and members the powers of leadership without responsibility for management, our Congress and assemblies proceeded to set up rules for the protection of these powers; to this end they forbade the executive the right to appear before them in open forum and organized standing committees to develop and protect their own leadership. It was to protect the leadership of its own members that the House of Representatives of the Congress refused to permit Alexander Hamilton to appear before it to present the plans of finance and administration approved by Washington and made his own. It was to protect the leadership of its own members that the Senate of the Congress took the attitude toward Washington himself which caused him to turn away in disgust. It was for like reason that the State Assembly refused the governors and their cabinets the privilege of the floor to explain and defend their acts and proposals. And this is the reason that our executives are not permitted to come before our representative bodies to-day. It is not for constitutional reasons; it is for the protection of the leadership of the committee chairmen.

" Invisible " Government — Electorate Left Helpless

Failure to recognize the President and the governors as leaders might have been made consistent with principles of responsible government if they had placed on the chairmen of their committees executive responsibility. But they did not. Instead of linking up executive responsibility with their committee leadership, as in a parliamentary cabinet system, or of accepting the alternative of bringing the elected executive before the representative body to give an account of past acts and to explain future proposals before supplies were granted, the Congress and the assemblies turned over their powers of inquest and discussion, their function as one of the two essential organs of popular control, to the standing committees which had been organized by them to be exercised in a secret irresponsible manner. And this is the reason that we have " invisible " and irresponsible government.

Organization by Irresponsible Bosses to Control the Electorate

With leadership exercised by a multitude of chairmen of standing committees some provision must be made for central control, otherwise there could be no coördination of action. At first this function was performed by a " *junta* " within the representative body itself. But after the electorate had been made broadly democratic, centralized control came to be organized outside the government. Because there was no issue raised and no appeal taken direct to the people by a responsible leader, the way was open for direct appeal by designing office seekers under control of " bosess." And so it has happened that for nearly a century we have had in this country the strange phenomenon of leadership in quest for votes being organized as a business for profit. In violation of every ideal of democracy and every principle of responsible government, private organizations have grown up, calling themselves political parties, which have undertaken to frame up issues (they call them platforms) as a basis for appeal, and to nominate and elect both executive officers and members of the representative body which will do the bidding of irresponsible leaders, the heads of these organizations, popularly known as bosses. Thus our democratic electorates are made the tools of a commercialized oligarchy that gains its support through the patronage of elections and appointments and thrives by dividing the spoils derived from the diversion of public power and the trust estate gathered for the promotion of the common welfare to private and partisan uses.

This is the " system " which has come to take the place of the representative government as conceived by those who framed our charters of liberty and our constitutions for the exercise of popular sovereignty.

During the last ten years the American people have come to realize that all their efforts to establish popular control and thereby make their government responsible must come to naught unless this " system " which has grown up and surrounded this maladjustment, this dissevering of responsibility from leadership is made the issue of the day. This is the meaning of the steps taken to reorganize the administrations around a responsible executive; this is the meaning of the new interest taken in a procedure of control over the purse which will make this power granted to legislative bodies the means of defining issues and enforcing executive responsibility.

Protest Against Irresponsible Leadership

It was because the " system " had become so fully intrenched and has gained such complete control over both parts of the mechanism of popular control — the representative " assemblies " and the " electorate " — that civic bodies interested in building up the public service decided to abandon the representative principle. They had run up against the system. They found that all the machinery of nomination and election was in the hands of these private profit-sharing organizations. They themselves were not able to cope with these "parties." And they started an active propaganda, carried out with the support of independent voters, to put each of the public services which they undertook to build up, one after another, into the hands of the trustees. Thus it came about that during our generation the administration has been broken up into a multitude of boards and commissions with long and overlapping terms, responsible to no one, but free from the domination of the bosses — public opinion responding to the appeal that it was better to rely on the "conscience" of these trustees, as they had come to rely on the "conscience" of their courts, instead of trusting to the abortive processes of representative and electoral control. All the state administrations having thus been disposed of in the main, the hold of the boss thus being weakened, there followed a movement to reëstablish the representative principle on such a basis that both of the essential organs of popular control (the representative "assembly" and the "electorate") could function — the one to bring the executive to account and define issues, and the other to serve as a court of last resort to decide whether the indictment of a majority of the representative body, acting as a grand jury, should be sustained or the accused executive would be acquitted and continued in office as the trusted servant of the people — their chosen leader to manage their affairs.

Recent Acts Looking Toward Establishing Responsible Government in the States

In the recent organic acts and budget procedures adopted by the states, opinion has been divided between those who would retain "government-by-commission" and

those who would reëstablish the representative principle.
Nineteen of the states have declared for irresponsible
trusteeships.   In effect they have said: We will continue
" government-by-commission " because by this means we
have succeeded in achieving results which we could not
achieve through the boss-ruled machinery of representative government as it has developed under the standing-
committee system; we see no end of irresponsible " party "
domination.   Twenty-three of the states have accepted
the view that the best way to get rid of the irresponsible
party and its boss is to elect a responsible leader and then
provide the means for making his acts and proposals
" visible " so that he may be held accountable to the electorate.   Two states, New York and Arkansas, have declared for an enlargement of the powers of the standing
committees of the representative bodies — preferring to
retain the multifarious irresponsible trustees and the irresponsible party boss to a responsible executive.

The Contest Now Before Congress

The contest is now on in Congress as to whether its
rules will be so changed that the popularly elected executive will be made responsible and accountable to the electorate, or the processes of invisible government will still
continue.   The contest between the opposing factions
takes concrete form in proposals to change the rules and
statutes governing the exercise of control over the purse.
The select committee of the House of Representatives to
which this subject was referred on October 8th reported
in favor of continuing the processes by which we have had
a hundred and twenty years of invisible government.   The
report is in favor of still maintaining the separation between responsibility for administering the public business
and leadership — making a concession to the President,
however, that he may prepare and submit a service
plan with no opportunity to meet his opposition face

to face. This is a right that the President has always had, but he has refused to exercise it under conditions that give to him no protection. In 1909 Congress tried to force this on the President by the Smith law, but still he refuses to act — and rightly so, for no man who has the judgment to command the respect of a broad electorate would think of submitting himself to trial for official acts and proposals by star-chamber proceedings.

Fight Over Using Power to Control the Purse to Protect Irresponsible Leadership

The committee of the Senate has not yet reached a conclusion — it has not reported what stand it will take. But the real question is this: Shall a procedure of control be established which will do away with irresponsible " parties " and irresponsible leaders? Shall the proceedings of Congress be such that the people may know what the responsible head of the government and those under him have been doing and what he proposes to do, so that the very inquiries and discussion of finance and administrative measures will bring issues and leaders before the electorate; or shall Congress still continue to bar its doors against the executive and develop a leadership of its own in the secret confines of the committee room, leaving issues to be framed and candidates to be nominated by an irresponsible oligarchy that has no acts to defend? All of the other questions raised about " executive " budgets and " legislative " budgets, staff organizations, accounting, reporting, are mere details — necessary, but, nevertheless, details to be settled after it is decided what kind of an instrument of control we are to have.

The Cause of the Independent Voter

The system reaches out to every branch and root of the government. It is intrenched in the lifelong habits of men who have given themselves to politics. It is the only thing known to citizens and to the business world in its dealings with the government. To require the President to come before Congress with a budget, and to give the cabinet the privileges of the floor to explain and defend their acts and proposals would in the end, if carried out on a basis to make popular control effective, upset all of the traditions and practices of Congress — it would make the executives who went before Congress and the leaders of the opposition who stood up against them the outstanding men before the country. Much has been said about the development of the " independent voter " in this country, especially since women have been given the suffrage. If the floor of Congress were made an open forum in which the responsible heads of the administration would meet their critics in full view and hearing of the nation, this would change the whole electorate into " independent " voters; and " parties " as we now know them could not exist. In place of " bosses " we would have " leaders "; and in place of " parties " we would have divisions " for " and " against " leaders whose public acts and proposals would be their " platforms." In such circumstances parties would necessarily be constituencies which take sides on real issues. It is not to be expected that a change of such fundamental importance as this which strikes at the very life of the " party " system will be advocated by any who are not independent.

The Irresponsible Party One of the Questions in Issue

This is the real issue before the American people. The fundamental question is whether we are going to have responsible or irresponsible leaders. Since the irresponsible " party " organization is the thing which stands out large in the minds of the people we need not rely entirely on the negative action taken by those who advocate government-by-commission as an antidote. Within a week after the select committee on the budget reported to the House, the committee on elections and qualifications of members reported a condition which rings true to the lifelong experience of every citizen. Recommending the unseating of Congressman Fitzgerald of Massachusetts, the members of the majority give this picture of conditions as they existed in the year of Our Lord, 1918:

"Your committee finds and reports that Martin Lomasney is the political boss of the Fifth Ward; that he and his lieutenants work through an organization located in the Fifth Ward known as the Hendricks Club; that he has built up his power through a number of years largely by means of fraudulent votes of the liquor dealers, bartenders, and city job holders, illegally registered in his ward, and in the padded returns of alleged residents in cheap lodging houses."

Following this is an extended review of evidence which tells the story in detail of how the boss and the "organization" managed by him works to subvert the electorate to the uses of the "party." The members of the congressional committee who belong to the same "party" as the contestant, recommended that the seat now occupied by Mr. Fitzgerald be given to Mr. Tague; the members of the congressional committee who belong to Mr. Fitzgerald's "party" agreed with their political adversaries that Mr. Fitzgerald should not continue to represent the people of Massachusetts after such fraudulent acts have been brought to light, and they urge a new election for this reason:

"For many years it has been common knowledge in Boston that many men whose real homes are in the suburbs make an annual pretense of living in the locality here concerned for financial, political, or social reasons. It has also been commonly known that men in unreasonably large numbers have been registered from lodging houses, with the effect of making impersonation easy, inasmuch as repeaters can vote on the names of such men with little fear of detection.

"Mr. Tague took no offense at this state of affairs while it accrued to his advantage. He then made no request to the election commissioners that lists should be purged. He employed no investigators, no challengers. He did not assume it to be a part of good citizenship to lay the facts before the legislature and suggest a remedy. He acquiesced in what he now declares to be fraud, because that was then to his benefit."

This report with its evidences of " party " practice to elect those who are subservient is not introduced here in the thought that taken by itself it is of more than passing interest. But it does not stand by itself. Its significance. is found in the fact that this is but one of a long list of similar or related occurrences that run back to the beginning of the business history of these " parties " which thrive on the profits of such traffic — and who find their opportunity because there is no responsible leader before the people whose acts and proposals have been gone into by an inquisitorial or deliberative body, charged with the duty of granting or withholding support. In the recent Massachusetts Constitutional Convention many days were spent in committee and out discussing the question as to how popular control could be made effective, but, when it came to the question of making the General Court a grand jury for the people to frame issues to be settled by the electorate, the delegates who had been elected on a " party " ticket shied. This system is still at work. It is still at work not alone in Boston; it is at work in New York, in Philadelphia, in Pittsburgh, in Cincinnati, in Chicago, in St. Louis, in San Francisco. And we may be assured that it will remain in operation throughout the length and breadth of the land so long as the people have no alternative before them — no issues and no candidates except those who are put before them by irresponsible profit-

sharing business organizations which have appropriated
the names of " parties."

Again be it said, that in a responsible government a
" party " is one side in a division on a question arising
over the acts or proposals of a responsible leader.   The
head of a responsible party is a responsible leader; the
head of an irresponsible party is a boss.   We now have
the irresponsible " party " system because no other form
of centralized control is possible in a democracy which
has permitted its mechanism of popular control to be made
ineffective.

Government by Chairmen of Irresponsible Committees Must Go

We need not go to Mr. Tomasney's ward to see the
effects of a system in which a representative " Congress "
or " assembly " shuts its doors to a responsible leader and
leaves the people in ignorance as to what is going on.
There has been an occurrence within the last two months
that challenges the attention of the world: An American
President, charged with the duty of negotiating treaties,
after two months in conference with the heads of the
Allied Powers, at the conclusion of a world war, going
to the Senate of the United States as his constitutional
advisers — every member of which is bound by his oath of
office to vote for or against a proposed covenant that must
seriously affect national life for all time to come — is
turned away.   When he knocks at the Senate door he
finds it closed, and standing in front of it is a " party "
leader who tells him that if he has anything to say he can
take it up with a committee of which this " party " leader
is the head.   The President says that he has no business
with a committee; that his business is with the Senate;
that he comes as the responsible head of the government,
elected by the voters of the nation, to confer with the

representative body selected by forty-eight sovereign states to approve or disapprove the negotiation which he has on hand. But the Senate refuses, as has been its custom for a hundred years. Its members do not wish to ask any questions of President Wilson; they do not wish to have the head of the nation come into their sacred chamber. Why? This would put " party " leadership and the committee system into the discard. It would make it a matter between President Wilson and the members. They don't want to hear from President Wilson; they want to hear from their committee, after they have worked the whole matter out in secret session; they want to hear from their committee leaders, too, when the President is not present; they want to cast their votes " for " or " against " the measure with no chance given to ask questions of the one who is best informed, or to listen to his defense when attacked by an organized opposition. Then President Wilson, being denied access to the Senate, decides to tell the people of the United States about the treaty. He starts out; leaves the executive office; makes a trip across the continent. And several senators trail after him seeking opportunities to go before the popular audiences where he has been to answer his arguments. Does history record a greater travesty? This is a caricature on representative government.

The incident, ludicrous as it is, is not an exception. It is typical. It is true to form. It is the necessary and normal result of the action taken in 1789 to protect the committee system established as a revolutionary measure and which in turn produced our irresponsible party system. The exceptional feature about it is that the President considered the matter of such exceptional importance that he took his proposal out of the closet and went before the people with it instead of waiting to have it mauled about the Senate in his absence; it is exceptional in that President Wilson insisted on giving to the American people his side of the case before it was put to a party vote. But how much more fully might the people be informed if the Senate had opened its doors, given the full membership a chance to ask questions, and the President a chance to meet his critics face to face.   Is there any other way that the conscience and the judgment of a nation can assert itself?   Is there any other way that public opinion can be informed and popular control can assert itself deliberately?

Mr. Cannon's Defense

Congressman Cannon in his recent article on the national budget in defense of leadership by standing committee says:

"The multifarious duties of the members of Congress in considering 25,000 bills justifies them in following the committees having jurisdiction."

What are all these 25,000 measures about?   Does any one know? — either before or after the committees have got through with them?   Can any indictment be brought against our legislative system which is more severe than this statement made in defense?   If Congress passed a hundred measures a year which were well considered and fully understood by members and the people, this would satisfy all the requirements of a progressive people.   But to pass bills by the thousand and vote money by the billions without any one knowing what are the reasons which lie back of this exercise of sovereign power except a few members of one or another of half a hundred or more committees this is the " system "; this is the cause of those " fits of popular rage " that become the moving cause with a greater democratic electorate that has been made our constitutional organ for voicing the will that determines the destinies of one hundred million Americans.

The Outlook for Responsible Government

This brings us to a consideration of the present outlook for responsible government in the United States. What are the conditions which cause hope to rise in the minds and hearts of those whose civic interest centers in their faith in democratic institutions?

First, there is this great outstanding fact: that from the day of our independence the soul of the American people has been growing more and more democratic, and where the spirit of democracy is, whatever the institutional maladjustment, even a kleptarchy cannot go far wrong. The spirit of rightness in a democratic people must in the end prevail, however maddening may be the conditions which stand between the spirit and its goal. The spirit of the nation cannot be reconciled with "invisible government" in any of its forms. If we read the signs of the times aright the great American democratic electorate will not much longer continue to accept the domination of an irresponsible oligarchy in matters of election and appointment because American democracy has come to look to the Government and its leadership as something vital to the people. Government is no longer a necessary evil; it is the needed servant of the people. Public offices are no longer to be filled by those who are " smart " at playing a game of deceit and treachery. The people are beginning to demand real, genuine, wholesouled leadership which rests on the good will of citizenship built up through long years of service.

A second fact gives us courage and challenges attention. For the first time in our history the people are beginning to think in terms of the underlying principles of the mechanism of popular control. The people are beginning to demand that the acts of the government be made " visible "; that obstructions to the effective use and maladjustments of the mechanism of popular control be re-

CPSIA information can be obtained
at www.ICGtesting.com
Printed in the USA
BVHW051231210721
612411BV00006B/1249

9 780344 149177